BISMARCK

THE MAN & THE STATESMAN

VOLUME ONE

BISMARCK
THE MAN & THE STATESMAN
VOLUME ONE

OTTO VON BISMARCK

COSIMO CLASSICS

NEW YORK

Bismarck: The Man & the Statesman, Volume One
© 2005 Cosimo, Inc.

Cosimo, P.O. Box 416
Old Chelsea Station
New York, NY 10113-0416

or visit our website at:
www.cosimobooks.com

Bismarck: The Man & the Statesman, Volume One originally published by Harper & Brothers in 1889.

Library of Congress Cataloging-in-Publication Data
A catalog record for this book is available from the Library of Congress

Cover design by www.wiselephant.com

ISBN: 1-59605-184-1

EDITOR'S PREFACE.

PRINCE BISMARCK began his notes soon after his dismissal from the offices he had so gloriously filled had removed the espalier—as he himself repeatedly said—over which his life had hitherto climbed. The first suggestion came to him in an inquiry from Messrs. Cotta, coupled with an offer of publication; and as early as June 6, 1890, an agreement was made between the Prince and the representatives of the publishing firm of Cotta, by which, in the event of any Reminiscences being written by the Prince, the right of publication was conveyed to that house. To Lothar Bucher, the historian and diplomatist, who after the Prince's resignation lived for years, with short intervals, as a quiet inmate now at Friedrichsruh, now at Varzin, belongs the merit of having confirmed Prince Bismarck in his resolution to set down in writing his recollections and political thoughts, and of having in daily conversations kept him to the task when begun. Bucher's shorthand notes from the Prince's dictation formed the groundwork of the first draft. This for years the Prince zealously worked at, constantly revising the notes as divided into chapters and systematically arranged, and supplementing them with his own hand. In order to lighten his labour the ' Reflections and Reminiscences ' were privately printed as early as 1893, with all the alterations which the Prince

had made in the first draft. He then went over this printed
' copy ' again two or three times, and subjected it to careful verification, in which his almost unerring memory
was of the greatest service to him. Even within the last
two years he entirely recast whole chapters.

The increasing burden of years and a certain shrinking from the trouble of writing occasionally brought the
work to a standstill; but a great portion was finished and
now forms a precious inheritance for the German nation.
Our Statesmen and Historians will in centuries yet to
come draw instruction from this source, while our whole
people, even to the remotest times, will, as from the works
of their classical writers, derive edification from the book
which Bismarck has bequeathed to them.

It has been the Editor's duty, in pursuance of injunc-
tions emanating from Prince Bismarck himself, to correct
by the originals the various documents, which were often
taken from defective printed versions; to correct trifling
errors in dates, or in the spelling of names, due to want of
official material; and to draw attention in foot-notes to
similar expressions used by the Prince in his political
speeches, as well as to give literary references. Nowhere,
however, has the text been altered or abridged—where the
dead is of such sort, piety bids us refrain.

Annotations from the Prince's hand are indicated by
asterisks, etc. (* †), those of the Editor by numerals.

HORST KOHL.

CHEMNITZ: *October* 17, 1898.

*_** The English editor of this work, which from unavoidable causes has been produced under severe pressure
of time, wishes to offer his acknowledgments to those who
have taken part in the labour of translation; and more
particularly to Mr. J. W. HEADLAM, late Fellow of King's
College, Cambridge, whose special acquaintance with recent German history has been of the greatest service in
the somewhat arduous labour of revision.   The few notes
that have been added in the English edition are distinguished by square brackets [ ].

November 12, 1898.

CONTENTS

OF

THE FIRST VOLUME

PAGE

EDITOR'S PREFACE v

CHAPTER I

UP TO THE UNITED DIET

Political views of youth 1
Reaction of the Hambach Festival and the Frankfort outbreak on the
    German National idea and the Liberalism of Bismarck . . . 2
Thoughts in youth on foreign policy 3
Inclination to a diplomatic career 3
Ancillon's ideal of a diplomatist 3
Want of suitable material for the Diplomatic Service in the Prussian
    country gentry, and causes of this phenomenon 5
Foreigners in the Diplomatic Service and in the Army . . . 5
Personnel and institutions of the Prussian justice of the day . . 6
As *Auscultator* in the Criminal and Municipal Court 7
'I vote with my colleague Tempelhof' 8
Herr Prätorius's attempt at reconciliation 8
Need of a regulation in divorce procedure 9
Employment in the Division for Petty Suits 9
Transfer to the Administration 10
The Rhine Government Board; staff and business 10
Continuation of functions as *Referendarius* in the Government Office
    at Potsdam 11
Aversion to the 'pigtail and periwig' bureaucracy of the day . . 11
Unjust views taken of that time as compared with bureaucracy now . 11
The *Landrath* then and now 12

ix

BISMARCK

PAGE

Greater impartiality of the earlier Government officials ; political party
    influence upon the Judges in our time 13
Renunciation of an official career ; entrance on the management of the
    Pomeranian Estates 15
Bismarck's so-called ' Junkerthum ' 16
Unlimited authority of the old Prussian regal power not the last word
    of his convictions 17
Bismarck's ideal of monarchical power 18
Conflict with the bureaucracy 19
Bismarck *versus* Bismarck 19
The Opposition in the first United Diet 20
Bismarck's conflict with the Opposition 20
Frederick William IV and Bismarck 21

CHAPTER II

THE YEAR 1848

First impression of the events of March 18 and 19 22
Expulsion by the Schönhausen peasants of the Deputies from Tanger-
    münde 22
Their readiness to march to Berlin 23
Bismarck in Potsdam ; interview with Bodelschwingh, Möllendorf, and
    Prittwitz 23
Bismarck with the Princess of Prussia 25
With Prince Frederick Charles 25
Bismarck attempts to enter the Palace at Berlin ; is repulsed . . 26
Bismarck's letter to the King ; the first demonstration of sympathy . 26
In the streets of Berlin 27
Interview with Prittwitz and Möllendorf upon the possibility of inde-
    pendent military action 27
Bismarck threatened with arrest at Magdeburg 28
Bismarck with a deputation of Schönhausen peasants at Potsdam . 29
Address of the King to the Officers of the Body Guard . . . 29
Bismarck's letter to Lieutenant-General von Prittwitz 29
Contributions towards the history of the March-movement from conver-
    sations with Police-Commissioner von Minutoli and General von
    Prittwitz 32
Prince Lichnowski 34
Bismarck's declaration against the Address 34
Letter to a Magdeburg newspaper 36
A newspaper article : ' From the " Altmark " ' 37
Bismarck against the proposal of Vincke respecting the abdication of the
    King and invitation of the Princess of Prussia to take the Regency 40
Meeting with the Prince of Prussia on his return from England . . 41

CONTENTS

	PAGE
First meeting with the Prince	42
With the Prince at Babelsberg	42
First-relations with the Princess of Prussia and Prince Frederick William	44
The need of defence of the German Princes against the Revolution utilised by Frederick William IV not in the direction of union	44
Procession of March 21	46
Would a victory of Frederick William IV over the Revolution have had lasting effects on the German National question?	47
First visit to Sans-Souci	47
Conversation with the King	48
The King's legal views	49
Possible mental reservations of the King in his attitude towards the National Assembly	50
The Camarilla	51
Leopold and Ludwig von Gerlach	51
General von Rauch	53
On the quest of a new Ministry	54
The Presidency undertaken by Count Brandenburg	55
Otto von Manteuffel is induced by Bismarck to enter the Brandenburg Ministry	56
The new Ministers before the National Assembly	56
Precautions for their safety	56
Military occupation of Count Kniphausen's residence	57
Criticism of Wrangel's conduct	58
Secret thoughts of the King on the removal of the National Assembly	58

CHAPTER III

ERFURT, OLMÜTZ, DRESDEN

The latent German ideas of Frederick William IV were responsible for the failures of Prussian policy after 1848	59
Phrases about the German vocation of Prussia, and moral conquests	60
The dynasties and the barricades	60
Self-deception of the Frankfort Assembly	61
Strength of the dynastic feeling in Prussia	62
Refusal of the Imperial Crown by Frederick William IV	62
Bismarck's judgment upon the position at the time, and in 1849	63
His views of that time founded on party judgment	64
Party life formerly and now	64
The League of the Three Kings	65
Advantage of the situation for Prussia	65
Delusion of the leading circles in Prussia about the real comparative strength	66

BISMARCK

	PAGE
Hesitation of Frederick William IV	68
Prussian troops in the Palatinate and Baden	68
Bismarck's confidence in Prussia's military force in the struggle against the Revolution	69
Half-heartedness of Prussian policy at that time	70
General von Radowitz, groom of the stole to the King's mediæval fancy	71
The Erfurt Parliament : Count Brandenburg tries to win Bismarck to the Erfurt policy	72
Bismarck and Gagern	73
The Gagern and Auerswald families	74
Stockhausen, Minister for War, quiets Bismarck down . . .	75
Prussia's military helplessness and its causes	76
Bismarck's speech of December 3, 1850	78
Leading thought of the speech	81
Quieter views of the German Revolution in St. Petersburg in November 1850	82
Baron von Budberg	82
Trifling profits from the Dresden negotiations	83
Prince von Schwarzenberg and Herr von Manteuffel at Dresden .	84
Fundamental error of Prussian policy at that time . . .	84

CHAPTER IV

DIPLOMATIST

Appointment as Envoy to the Federal Diet	85
Ill-temper of Herr von Rochow	87
First studies in decorations, made upon General von Peucker .	87
Bismarck's indifference to decorations	88
The *Monsieur décoré* in Paris and St. Petersburg . . .	89
Dance-loving Frankfort	90
Dislike of King William I to dancing Ministers	90
Mission to the ' High School of Diplomacy ' at Vienna . .	91
Letter of introduction of June 5, 1852	91
Reception in Vienna	93
Difficulties of a Customs-union with Austria . . .	93
Klentze's calumnies	95
Bismarck's aversion to the Vienna post and the post of Minister .	95
Difficulties of a Minister's position under Frederick William IV .	96
Bismarck with King George V of Hanover	97
Dereliction of George V	98
A Prussian Consul as Austrian Agent	99

CONTENTS

CHAPTER V

PARTY OF THE 'WOCHENBLATT.' THE CRIMEAN WAR

PAGE

The Bethmann-Holweg group and the Prince of Prussia . . . 100
Count Charles von der Goltz 100
Count Robert von der Goltz as impresario of the Bethmann-Holweg
    group 101
The 'Preussisches Wochenblatt' 101
Rudolf von Auerswald 102
Bismarck declines to join the Wochenblatt party 103
Olmütz as felt by the Prince of Prussia 103
Manteuffel's aversion to a breach with Austria 105
The Prusso-Austrian offensive and defensive alliance of April 20, 1854 105
Bismarck represents to the King the opportunity afforded of raising
    Prussian prestige in Europe by utilising the war between Russia and
    the Western Powers as an excuse for stationing troops in Upper
    Silesia 106
The German Confederation under pressure from a French-Austrian
    Alliance 107
Saying of King William I of Wurtemberg, 'My dear boy, that is very
    fine, but too dear for me' 108
Extracts from letters of General von Gerlach 109
A letter from Niebuhr 112
Further extracts from Gerlach's letters 113
Usual course of Cabinet crises 118
Count Alvensleben as candidate for the Ministry. . . . 119
Double game of the Wochenblatt party 119
Their political programme 120
Criticism of it 121
A forged memorandum 122
Bunsen's Memorandum on the reconstruction of the Map of Europe . 122
Interview of the Prince of Prussia with Bismarck on the position of
    Prussia in the Crimean War, especially towards Russia . . 123
Objection to Prussia fighting Russia 124
The theft of dispatches and letters 125
Hinckeldey betrays himself 126
A letter from Bismarck to Gerlach upon the abdication by Prussia of
    her European position 126

BISMARCK

CHAPTER VI

SANS-SOUCI AND COBLENZ

PAGE

The Prince of Prussia under the influence of his wife 132
Inclination of the Princess (and Empress) Augusta to everything French
and English 132
Her dislike of everything Russian 133
Herr von Schleinitz 134
Breakfast discourses of the Princess (and Empress) Augusta, and their
influences 134
Hostility between the Courts of Sans-Souci and Coblenz . . . 135
Queen Elizabeth 135
Inclination of the Princess (and Empress) Augusta towards Catholicism 136
Her differences with Oberpräsident von Kleist-Retzow . . . 138
The Staff of the Court of Sans-Souci 138
Gustav von Alvensleben as champion of State interests at the Court of
Coblenz 139

CHAPTER VII

ON THE ROAD BETWEEN FRANKFORT AND BERLIN

Bismarck summoned to frighten Manteuffel 140
Marquis Moustier tries to influence Bismarck in the direction of the
Western Powers 141
Goltz and Pourtalès as occasional confidants of the King against
Manteuffel 141
Manteuffel in conflict with the ' Kreuzzeitung ' party respecting
Rhino Quehl 142
Letters from Gerlach relating to this dispute 144
Manteuffel sulks 149
Count Albert von Alvensleben as ' bogey ' 150
Bismarck as herald of peace 150
Bismarck releases Manteuffel from Quehl, and the agents employed for
stealing the dispatches 151
Frederick William IV's idea of the position of a Minister . . . 151 .
A paper of Manteuffel's and one of Frederick William IV's upon the
composition of the First Chamber 152
Bismarck as Royal confidant in the transactions with the Conservative
party of the Second Chamber 153
The King's wrath at Bismarck's delay 154
Interned in the Castle of Charlottenburg 154
Alteration of tone in the Conservative party through Bismarck . . 155
xiv

CONTENTS

	PAGE
First Chamber or House of Lords?	156
Bismarck's proposal for the formation of the House of Lords	158
Opposition of Manteuffel and the Camarilla to Bismarck's appointment as Minister	159
Bismarck and the leaders of the Conservative party	159
Bismarck as the King's editor	160
Slight causes, great effects	162

CHAPTER VIII

VISIT TO PARIS

Count Hatzfeldt invites Bismarck to Paris	163
Change in the King's mood	163
Queen Victoria and Prince Albert in Paris	163
Prejudice of Prince Albert and the Princess Royal Victoria against Bismarck	164
Conversation with the Crown Princess upon the future of the Monarchy	164
Attitude of Queen Victoria	165
A supper at Versailles; Bismarck as distributor of tickets	166
Plebeian manners of French Court-society under the Second Empire	167
Meeting with the Emperor Napoleon III	168
The Court of Berlin is out of temper with Bismarck on account of his visit to Paris	169
Expression of this ill-temper	169
Bismarck's judgment of Napoleon III	169
Acceptance of this opinion by Frederick William IV	170
The conception of Legitimacy	170
Extacts from Bismarck's correspondence with Gerlach on the relations of Prussia to Napoleon III	171

CHAPTER IX

TRAVELS. REGENCY

Fresh advances of the King	211
Herr von Bismarck is offered the Ministry of Finance	211
Napoleon's idea of a Franco-Prussian understanding for securing Prussian neutrality in case of a war with Austria about Italy	212
Bismarck's reply to Napoleon's proposal	214
Hunting-trip to Denmark and Sweden	215
Audience of King Frederick VII of Denmark	215
Aversion of the Schleswig-Holsteiners to the formation of a new Small State	216

BISMARCK

PAGE

Fall in Sweden ; return to Berlin ; hunting expedition to Courland . 216
The King's first illness 216
Apoplectic fit 217
Interview with the Prince of Prussia 217
Bismarck dissuades the Prince from entering upon his Regency with a
refusal of the Constitution 217
The Prince as the King's representative 218
Intrigue against the Prince 218
The Prince appointed Regent 222
Manteuffel's dismissal 222
Interview with the Prince of Prussia respecting the appointment as
Ambassador to St. Petersburg 223
Usedom and his wife 224
Episode : the endeavor to retire in 1869 225
Letters of King William to Bismarck 226
Arrangement of the difference 227
Interview with the Prince of Prussia (*continuation*); the Ministry of the
New Era 232
Princess Augusta 233
Count Schwerin 233
The banker Levinstein as Austrian agent, and as confidant of Man-
teuffel's Ministry 234
Corruption in the Foreign Office 237

CHAPTER X

ST. PETERSBURG

Friendship of the Emperor Nicholas I for Austria in 1849, and at
Olmütz 239
The Czar's distrust of his own subjects 240
Nicholas and Frederick William IV 240
St. Petersburg society at the time 241
The *Monsieur décoré* in Paris and St. Petersburg once more . 244
Life in the streets at St. Petersburg 245
Social tone of the younger generation 246
Their anti-German spirit perceptible in political relations . . 246
Prince Gortchakoff as Bismarck's patron and adversary . . 246
Causes of Gortchakoff's ill-temper 247
Does Germany need a war with Russia ? 247
Hospitality at the Imperial Palaces . . . , . . 247
A Grand Ducal *enfant terrible* 249
Peculation of the Court servants 249
An Imperial tallow bill 249

CONTENTS

PAGE

Russian persistency : the sentinel dating from Catherine II. . . 250
Bismarck's want of influence on the decisions in Berlin . . . 251
The accuracy of his reports is impugned to the Regent . . . 251
Count Münster as Bismarck's overseer at St. Petersburg . . . 251
Political moves of Russian diplomacy 252
Violation of postal secrecy a royal privilege 252
Austrian practice 252
The ordinary postal letter to the Prussian Ambassador in Vienna or St.
    Petersburg as a method of conveying unpleasant communications to
    the Austrian or Russian Government 253
Secrecy of letters in the Thurn and Taxis Post 253
Customary abuses in the Prussian Embassy at Vienna up to 1852 . 254
Severe Austrian measures against unfaithful employés in the Foreign
    Service 254
Russian means for satisfying discontented employés 254
Recollections of the visit ιo Moscow 255
Correspondence with Prince Obolenski 256
Illness and treatment by a Russian ' physician ' 258
At the baths of Nauheim 260
Long illness from inflammation of the lungs at Hohendorf . . . 260

CHAPTER XI

INTERMEDIATE POSITION

Bismarck is proposed to the Regent as Foreign Minister . . . 261
Bismarck develops his programme 262
The Regent declares himself in favour of the views of Schleinitz . . 263
Princess Augusta as Herr von Schleinitz's guardian angel . . 264
R. von Auerswald 264
Ministerial crisis occasioned by the Homage question . . . 264
Roon's letter of June 27, 1861 264
Bismarck's answer 266
His journey to Berlin 270
Progress of the crisis after Roon's letter of July 24, 1861 . . . 270
Coronation of William I 273
Conversation with Queen Augusta upon the German policy of Prussia 274
Ministerial Bill-jobbing 274
Prince Hohenlohe-Ingelfingen as Deputy Minister President . . 275
Summons of Bismarck from St. Petersburg to Berlin, April, 1862 . 276
His appointment to Paris 276
Bismarck's letter to Roon 277
Roon's letter to Bismarck 278
Bismarck's answer 279

BISMARCK

PAGE

Interview with Napoleon III ; Proposal of a Franco-Prussian Alliance 282
Austria's propositions to Napoleon III 283
Journey to the South of France ; correspondence with Roon . . 284
Telegraphic summons of September 18 293
Audience of the Crown Prince 294
Audience at Babelsberg 295
Appointment of Bismarck as Minister and provisional President of the Ministry of State 297

CHAPTER XII

RETROSPECT OF PRUSSIAN POLICY

Want of independence and energy in the Foreign and German policy of Prussia since the time of Frederick the Great 298
Particularist character of Prussian policy 298
Determining influence of the Polish question 299
The Reichenbach Convention and its signification . . . 299
Neglected opportunities in the history of Prussia . . . 300
Mistake of the interposition of 1805 301
Prussia as vassal State of Russia under Nicholas I . . . 302
Prussia becomes Russia's creditor by her attitude in the Crimean War, and during the Polish Insurrection in 1863 303
Causes of the feeling of independence at the Court of Berlin . 303
Superiority of Prussia to Russia and Austria in military preparations 304
Prussia waits in the ante-chamber at Paris, for admission to sign as a Great Power 305
Mistaken nature of policy at that time 306
The inheritance of Frederick the Great in the hands of his *Epigoni* . 307
Who bears the political responsibility in an absolute monarchy ? . 307
Ministerial responsibility in a Constitutional State . . . 308
The person responsible for Prussian policy under Frederick William IV 308
Why Bismarck could not become a Minister of Frederick William IV 309
Preference of pure absolutism without a Parliament to absolutism supported by a docile one 310
The Italian war 310
Want of plan in the Prussian policy of the time under the domination of Princess Augusta and Herr von Schleinitz . . . 311
Cross-movements against Bismarck's direction of foreign policy . 312
Blood and iron 313
Bismarck strengthens the desponding King by reminding him of the sword-belt of the Prussian officer 315
Seriousness of the situation 316

CONTENTS

CHAPTER XIII

DYNASTIES AND STOCKS

PAGE

The dynasties in their attitude towards the German National question 318

Prussia's position in the Confederation 318

The dream of a Dualistic policy based on the agreement of Austria and Prussia is destroyed by Schwarzenberg's dispatch of December 7, 1850 : a turning-point in Bismarck's views 319

Prussia as a Great Power 320

German patriotism requires the intervention of dynastic attachment . 320

Strength of the National feeling in other nations . . . 321

German stock-Particularism 322

The dynastic attachment of the Guelfs 324

For Bismarck German National feeling is the stronger force . . 325

How far are dynastic interests justified in Germany ? . . . 325

Bismarck's struggles with Prussian Particularism . . . 326

The unlimited political sovereignty of the dynasties acquired by revolution at the cost of the nation and its unity 326

Unnatural dismemberment of the German people by dynastic boundaries 327

CHAPTER XIV

THE MINISTRY OF CONFLICT

Karl von Bodelschwingh 328

Count Itzenplitz 329

Von Jagow 329

Von Selchow 330

Count Fr. zu Eulenburg 331

Von Roon 331

Von Mühler 333

Count zur Lippe 334

Letter from the King to von Vincke of Olbendorf . . 345

CHAPTER XV

THE ALVENSLEBEN CONVENTION

Polonism and absolutism in conflict at the Russian Court . . 338

Russo-Polish efforts for fraternisation 339

Alexander II on the insecurity of the Polish possessions . . 340

Alexander II invites Bismarck to enter the Russian service. . 341

BISMARCK

PAGE

Advantages of Russian friendship for German struggles towards unity 342
Attitude of Austria during the Pclish Insurrection 343
Napoleon III's attitude in the Polish question 344
Difficulty of the Polish question for Prussia 346
Significance of the Alvensleben Military Convention 346
Prince Gortchakoff 347
First meeting with Herr Hintzpeter 347

CHAPTER XVI

THE DANTZIC EPISODE

Bismarck and the Emperor Frederick 349
Relaxation of the Press regulations 349
The Crown Prince's Dantzic speech 350
His expostulatory letter and the King's answer 351
Bismarck withholds the King from taking extreme steps against his son 351
Indiscretions of the 'Times' 352
Conjectures as to the authors of this publication 353
Conference with the Crown Prince at Gastein 355
Fresh protest of the Crown Prince 355
Tension between the King and the Crown Prince 356
Expressions used by Bismarck to the Crown Prince 357
Memorandum of the Crown Prince and correspondence between the
    King and Bismarck connected with it 358

CHAPTER XVII

THE FRANKFORT DIET OF PRINCES

Count Rechberg 366
How Bismarck won Rechberg's confidence 367
Attempt at a union of all Germany on the basis of Dualism . . . 368
Probable effect of such an arrangement 368
What effect would the establishment of Austrian predominance have
    had ? 369
Agreement of Prussia and Austria the preliminary condition to prevent
    English and European interference in the Danish question . . 370
Discussion between Bismarck and Count Karolyi on the relations of
    Prussia and Austria 370
Contempt for Prussia in Vienna 371
Differences in character between Frederick William IV and William I 371
Over-estimate of the weakening effect of the conflict on Prussia's foreign
    poiicy and military capacity 372

CONTENTS

	PAGE
Belief in the military superiority of Austria	. 373
Disinclination of Austria to a peaceable Dualism . . .	. 373
Invitation to the Frankfort Diet of Princes . . .	. 374
The Emperor Francis Joseph at Gastein	. 375
First impression of the invitation on the King	. 375
Bismarck against going to the Diet of Princes	. 376
King John of Saxony at Baden	. 376
Effect upon the German Middle States of Prussia's holding aloof	. 377
Rechberg approaches Prussia	. 378
Death of Frederick VII of Denmark	. 378
Brilliant commencement of the Dual policy	. 379
Joint action with Austria endangered by military influences .	. 379
Culmination and turning-point of the attempt at a friendly Dualism	. 380
Conference of the two Monarchs and their Ministers at Schönbrunn	. 380
Rechberg's position attacked	. 382
Negotiations as to a future admission of Austria into the Zollverein	. 383
Bismarck is in favor of a *pactum de contrahendo* on political grounds, but opposed to a Customs-union	. 383
Thwarting of Bismarck's policy by Bodelschwingh, Itzenplitz, and Delbrück	. 384
Rechberg is dismissed and replaced by Count Mensdorff . .	. 384
Extracts from letters of Thile, Abeken, and Goltz . . .	. 385
Uncertainty and changeableness of Austrian friendship . .	. 385

CHAPTER XVIII

KING LEWIS II OF BAVARIA

At the Court of Munich	. 388
Crown Prince Lewis	. 388
Characteristics of King Lewis II	. 389
Passages from the correspondence of King Lewis with Bismarck .	. 399

PORTRAIT OF OTTO VON BISMARCK IN 1834 . . . *Frontispiece*

FACSIMILE OF PRINCE BISMARCK'S HANDWRITING , . *To face p.* 13

BISMARCK

CHAPTER I

TO THE FIRST UNITED DIET

I LEFT school at Easter 1832, a normal product of our state system of education; a Pantheist, and, if not a Republican, at least with the persuasion that the Republic was the most rational form of government; reflecting too upon the causes which could decide millions of men permanently to obey *one man*, when all the while I was hearing from grown up people much bitter or contemptuous criticism of their rulers. Moreover, I had brought away with me 'German-National' impressions from Plamann's preparatory school, conducted on Jahn's drill-system, in which I lived from my sixth to my twelfth year. These impressions remained in the stage of theoretical reflections, and were not strong enough to extirpate my innate Prussian monarchical sentiments. My historical sympathies remained on the side of authority. To my childish ideas of justice Harmodius and Aristogeiton, as well as Brutus, were criminals, and Tell a rebel and murderer. Every German prince who resisted the Emperor before the Thirty Years' war roused my ire; but from the Great Elector onwards I was partisan enough to take an anti-

I

BISMARCK

imperial view, and to find it natural that things should
have been in readiness for the Seven Years' war. Yet
the German-National feeling remained so strong in me
that, at the beginning of my University life, I at once entered into relations with *Burschenschaft*, or group of students which made the promotion of a national sentiment
its aim. But after personal intimacy with its members, I
disliked their refusal to 'give satisfaction,' as well as
their want of breeding in externals and of acquaintance
with the forms and manners of good society; and a still
closer acquaintance bred an aversion to the extravagance of
their political views, based upon a lack of either culture or
knowledge of the conditions of life which historical causes
had brought into existence, and which I, with my seventeen
years, had had more opportunities of observing than most
of these students, for the most part older than myself.
Their ideas gave me the impression of an association between Utopian theories and defective breeding. Nevertheless, I retained my own private National sentiments, and
my belief that in the near future events would lead to German unity; in fact, I made a bet with my American friend
Coffin that this aim would be attained in twenty years.

In my first half-year at Göttingen occurred the Hambach festival * (May 27, 1832), the 'festal ode' of which
still remains in my memory; in my third the Frankfort
outbreak † (April 3, 1833). These manifestations revolted
me. Mob interference with political authority conflicted

* [A gathering of, it is said, 30,000 at the Castle of Hambach in the
Palatinate ; where speeches were made in favour of Germany, unity, and the
Republic.]

† [An attempt made by a handful of students and peasants to blow up
the Federal Diet in revenge for some Press regulations passed by it. They
stormed the guard house, but were then suppressed.]

2

with my Prussian schooling, and I returned to Berlin with less liberal opinions than when I quitted it; but this reaction was again somewhat mitigated when I was brought into immediate connexion with the workings of the political machine. Upon foreign politics, with which the public at that time occupied itself but little, my views, as regards the War of Liberation, were taken from the standpoint of a Prussian officer. On looking at the map, the possession of Strasburg by France exasperated me, and a visit to Heidelberg, Spires and the Palatinate made me feel revengeful and militant. In the period before 1848 there was scarcely any prospect for a *Kammergerichts-Auskultator* and *Regirungs-Referendar*, who had no relations whatever with the ministerial and higher official circles, of partaking in Prussian politics until he had travelled the monotonous road which would lead him after decades of years through the grades of a bureaucratic career, to gain notice in the higher posts, and thereby win promotion. In the family circle in those days, men like Pommer-Esche and Delbrück were represented to me as model leaders on the official road, and work upon and within the Zollverein was recommended as the best line to strike into. So far as, at my then age, I seriously thought at all of an official career, I had diplomacy in view, even after my application to the minister Ancillon had evoked very little encouragement thereto from him. Not to me, but in exalted circles, he used to indicate Prince Felix Lichnowski as an example of what our diplomacy lacked, although it might have been surmised that this personage, as he exhibited himself at that time in Berlin, would not exactly come in the way of an appreciative estimate from a minister sprung from an Evangelical clerical stock.

3

BISMARCK

The minister had the impression that the category of our ' home-made ' Prussian squirearchy did not furnish him with the desirable material to draw upon for our diplomacy, and was not adapted to make up for the want of address which he found in the *personnel* of this branch of the service. This impression was not absolutely unjustified. As minister, I have always had a fellow-provincial's kindness for native-born Prussian diplomatists, but my official sense of duty has rarely allowed me to gratify this preference; as a rule only when the personages in question were transferred to a diplomatic from a military position. In purely Prussian civil-diplomats, who have never, or only inadequately, come under the influence of military discipline, I have as a rule observed too strong a tendency to criticism, to ' cocksureness,' to opposition and personal touchiness, intensified by the discontent which the Old Prussian gentleman's feeling of equality experiences when a man of his own rank is put over his head, or becomes his superior otherwise than under military conditions. In the army, men in a similar position have been for centuries accustomed to seeing this happen; and when they themselves have reached higher positions, they pour the dregs of their ill-temper towards former superiors upon the heads of those who afterwards become their subordinates. Moreover, in diplomacy there is this to be considered, that those among the aspirants who possess means or a chance knowledge of foreign languages (especially of French) regard those very circumstances as a ground for preference, and therefore make more claims upon those highest in authority and are more inclined than others to criticise them. An acquaintance with languages (after the fashion in which it is possessed even by head-waiters) was

4

with us readily made the basis for a belief in diplomacy as one's vocation, especially so long as our Ambassadorial reports, particularly those *ad regem*, had to be in French; as was the official rule in force (though not always followed), till I became minister. I have known many among our older ambassadors step into the highest positions simply on account of their proficiency in French, without any knowledge of politics; they only included in their dispatches, too, what they could put fluently into French. Even as late as 1862 I had to report officially in French from St. Petersburg; and the Ambassadors who wrote even their private letters to the Minister in French recommended themselves thereby as having a special vocation for the diplomatic career, even when they were notoriously deficient in political judgment.

Moreover, I cannot say that Ancillon was wrong in having the impression, with regard to most of the candidates from our squirearchy, that they found difficulty in escaping from the narrow horizon which bounded Berliners of those days, or, as one might say, from their 'provincial' views, and that in diplomatic matters they would not easily succeed in laying a coat of European varnish over the specifically Prussian bureaucrat. How these observations acted in practice is clearly shown when we go through the list of our diplomatists of those days: one is astonished to find so few native Prussians among them. The fact of being the son of a foreign ambassador accredited to Berlin was of itself ground for preference. The diplomatists who had grown up in small courts and had been taken into the Prussian service had not infrequently the advantage over natives of greater assurance in Court circles and a greater absence of shyness. An especial example of this tendency

5

was Herr von Schleinitz. In the list we find also members of noble houses in whom descent supplied the place of talent. I scarcely remember from the period when I was appointed to Frankfort anyone of Prussian descent being appointed chief of an important mission, except myself, Baron Carl von Werther, Canitz, and Count Max Hatzfeldt (who had a French wife). Foreign names were at a premium: Brassier, Perponcher, Savigny, Oriola. It was presumed that they had greater fluency in French, and they were more out of the common. Another feature was the disinclination to accept personal responsibility when not covered by unmistakable instructions, just as was the case in the military service in 1806 in the old school of the Frederickian period. Even in those days we were breeding stuff for officers, even as high as the rank of regimental commander, to a pitch of perfection attained by no other state; but beyond that rank the native Prussian blood was no longer fertile in talents, as in the time of Frederick the Great. Our most successful commanders, Blücher, Gneisenau, Moltke, Goeben, were not original Prussian products, any more than Stein, Hardenberg, Motz, and Grolman in the Civil Service. It is as though our statesmen, like the trees in nurseries, needed transplanting in order that their roots might find full development.

Ancillon advised me first of all to pass my examination as *Regirungs-Assessor*, and then, by the circuitous route of employment in the Zollverein to seek admittance into the *German* diplomacy of Prussia; he did not, it would seem, anticipate in a scion of the native squire-archy a vocation for European diplomacy. I took his hint to heart, and resolved first of all to go up for my examination as *Regirungs-Assessor*.

6

TO THE FIRST UNITED DIET

The persons and institutions of our judicial system with which I was in the first instance concerned gave my youthful conceptions more material for criticism than for respect. The practical education of the *Auscultator* began with keeping the minutes of the Criminal Courts, and to this post I was promoted out of my proper turn by the *Rath*, Herr von Brauchitsch, under whom I worked, because in those days I wrote a more than usually quick and legible hand. Of the examinations, as criminal proceedings in the inquisitorial method of that day were called, the one that has made the most lasting impression upon me related to a widely ramifying association in Berlin for the purpose of unnatural vice. The club arrangements of the accomplices, the agenda books, the levelling effect through all classes of a common pursuit of the forbidden —all this, even in 1835, pointed to a demoralisation in no whit less than that evidenced by the proceedings against the Heinzes, husband and wife, in October 1891. The ramifications of this society extended even into the highest circles. It was ascribed to the influence of Prince Wittgenstein that the reports of the case were demanded from the Ministry of Justice, and were never returned—at least, during the time I served on the tribunal.

After I had been keeping the records for four months, I was transferred to the City Court, before which civil causes are tried, and was suddenly promoted from the mechanical occupation of writing from dictation to an independent post, which, having regard to my inexperience and my sentiments, made my position difficult. The first stage in which the legal novice was called to a more independent sphere of activity was in connexion with divorce proceedings. Obviously regarded as the least important,

7

they were entrusted to the most incapable *Rath*, Prätorius
by name, and under him were left to the tender mercies of
unfledged *Auscultators*, who had to make upon this *corpus
vile* their first experiments in the part of judges—of course,
under the nominal responsibility of Herr Prätorius, who
nevertheless took no part in their proceedings. By way
of indicating this gentleman's character, it was told to us
young people that when, in the course of a sitting, he was
roused from a light slumber to give his vote, he used to
say, ' I vote with my colleague Tempelhof '—whereupon it
was sometimes necessary to point out to him that Herr
Tempelhof was not present.

On one occasion I represented to him my embarrassment at having, though only a few months more than
twenty years old, to undertake the attempt at a reconciliation between an agitated couple : a matter crowned, according to my view, with a certain ecclesiastical and moral
' nimbus,' with which in my state of mind I did not feel
able to cope. I found Prätorius in the irritable mood of
an old man awakened at an untimely moment, who had
besides all the aversion of an old bureaucrat to a young
man of birth. He said, with a contemptuous smile, ' It
is very annoying, Herr *Referendarius*, when a man can do
nothing for himself ; I will show you how to do it.' I returned with him into the judge's room. The case was
one in which the husband wanted a divorce and the wife
not. The husband accused her of adultery ; the wife,
tearful and declamatory, asserted her innocence ; and despite all manner of ill-treatment from the man, wanted to
remain with him. Prätorius, with his peculiar clicking
lisp, thus addressed the woman : ' But, my good woman,
don't be so stupid. What good will it do you ? When

you get home, you husband will give you a jacketing until you can stand no more. Come now, simply say "yes," and then you will be quit of the sot.' To which the wife, crying hysterically, replied : ' 1 am an honest woman! I will not have that indignity put upon me! I don't want to be divorced!' After manifold retorts and rejoinders in this tone, Prätorius turned to me with the words : ' As she will not listen to reason, write as follows, Herr *Referendarius*,' and dictated to me some words which, owing to the deep impression they made upon me, I remember to this day. ' Inasmuch as the attempt at reconciliation has been made, and arguments drawn from the sphere of religion and morality have proved fruitless, further proceedings were taken as follows.' My chief then rose and said, 'Now, you see how it is done, and in future leave me in peace about such things.' I accompanied him to the door, and went on with the case. The Divorce Court stage of my career lasted, so far as I can remember, from four to six weeks; a reconciliation case never came before me again. There was a certain necessity for the ordinance respecting proceedings in divorce cases, to which Frederick William IV was obliged to confine himself after his attempts to introduce a *law* for the substantial alteration of the Marriage Law had foundered upon the opposition of the Council of State. With regard to this matter it may be mentioned that, as a result of this ordinance, the Attorney-General was first introduced into those provinces in which the old Prussian common law prevailed as *defensor matrimonii*, and to prevent collusion between the parties.

More inviting was the subsequent stage of petty cases, where the untrained young jurist at least acquired practice in listening to pleadings and examining witnesses, but where more use was made of him as a drudge than was met by the resulting benefit to his instruction. The locality and the procedure partook somewhat of the restless bustle of a railway manager's work. The space in which the leading *Rath* and the three or four *Auscultators* sat with their backs to the public was surrounded by a wooden screen, and round about the four-cornered recess formed thereby surged an ever-changing and more or less noisy mob of parties to the suits.

My impression of institutions and persons was not essentially modified when I had been transferred to the Administration. In order to abbreviate the detour to diplomacy, I applied to a Rhenish government, that of Aachen, where the course could be gone through in two years, whereas in the ' old ' provinces at least three years were required.[1]

I can well imagine that in making the appointments to the Rhenish Governing Board in 1816 the same procedure was adopted as at the organisation of Elsass-Lothringen in 1871. The authorities who had to contribute a portion of their staff would not be likely to respond to the call of state requirements by putting their best foot foremost to accomplish the difficult task of assimilating a newly acquired population, but would have chosen those members of their offices whose departure was desired by their superiors or wished by themselves; in the board were to be found former secretaries of prefectures and other relics of the French administration. The *personnel* did not all correspond to the ideal which floated unwarrantably enough before my eyes at twenty-one, and still less was this the

[1] See the ' Proceedings during my stay at Aachen ' in *Bismarck-Jahrbuch III.*, and the ' Samples of Examination for the Referendariat ' in *Bismarck-Jahrbuch II.*

case with the details of the current business. I recollect that, what with the many differences of opinion between officials and governed, or with internal differences of opinion among each of these two categories, whose polemics for many years considerably swelled the bulk of the records, my habitual impression was, ' Well, yes, that is *one* way of doing it ; ' and that questions, the decision of which one way or the other was not worth the paper wasted upon them, created a mass of business which a single prefect could have disposed of with the fourth part of the energy bestowed upon them. Nevertheless, except for the subordinate officials, the day's work was slight ; as regards heads of departments especially, a mere sinecure. I quitted Aachen with a very poor opinion of our bureaucracy, in detail and collectively, with the exception of the gifted President, Count Arnim-Boitzenburg. My opinion of the detail became more favourable owing to my next subsequent experience in the government at Potsdam, to which I got transferred in the year 1837 ; because there, unlike the arrangement in other provinces, the indirect taxes were at the disposal of the government, and it was just these that were important to me if I wanted to make customs-policy the basis of my future.

The members of the board made a better impression upon me than those at Aachen ; but yet, taking them as a whole, it was an impression of pigtail and periwig, in which category my youthful presumption also placed the paternal dignified President-in-Chief, von Bassewitz ; while the President of the Aachen Government, Count Arnim, wore the generic wig of the state service, it is true, but no intellectual pigtail. When therefore I quitted the service of the state for a country life, I imported into the relations which as a landed proprietor I had with the officials, an opinion, which I now see to have been too mean, of the value of our bureaucracy, and perhaps too great an inclination to criticise them. I remember that as substitute provincial president I had to give my verdict on a plan for abolishing the election of those officials; I expressed myself to the effect that the bureaucracy, as it ascended from the provincial president, sank in the general esteem; it had preserved it only in the person of the provincial president, who wore a Janus head, one face turned towards the bureaucracy, the other towards the country.

The tendency to interference in the most various relations of life was, under the paternal government of those days, perhaps greater than now; but the instruments of such interference were less numerous, and, as regards culture and breeding, stood much higher than do some of those of to-day. The officials of the right worshipful royal Prussian government were honest, well-read and well-bred officials; but their benevolent activity did not always meet with recognition, because from want of local experience they went to pieces on matters of detail, in regard to which the views of the learned citizen at the green table were not always superior to the healthy common-sense criticism of the peasant intelligence. The members of the Governing Boards had in those days *multa*, not *multum*, to do; and the lack of higher duties resulted in their not finding a sufficient quantity of important business, and led them in their zeal for duty to go beyond the needs of the governed, into a tendency to over-regulation—in a word, into what the Swiss calls *Befehlerle*.[1] To glance at a comparison with present conditions, it had been hoped that the

[1] [Say 'red tape.']

state authorities would have been relieved of business and of officials by the introduction of the local self-government of to-day; but, on the contrary, the number of the officials and their load of business have been very considerably increased by correspondence, and friction with the machinery of self-government, from the provincial councillor down to the rural parish administration. Sooner or later the flaw must be reached, and we shall be crushed by the burden of clerkdom, especially in the subordinate bureaucracy.

Moreover, bureaucratic pressure upon private life is intensified by the mode in which self-government works in practice and encroaches more sharply than before on the rural parishes. Formerly the provincial president, who stood in as close relations with the people as with the state, formed the lowest step in the state bureaucracy. Below him were local authorities, who were no doubt subject to control, but not in the same measure as nowadays to the disciplinary powers of the district, or the ministerial, bureaucracy. The rural population enjoys to-day, by virtue of the measure of self-government conceded to it, an autonomy, not perhaps similar to that which the towns had long ago; but it has received, in the shape of the official commissioner, a chief who is kept in disciplinary check by superior instructions proceeding from the provincial president, under the threat of penalties, and compelled to burden his fellow-citizens in his district with lists, notifications, and inquisitions as the political hierarchy thinks good. The governed *contribuens plebs* no longer possess, in the court of the provincial president, that guarantee against blundering encroachment which, at an earlier period, was to be found in the circumstance that people resident in the district who became provincial presidents, as a rule resolved to remain so in their own districts all their life long, and sympathised with the joys and sorrows of the district. To-day the post of provincial president is the lowest step in the ladder of the higher administration, sought after by young ' assessors' who have a justifiable ambition to make a career. To obtain it they have more need of ministerial favour than of the goodwill of the local population, and they attempt to win this favour by conspicuous zeal, and by ' taking it out of' the official commissioners of the so-called local administration, or by carrying out valueless bureaucratic experiments. Therein lies for the most part the inducement to overburden their subordinates in the local self-government system. Thus self-government means the aggravation of bureaucracy, increase in the number of officials, and of their powers and interference in private life.

It is only human nature to be more keenly sensitive to the thorns than to the roses of every institution, and that the thorns should irritate one against the existing state of things. The old government officials, when they came into direct contact with the governed population, showed themselves to be pedantic, and estranged from the practical working of life by their occupation at the green table; but they left behind them the impression of toiling honestly and conscientiously for justice. The same thing cannot be assumed in all their degrees of the wheels in the machine of the self-government of to-day in those country districts where the parties stand in acute opposition to each other; goodwill towards political friends, frame of mind as regards opponents, readily become a hindrance to the impartial maintenance of institutions. According to my experiences in earlier and more recent times, I should, for the rest, not like to allow impartiality, when comparing judicial and administrative decisions, to the former alone, not at least in every instance. On the contrary, I have preserved an impression that judges of small local courts succumb more easily to strong party influences than do administrative officials; nor need we invent any psychological reason for the fact that, given equal culture, the latter should *à priori* be considered less just and conscientious in their official decisions than the former. But I certainly do assume that official decisions do not gain in honesty and moderation by being arrived at collectively; for apart from the fact that, in the case of voting by majority, arithmetic and chance take the place of logical reasoning, that feeling of personal responsibility, in which lies the essential guarantee for the conscientiousness of the decision, is lost directly it comes about by means of anonymous majorities.

The course of business in the two boards of Potsdam and Aachen was not very encouraging for my ambition. I found the business assigned to me petty and tedious, and my labours in the department of suits arising from the grist tax and from the compulsory contribution to the building of the embankment at Rotzi, near Wusterhausen, have left behind in me no sentimental regrets for my sphere of work in those days. Renouncing the ambition for an official career, I readily complied with the wishes of my parents by taking up the humdrum management of our Pomeranian estates. I had made up my mind to live and die in the country, after attaining successes in agriculture—perhaps in war also, if war should come. So far as my country life left me any ambition at all, it was that of a lieutenant in the Landwehr.

15

BISMARCK

The impressions that I had received in my childhood were little adapted to make a squire of me. In Plamann's educational establishment, conducted on the systems of Pestalozzi and Jahn, the ' von ' before my name was a disadvantage, so far as my childish comfort was concerned, in my intercourse with my fellow-pupils and my teachers. Even at the high school at the Grey Friars I had to suffer, as regards individual teachers, from that hatred of nobility which had clung to the greater part of the educated *bourgeoisie* as a reminiscence of the days before 1806. But even the aggressive tendency which occasionally appeared in *bourgeois* circles never gave me any inducement to advance in the opposite direction. My father was free from aristocratic prejudices, and his inward sense of equality had been modified, if at all, by his youthful impressions as an officer, but in no way by any over-estimate of inherited rank. My mother was the daughter of Mencken, Privy Councillor to Frederick the Great, Frederick William II, and Frederick William III, who sprang from a family of Leipzig professors, and was accounted in those days a Liberal. The later generations of the Menckens—those immediately preceding me—had found their way to Prussia in the Foreign Office and about the Court. Baron von Stein has quoted my grandfather Mencken as an honest, strongly Liberal official. Under these circumstances, the views which I imbibed with my mother's milk were Liberal rather than reactionary; and if my mother had lived to see my ministerial activity, she would scarcely have been in accord with its direction, even though she would have experienced great joy in the external results of my official career. She had grown up in bureaucratic and court circles; Frederick William IV spoke of her as ' Mienchen,' in memory of childish games. I can therefore declare it an unjust estimate of my views in my younger years, when ' the prejudices of my rank' are thrown in my teeth and it is maintained that a recollection of the privileges of the nobility has been the starting-point of my domestic policy.

Moreover, the unlimited authority of the old Prussian monarchy was not, and is not, the final word of my convictions. As to that, to be sure, this authority of the monarch constitutionally existed in the first United Diet, but accompanied by the wish and anticipation that the unlimited power of the King, without being overturned, might fix the measure of its own limitation. Absolutism primarily demands impartiality, honesty, devotion to duty, energy, and inward humility in the ruler. These may be present, and yet male and female favourites (in the best case thé lawful wife), the monarch's own vanity and susceptibility to flattery, will nevertheless diminish the fruits of his good intentions, inasmuch as the monarch is not omniscient and cannot have an equal understanding of all branches of his office. As early as 1847 I was in favour of an effort to secure the possibility of public criticism of the government in parliament and in the press, in order to shelter the monarch from the danger of having blinkers put on him by women, courtiers, sycophants, and visionaries, hindering him from taking a broad view of his duties as monarch, or from avoiding and correcting his mistakes. This conviction of mine became all the more deeply impressed upon me in proportion as I became better acquainted with Court circles, and had to defend the interest of the state from their influences and also from the opposition of a departmental patriotism. The interests of the state alone have guided me, and it has been a calumny when publicists, even well-meaning, have accused me of having ever advocated an aristocratic system. I have never regarded birth as a substitute for want of ability; whenever I have come forward on behalf of landed property, it has not been in the interests of proprietors of my own class, but because I see in the decline of agriculture one of the greatest dangers to our permanence as a state. The ideal that has always floated before me has been a monarchy which should be so far controlled by an independent national representation—according to my notion, representing classes or callings—that monarch or parliament would not be able to alter the existing statutory position before the law *separately* but only *communi consensu ;* with publicity, and public criticism, by press and Diet, of all political proceedings.

Whoever has the conviction that uncontrolled Absolutism, as it was first brought upon the stage by Louis XIV, was the most fitting form of government for German subjects, must lose it after making a special study in the history of Courts, and such critical observations as I was enabled to institute at the court of Frederick William IV (whom personally I loved and revered) in Manteuffel's days. The King was a religious absolutist with a divine vocation, and the ministers after Brandenburg were content as a rule if they were covered by the royal signature even when they could not have personally answered for the contents of what was signed. I remember that on one occasion a high Court official of absolutist opinions, on hearing of the news of the royalist rising at Neuchatel, observed, with some confusion, in the presence of myself and several of his colleagues : ' That is a royalism of which nowadays one has to go very far from Court to get experience.' Yet, as a rule, sarcasm was not a habit of this old gentleman.

Observations which I made in the country as to the venality and chicanery of the ' district sergeants' and other subordinate officials, and petty conflicts which I had with the government in Stettin as deputy of the ' Circle' and deputy for the provincial president, increased my aversion to the rule of the bureaucracy. I may mention one of these conflicts. While I was representing the president then on leave, I received an order from the government to compel the patron of Külz, that was myself, to undertake certain burdens. I put the order aside, meaning to give it to the president on his return, was repeatedly worried about it, and fined a thaler, to be forwarded through the post. I now drew up a statement, in which I figured as having appeared, first of all as representative of the *Landrath*, and secondly as patron of Külz. The party cited made the prescribed representations to himself in his capacity as No. 1, and then proceeded in his capacity of No. 2 to set forth the ground on which he had to decline the application; after which the statement was approved and subscribed by him in his double capacity. The government understood a joke, and ordered the fine to be refunded. In other cases, things resulted in less pleasant heckling. I had a critical disposition, and was consequently liberal, in the sense in which the word was then used among landed proprietors to imply discontent with the bureaucracy, the majority of whom on their side were men more liberal than myself, though in another sense.

I again slipped off the rails of my parliamentary liberal tendencies, with regard to which I found little understanding or sympathy in Pomerania, but which in Schönhausen met with the acquiescence of men in my own district, like Count Wartensleben of Karow, Schierstädt-Dahlen, and others (the same men of whom some were among the party of Church patrons in the New Era subsequently condemned). This was the result of the style, to me unsympathetic, in which the opposition was conducted in the first United Diet, to which I was summoned, only for the last six weeks of the session, as substitute for Deputy von Brauchitsch, who was laid up with illness. The speeches of the East Prussians, Saucken-Tarputschen and Alfred Auerswald, the sentimentality of Beckerath, the Gallo-Rhenish liberalism of Heydt and Mevissen, and the boisterous violence of Vincke's speeches, disgusted me; and even at this date when I read the proceedings they give me the impression of imported phrases made to pattern. I felt that the King was on the right track, and could claim to be allowed time, and not be hurried in his development.

I came into conflict with the Opposition the first time I made a longer speech than usual, on May 17, 1847, when I combated the legend that the Prussians had gone to war in 1813 to get a constitution, and gave free expression to my natural indignation at the idea that foreign domination was in itself no adequate reason for fighting.[1] It appeared to me undignified that the nation, as a set-off to its having freed itself, should hand in to the King an account payable in the paragraphs of a constitution. My performance produced a storm. I remained in the tribune turning over the leaves of a newspaper which lay there, and then, when the commotion had subsided, I finished my speech.

[1] *Politische Reden* (Cotta's edition), i. 9.

TO THE FIRST UNITED DIET

At the Court festivities, which took place during the session of the United Diet, I was avoided in a marked manner both by the King and the Princess of Prussia, though for different reasons: by the latter because I was neither Liberal nor popular; by the former for a reason which only became clear to me later. When, on the reception of the deputies, he avoided speaking to me—when, in the Court circle, after speaking to every one in turn, he broke off immediately he came to me, turned his back, or strolled away across the room—I considered myself justified in supposing that my attitude as a Royalist Hotspur had exceeded the limits which the King had fixed for himself. Only some months later, when I reached Venice on my honeymoon, did I discover that this explanation was incorrect. The King, who had recognised me in the theatre, commanded me on the following day to an audience and to dinner; and so unexpected was this to me that my light travelling luggage and the incapacity of the local tailor did not admit of my appearing in correct costume. My reception was so kindly, and the conversation, even on political subjects, of such a nature as to enable me to infer that my attitude in the Diet met with his encouraging approval. The King commanded me to call upon him in the course of the winter, and I did so. Both on this occasion and at smaller dinners at the palace I became persuaded that I stood high in the favour of both the King and the Queen, and that the former, in avoiding speaking to me in public, at the time of the session of the Diet, did not mean to criticise my political conduct, but at the time did not want to let others see his approval of me.

CHAPTER II

I RECEIVED the first intelligence of the events of March 18 and 19, 1848, while staying with my neighbour, Count Wartensleben, at Karow, whither ladies from Berlin had fled for refuge. At the first moment I was not so much alive to the political range of what was going on as filled with bitterness at the massacre of our soldiers in the streets. Politically, I thought the King would soon be master of the situation if only he were free; I saw that the first thing to be done was to liberate him, as he was said to be in the power of the insurgents.

On the 20th I was told by the peasants at Schönhausen that a deputation had arrived from Tangermünde with a demand that the black, red, and gold flag should be hoisted on the tower, as had already been done in the above-named town; threatening, in case of refusal, to visit us again with reinforcements. I asked the peasants if they were willing to defend themselves. They replied with a unanimous and brisk ' Yes,' and I advised them to drive the townspeople out of the village; which was attended to, the women zealously co-operating. I then had a white banner with a black cross in the shape of the Iron Cross, which happened to be in the church, hoisted on the tower, and ascertained what supply of weapons and ammunition was available in the village, when about fifty peasants' fowling-pieces came to light. Including ancient specimens, I myself possessed some twenty more, and had powder fetched by mounted messengers from Jerichow and Rathenow. Next, accompanied by my wife, I went the round of the villages and found the peasants already eager to march to the help of the King in Berlin. Especially enthusiastic was an old dyke-surveyor named Krause of Neuermark, who had been a sergeant in my father's regiment of carabineers. Only my next-door neighbour sympathised with the Berlin movement, accused me of hurling a firebrand into the country, and declared that if the peasants really prepared to march off, he would come forward and dissuade them. I replied, ' You know that I am a quiet man, but if you do that I shall shoot you.' ' I am sure you won't,' said he. ' I give you my word of honour that I will,' I replied, ' and you know that I keep my word: so drop that.'

I immediately went quite alone to Potsdam, where, in the railway station, I saw Herr von Bodelschwingh, who up to the 19th had been Minister of the Interior. It was plain that he had no desire to be seen in conversation with me, the reactionary. He returned my greeting in French, with the words, ' Do not speak to me.' ' The peasants are rising in our part,' I replied. ' For the King?' ' Yes.' ' That rope-dancer!' said he, pressing his hands to his eyes while the tears stood in them. In the town itself I found a bivouac of the Footguard among the trees adjoining the garrison church. I spoke to these men and found them enraged at the order to retire, and eager for more fighting. All the way back along the canal I was followed by civilians with the look of spies, who had attempted to parley with the troops, and used threatening language towards me. I had four rounds of ammunition in my pocket, but had no need to use them. I dismounted at the residence of my friend Roon, who, as governor to Prince Frederick Charles, occupied some rooms in the castle; and visited in the 'Deutsches Haus' General von Möllendorf, whom I found still stiff from the treatment he had suffered when negotiating with the insurgents, and General von Prittwitz, who had been in command in Berlin. I described to them the present temper of the country people; they in return gave me some particulars as to what had happened up to the morning of the 19th. What they had to relate, and the later information which came from Berlin, could only strengthen my belief that the King was not free.

Prittwitz, who was older than I, and judged more calmly, said: ' Send us none of your peasants, we don't want them. We have quite enough soldiers. Rather send us potatoes and corn, perhaps money too, for I do not know whether the maintenance and pay of the troops will be sufficiently provided for. If auxiliaries came up I should receive, and should have to carry out, an order from Berlin to drive them back.' ' Then fetch the King away,' I said. He replied: ' There will be no great difficulty about that; I am strong enough to take Berlin, but that means more fighting. What can we do after the King has commanded us to play the part of the vanquished? I cannot attack without orders.'

In this condition of affairs I hit upon the idea of obtaining from another quarter a command to act, which could not be expected from the King, who was not free, and tried to get at the Prince of Prussia. Referred to the Princess, whose consent thereto was necessary, I called upon her in order to discover the whereabouts of her consort, who, as I subsequently discovered, was on the Pfaueninsel.   She received me in a servant's room on the *entre-sol*, sitting on a wooden chair.   She refused the information I asked for, and declared, in a state of violent excitement, that it was her duty to guard the rights of her son.   What she said rested on the supposition that the King and her husband could not maintain their position, and naturally led to the conclusion that she meant to be regent during the minority of her son.   In order to obtain the co-operation of the Right in the Chambers to this end, formal overtures had been made to me by George von Vincke.   As I could not get at the Prince of Prussia, I tried my luck with Prince Frederick Charles, representing to him how necessary it was that the royal house should remain in touch with the army, and, if his Majesty were not free, should act in the cause without the King's command.   He replied, in a state of lively agitation, that however much my idea might appeal to him, he nevertheless felt himself too young to carry it out, and could not follow the example of those students who meddled with politics, for all he was no older than they.   I then determined to attempt to get at the King.

Prince Charles gave me at the palace at Potsdam, by way of passport and credentials, the following open letter: ' The bearer, with whom I am well acquainted, has the commission from me to inquire *personally* as to the health of his Majesty, my most gracious brother, and to bring me back word for what reason I have had *no* answer for thirty hours to the repeated inquiries I have written in my own hand, whether I ought not to come to Berlin.

' CHARLES, Prince of Prussia.

' Potsdam : March 21, 1848, 1 P.M.'

25

BISMARCK

I hastened to Berlin. Being known, since the days of the United Diet, to many people by sight, I considered it advisable to shave my beard and to put on a broad-brimmed hat with a coloured cockade. As I hoped for an audience I was in dress clothes. At the exit of the railway station a collecting box was set up, inviting contributions on behalf of those fighting on the barricades, and beside it stood a lanky civic champion with a musket on his shoulder. A cousin of mine, whom I had encountered on leaving the train, took out his purse. 'You surely are not going to give anything for those murderers?' said I; adding, in reply to the warning look he gave me, 'Surely you are not afraid of that lout?' I had already recognised the sentinel for Meier, of the Supreme Court of Justice, a friend of mine, who, on hearing the word 'lout,' turned round furiously and then exclaimed, 'Gad's my life, Bismarck! What a sight you look! Here's a pretty dirty job!'

The civic guard at the palace asked me what I wanted there. On my replying that I had to deliver a letter to the King from Prince Charles, the sentinel looked suspiciously at me and said that could not be so, as the Prince was with the King at that minute. He must therefore have set off from Potsdam before me. The guard asked to see the letter which I had; I showed it, as it was open and the contents harmless, and I was allowed to go, but not into the palace. At a window on the ground-floor of the Hotel Meinhard sat a doctor whom I knew, so I joined him. There I wrote to the King what I wanted to say to him. I went with the letter to Prince Boguslaw-Radziwill, who had the entrée to the court and could hand it to the King. In this letter I said, among other things, that the revolution was confined to the great cities, and that the

King would be master in the country as soon as ever he left Berlin. The King gave me no reply, but told me later that this letter, badly written on bad paper, had been carefully preserved by him as the first token of sympathy which he received at that time.

As I went about the streets to observe the traces of the contest, some unknown person whispered in my ear: 'Are you aware that you are being followed?' In Unter den Linden another unknown whispered to me: 'Come along with me.' I followed him into the Kleine Mauer-strasse, where he said: ' Be off, or you will be arrested.' ' Do you know me?' I asked. 'Yes,' he replied, ' you are Herr von Bismarck.' I have never discovered from what quarter danger threatened me, or from whom the warning came. The unknown quitted me at once. A street boy bawled out after me, 'Look, there goes another Frenchy!' an expression of which I have been sundry times reminded by later investigators. My long 'goatee,' which alone had escaped the razor, my slouch hat and dress suit, had made the youngsters take me for an exotic product. The streets were empty, no carriage was visible, and the only pedes-trians were some groups of men wearing blouses and car-rying banners, one of which, in the Friedrichstrasse, was escorting a laurel-crowned hero of the barricades to some ovation or other.

The same day I returned to Potsdam—not because of the warning, but because in Berlin I found no ground on which to operate—and consulted once more with Generals Möllendorf and Prittwitz as to the possibility of indepen-dent action. ' How shall we set about it?' said Prittwitz. I was sitting by the open piano, and began to strum the infantry charging-march. Möllendorf, who was stiff with his wounds, fell upon my neck with tears in his eyes, and exclaimed, 'If you could only manage that for us!' 'I cannot,' I replied, ' but if you do it without orders, what can happen to you? The country will thank you, and ultimately the King too.' ' Then,' said Prittwitz, 'can you get me any certainty that Wrangel and Hedemann will go along with us? We cannot allow dissension as well as insubordination to enter the army.' I promised to manage that; I promised to go to Magdeburg myself, and to send a confidential man to Stettin, in order to sound both the commanding generals. From Stettin came this message from General von Wrangel: ' Whatever Prittwitz does I will do also.' I myself was less fortunate at Magdeburg. First of all, I got access to General von Hedemann's aide-de-camp, a young major to whom I explained my errand and who expressed his sympathy. In a short time, however, he came to me at the inn, and begged me to depart immediately in order to save myself unpleasantness, and to prevent the old general from making a fool of himself, as it was his intention to have me arrested for high treason.

Herr Von Bonin, who was then chief president, and the highest authority in the province, had issued a proclamation to the following effect: 'A revolution has broken out in Berlin. I will take up a position above parties.' This ' pillar of the monarchy' was subsequently a minister, and filled high and influential positions. General Hedemann belonged to the Humboldt clique.

On my return to Schönhausen I tried to make the peasants understand that an armed expedition to Berlin was not feasible, and thereby incurred the suspicion of having been infected by the revolutionary mania in Berlin. I therefore made a proposal to them, which was accepted, that a deputation from Schönhausen and the other villages should set off with me to Potsdam to see for themselves, and to speak to General von Prittwitz, and perhaps to the Prince of Prussia also. On the 25th, when we reached the Potsdam station, the King had just arrived there, and been favourably received by a great mob of people. I said to my rustic companions: 'There is the King. I will present you; speak to him.' They, however, nervously declined the proposition, and speedily retired to the back of the crowd. I greeted the King respectfully; he acknowledged the salute without recognising me, and drove to the palace. I followed him, and there heard the address which he delivered to the officers of the guard in the Marble Saloon.[1] At the words ' I have never been freer or more secure than when under the protection of my citizens,' there arose a murmuring and the clash of sabres in their sheaths, such as no King of Prussia in the midst of his officers had ever heard before, and, I hope, will ever hear again.*

Deeply grieved, I returned to Schönhausen.

The recollection of the conversation which I had had at Potsdam with Lieut.-General von Prittwitz induced me to send him in May the following letter, which my friends in the Schönhausen district also signed.

' Every one who has a Prussian heart in his breast must, in common with us the undersigned, have read with

---

[1] It will be found as taken down by an officer in Gerlach's *Denkwürdigkeiten*, i. p.148.

* [The accounts given by the *Allgmeine Preussische Zeitung*, the *Vossische Zeitung*, and the *Schlesische Zeitung* lie before me, and contradict each other and my own recollection (Wolff, *Berliner Revolutions-Chronick*, vol. i. p. 424).]

indignation the attacks in the press, to which, in the weeks immediately following March 19, the royal troops were exposed; as a reward for having faithfully performed their duty in action, and for having given an unsurpassable example of military discipline and self-restraint when commanded to retire. If the press has of late taken up a more decent attitude, the reason of it lies not so much in a more correct appreciation, among the faction controlling it, of the actual state of affairs, as in the fact that the rapid march of later events has driven the recollection of preceding events into the background; and there is an affectation of a willingness to forgive the troops on account of their latest deeds * for what they did before. Even among the country people, who received the first tidings of what had happened at Berlin with an exasperation difficult to control, these misrepresentations began to gain in consistency —misrepresentations which had been spread on all sides, and that without any serious contradiction, partly by the press and partly by emissaries working upon the people on the occasion of the elections; so that the well-disposed section of the country people already believe it cannot be wholly unfounded that the street-fighting in Berlin was brought about by the troops in preconcerted fashion, with or without the knowledge or the wish of the much-calumniated heir to the throne, in order to wrest from the people the concessions which the King had made to them. As for any preparatory action on the other side, or any systematic tampering with the people, scarcely any one is willing any longer to believe in it. We fear that these lies will, for a long time to come, be treated, at any rate in the imagination of the lower orders, as history, unless

* On April 23 they had occupied Schleswig.

30

they are met by circumstantial representations, accompanied by proofs of the true course of events, and that as
soon as possible; inasmuch as, in the incalculable course
of things at this time, fresh events may happen—to-day
or to-morrow—important enough so fully to engross the
public attention that explanations as to the past will no
longer excite any interest.

' In our opinion it would have the most beneficial influence on the political views of the population if they could
in some way be enlightened upon the tainted source of the
Berlin movement, as well as upon the fact that the struggle
of the March heroes was not needed to attain their *alleged*
object, namely, the defence of the constitutional institutions promised by his Majesty. Your Excellency, as commander of the glorious troops who took part in these
events, is, in our opinion, pre-eminently called and in a
position to bring to light the truth as to these things in
the most convincing manner. The persuasion of the importance of this to our country, and of the extent to which
the renown of the army will gain thereby, must serve as
our excuse if, with equal urgency and respect, we beg your
Excellency to publish, as soon as possible, as exact an
account of the events at Berlin, substantiated from the
military point of view, as is warranted by the exigencies
of the service.'

General von Prittwitz did not respond to this appeal.
Not till March 18, 1891, did retired Lieut.-General von
Meyerinck, in the supplement to the ' Militär-Wochen-
blatt,' furnish an account with the same object as that
just indicated by me, but, alas! too late; since the most
important witnesses, Edwin von Manteuffel and Count
Oriola, had died in the meantime.

BISMARCK

As a contribution to the history of the March days, I may here mention conversations which I had some weeks afterwards with persons who sought me out because they looked upon me as in the confidence of the Conservatives —some of them to justify their conduct before and on March 18, others to relate to me their experiences on that occasion. The Chief Commissioner of Police, von Minutoli, complained that he had been reproached with having foreseen the rising and taken no steps to prevent it, and denied that any marked symptoms of it had ever come to his knowledge. To my rejoinder that I had been told at Genthin by eye-witnesses that, during the day preceding March 18, foreign-looking men, most of them speaking Polish, some of them openly carrying weapons, and others with heavy baggage, had proceeded in the direction of Berlin—Minutoli said that von Bodelschwingh, the minister, had sent for him in the middle of March and expressed his alarm at the prevailing commotion, whereupon he had taken him to a crowd assembled in front of the Zelten. After Bodelschwingh had listened for some time to the speeches there delivered, he had said: ' After all, the men talk very sensibly. I thank you for having saved me from committing a foolish act.' It was a rather suspicious circumstance in Minutoli's case that he was so popular in the days immediately succeeding the street-fighting. For a Chief Commissioner of Police, such a result of a riot was unnatural.

General von Prittwitz, too, who had commanded the troops round the palace, called on me and thus explained the particulars of their retreat. After he had been notified of the proclamation ' to my beloved Berliners,' he had stopped the fighting, but occupied the palace square, the arsenal, and all the streets leading to them in order to protect the palace. Then Bodelschwingh came to him with the demand that he should evacuate the palace square. 'That is impossible,' he had answered; 'by doing so I should give up the King.' Whereupon Bodelschwingh said: 'The King has commanded in his proclamation that all "public places"* be evacuated. Is the palace square a public place or is it not? Besides, I am a minister of state, and I have learnt by heart my duty as such. I command you to evacuate the palace square.'

'What else could I do but march off?' concluded Pritt-witz. I replied: 'I should have considered it best to give a sergeant the order, "Arrest that civilian!"' Pritt-witz rejoined: 'It is easy to prophesy when you know. You judge as a politician. I acted exclusively as a soldier at the direction of a minister actually in power who relied upon a proclamation subscribed by the sovereign.' From another quarter I have heard that Prittwitz, purple in the face with rage, had interrupted this, his last open-air conversation with Bodelschwingh, by ramming his sword into its sheath, and muttering the challenge that Götz von Berlichingen shouted through the window to the imperial commissioner. Then he had turned his horse to the left and ridden silently at a foot's pace through the precincts of the palace. On being asked by an officer sent from the palace as to the whereabouts of the troops he had given the biting reply: 'They have slipped through my hands, and gone where every one has a finger in the pie.' †

From the officers in his Majesty's immediate *entourage*

---

* [The proclamation says 'all streets and places.']

† [I am acquainted with the letter of Pastor von Bodelschwingh of November 8, 1891, in the *Kreuzzeitung* of November 18, 1891, No. 539, and the *Memoirs of the Life of Leopold von Gerlach*.]

I have heard the following. They searched for the King, who was for the moment invisible, having withdrawn owing to a call of nature. When he again made his appearance and was asked, ' Has your Majesty commanded the troops to be withdrawn?' he replied ' No.' ' But they are already marching off,' said the aide-de-camp, leading the King to a window. The palace square was black with civilians, behind whom the last bayonets of the retiring soldiers were still visible. ' I did not command this! This cannot be!' exclaimed the King; and his expression was one of consternation and indignation.

As to Prince Lichnowski, I was told that he was alternately circulating terrifying rumours in the palace as to the weakness of the troops and their lack of ammunition and provisions, and in the square below exhorting the insurgents in German and Polish to hold out; ' upstairs,' he said, ' they had lost all courage.'

In the short session of the second United Diet I said, on April 2 :

' I am one of the few people who intend to vote against the Address; and I have asked leave to speak in order to justify my vote, and to explain to you that I accept the Address without reserve in so far as it is a programme for the future, for the sole reason that I cannot help myself. I do so, not voluntarily, but because I am compelled to do so by force of circumstances, for I have not changed my views during the last six months. I believe this ministry to be the only one that can bring us back out of our present position into a well-ordered and law-abiding state of things; and for this reason I will always give it my poor support wherever it is possible. What moves me, however, to vote against the Address are the expressions of joy and thankfulness for what has happened during the last few days. The past is buried; and it is a matter of more poignant grief to me than to many of you that no human power can raise it up again, since the Crown itself has thrown the earth upon its coffin. But if, constrained by the force of circumstances, I accept this, nevertheless I cannot bid adieu to my activity in the United Diet with the lie on my lips that I rejoice and am thankful for what I cannot but consider at the very least to have been a mistaken course. If by the new road we have now taken we really succeed in reaching the goal of a united German fatherland; if we reach a happy, or even a law-abiding and orderly condition of affairs, then the moment will have come when I can express my thanks to the originator of the new order of things; at present, however, it is impossible.'

I would have said more, but my emotion made it impossible to speak any longer, and I burst into a paroxysm of tears, which compelled me to leave the tribune.

A few days previously an attack in a Magdeburg paper had given me occasion to address its editor in the following letter, in which I claimed for myself also the benefit of one of the hardly won privileges, namely, the tumultuously-demanded ' right of free expression of opinion ' which had been conceded by the abolition of the censorship; never anticipating that forty-two years later the same would be denied to me.[1]

[1] By the decree of Caprivi, of May 23, 1890.

35

BISMARCK

'Schönhausen, near Jerichow: March 30, 1848.

' SIR,—I have noticed in to-day's issue of your paper
an article dated " From the Altmark," which casts suspicion upon certain personages, and also indirectly upon
me; and I therefore appeal to your sense of justice to
insert the following reply. I am not, indeed, the gentleman mentioned in the article, who is supposed to have
come from Potsdam to Stendal; but none the less I declared
last week in my own neighbourhood, that I did not consider the King in Berlin to be a free agent, and I suggested to my hearers that they should send a deputation
to the proper quarter. Yet I do not on this account want
to have imputed to me the selfish motives insinuated by
your correspondent. Firstly, it is quite intelligible that
any one acquainted with all that took place in regard to
his Majesty's person after the departure of the troops,
should adopt the opinion that the King was not master to
act as he would. Secondly, I consider that every citizen
of a free state is justified in expressing his own opinions
among his fellow-citizens, even when they conflict with
the public opinion of the moment : nay, judging from what
has happened lately, it might be difficult to contest any
one's right to support his political views by mob agitation. Thirdly, if all the actions of his Majesty during
the last fortnight were absolutely voluntary, which neither
I nor your correspondent can know with certainty, what
was it the Berliners had won? In that case, the struggle
on the 18th and 19th was at the very least aimless and
superfluous, and all the bloodshed without occasion and
without result. Fourthly, I believe I may express it as
the opinion of the great majority of the gentry, that at
a time when the social and political existence of Prussia

is at stake, when Germany is threatened with schism in more than one direction, we have neither the time nor the inclination to squander our strength in reactionary experiments, or in the defence of insignificant and hitherto intact rights of landlords. We are, however, ready and willing to transfer these to worthier hands, inasmuch as we consider all this a subordinate question; regarding the restoration of law and order in Germany, the maintenance of the honour and inviolability of our fatherland, as the sole task of every one whose views of our political situation have not been troubled by party spirit.

' If you will insert the foregoing I have no objection to the publication of my name.

'I am, sir, your obedient servant,

' BISMARCK.'

I may observe in reference to the above, that I always from my younger days signed my name without the ' von,' and only adopted my present signature, ' von Bismarck,' as a protest against the proposal for the abolition of the nobility in 1848.

The following article, the draft manuscript of which is still in my possession, was, as its contents show, composed in the period between the second United Diet and the Elections to the National Assembly. I have not been able to find out in which journal it appeared.

'From the Altmark.

'A portion of our fellow-citizens who, under the system of division into Estates, enjoyed a large share in the representation—I mean the inhabitants of the towns—are beginning to feel that by the new mode of election (according to which, in almost all districts, the civic population

will have to compete with an overwhelming majority of the
agricultural) their interests must suffer in comparison with
those of the great masses of the rural population. We live
in the age of material interests; and, after the consolida-
tion of the new constitution, after the settling of the present ferment, the strife of parties will turn upon the point
whether the burdens of the state shall be borne proportionately to the ability to bear them, or whether they shall be
disproportionately imposed upon landed property, always
open as it is to taxation, the safest and most convenient
source of revenue inasmuch as it is impossible to conceal
its extent. It is natural that the townsfolk should strive
to keep the tax-collector as far as possible from the manufactures, from town house property, and from the *rentier*
and the capitalist; and should prefer to direct his attention
to fields and meadows and their produce. A beginning has
been made by exempting from the new direct impost the
lowest classes in towns hitherto liable to the grist tax;
whilst in the country they pay now, as formerly, on the
class taxation system.* We hear, moreover, of measures
for the support of industry at the expense of the state exchequer; but we do not hear of anything being done for the
relief of the country folk, who, on account of the warlike
outlook, cannot find a market overseas for their produce;
while at the same time they are obliged in these poverty-
stricken times to sell their farms to meet calls for capital. With regard to indirect taxation, in the same way we
hear far more of the protective system which favours our
home manufactures and trade, than of the Free Trade necessary to the agricultural population. It is, as I have said, nat-

---

* [The 'Classen-Steuer' was a system by which the population was
divided into groups, and every member of each group was taxed equally,
whatever his income.]

ural that a portion of the inhabitants of the towns should on the occasion of the impending elections, as regards the point in question, shun no means to promote their own interests and weaken the representation of the country-folk. A very effective lever for the accomplishment of the latter object lies in the endeavours to make the country population suspicious of those among them whose culture and intelligence might enable them successfully to represent the interests of the soil in the National Assembly. Hence trouble is taken artificially to promote ill-feeling against the landed gentry, in the persuasion that, the influence of this class once destroyed, the rural population will then be obliged to elect either lawyers or other townsfolk who have agricultural interests but little at heart; either this, or the country will be represented by simple rustics whose action, it is hoped, can be imperceptibly guided by the eloquence and crafty policy of the party leaders in the National Assembly. They therefore try to represent the gentry who have hitherto been, as men who would seek to maintain and bring back antiquated conditions; whilst in reality the country gentlemen, like every other reasonable man, say themselves that it would be senseless and impossible to stop or dam back the stream of time. Efforts are also made in the villages to excite and encourage the idea that the time has now come for the people to free themselves, without giving compensation, from all the payments which, according to the ' Separation compacts ' * are due from them to the landed proprietors. The fact, however, is ignored that a government which is to maintain order and justice

* [A technical term in German law for the payments made by the peasants to the landowners, under the Enclosure Acts, as compensation for the old feudal service.]

cannot begin by plundering one class of citizens in order
to endow another; that all rights based on law, custom or
contract, all demands which one man may have to make
upon another, all claims to interest on securities and to capital, could be taken away from those who enjoy them with
the same degree of right with which they would deprive
the landed gentry of their rents without full satisfaction.
They try to blind the countryman to the fact that he has the
same interest in agriculture as the landed proprietor, and
the same opponent in an exclusive industrial system which
is stretching out its hand for domination in the Prussian
state; if this deception succeeds, let us hope it will not
last long, and that an end will be made to it by quickly
and legally abolishing the rights hitherto enjoyed by the
landed proprietors; also that the agricultural population
will not first find out when they have to pay the reckoning
(in other words, when it is too late) how neatly they have
been imposed upon by the clever people of the towns.'

During the session of the Second United Diet, George
von Vincke, in the name of his colleagues, and, as it was
alleged, by instruction from a high quarter, asked my co-
operation in a plan requesting the King, through the Diet,
to abdicate, and, passing over the Prince of Prussia—but,
as it was stated, with his concurrence—to bring about the
regency of the Princess on behalf of her son, who was a
minor. I promptly declined, and declared that I would
meet such a motion with another proposing criminal proceedings on a charge of high treason. Vincke defended his
suggestion as a well-thought-out, well-prepared measure
that was dictated by policy. He considered the Prince
impossible, by reason of his nickname (alas! undeserved)
of 'Prince Cartridge,' and asserted that his assent to the

proposal had already been obtained in writing. He also had a declaration ready, to the effect—that chivalrous gentleman was said to have so expressed himself—that he was ready to renounce his right to the succession if his King could thereby be protected from danger. I have never seen this declaration, and his Highness never mentioned it to me. Herr von Vincke finally gave up his attempt to win my adhesion to the scheme of the Princess's regency coolly and easily, with the statement that without the co-operation of the Extreme Right, which he regarded me as representing, the King could not be prevailed upon to abdicate. This negotiation took place at my residence at the Hotel des Princes (ground floor, right), and included more on both sides than can be committed to writing.

I never spoke to the Emperor William of this occurrence or of the expression which I happened to hear from his consort during the March days in the Potsdam Stadtschloss, nor do I know if others did. I concealed these events from him, even in such times as the period of the four years' conflict, the Austrian war, and the ' Kulturkampf,' when I was obliged to recognise in Queen Augusta an opponent who put both my ability to do what I considered my duty, and my nerve, to the severest test they ever experienced.

On the other hand, she must have written to her husband in England that I had attempted to get at him in order to win his support to a counter-revolutionary movement for liberating the King; for when, on his return on June 7, he stopped for a few moments at the Genthin station, and I had retired into the background because I did not know whether in his capacity as ' deputy for Wirsitz ' he would like to be seen with me, he recognised me in the hindmost ranks of the crowd, pushed his way through those in front of me, held out his hand to me and said : ' I know you have been active on my behalf, and will never forget you were so.'

My first meeting with him had been in the winter of 1834–35, at a court ball. I was standing beside a certain Herr von Schack, from Mecklenburg, a tall man like myself, dressed as I was, in the uniform of a *Referendarius*, which prompted the Prince to observe jocosely that Justice must be looking for her recruits by the standard of the Guards; then, turning to me, he asked why I had not become a soldier. ' I had the wish,' I replied, ' but my parents were against it, because the prospect was too unfavourable.' Whereupon the Prince remarked : ' The career is certainly not brilliant, but the judicial career is not more so.' During the first United Diet, to which he belonged as a member of the Upper House, he spoke to me repeatedly in the joint sittings in a way which showed that he approved of the political attitude which I had adopted.

Soon after the meeting at Genthin he invited me to Babelsberg. I told him of many things concerning the March days, partly from my own experience and partly from what I had heard from the officers, especially as to the temper in which the troops began the retreat from Berlin, and vented in bitter songs which they sung on the march. I was cruel enough to read him the verses, which may be called historical, as indicating the temper of the troops on the retreat they were ordered to make from Berlin.

> Prussians they were, and black and white their colours,
> When o'er the ranks once more the banner spread,
> As for their King with loyal hearts rejoicing
> His faithful troops fell one by one in death.

THE YEAR 1848

Without a tear we saw them
Carry the slain away ;
But hark ! a cry pierces our loyal breasts.
' Prussians no longer, ye must Germans be.'

His throne with loving service we surrounded,
Still strong in faith, in confidence secure ;
And now we see how loyalty is valued,
When to his Prussians' cries our King is deaf.
All ties are burst asunder now ;
Woe to our country ! since its King
Rejects his loyal friends and breaks our hearts,
And with them shatters what upheld his throne.

There, as the storm raged round his sacred head,
It was his soldiers' courage held him safe
From the fierce rage of his accusing people,
Who now claim victory that should be ours.
Unwavering they stood their ground
And for their master and their King
Poured out their life-blood with one willing mind.
Their death was sweet, and nought their honour stained.

And where they fell, thy true and valiant soldiers—
Mark but the shame, thou holy Fatherland!—
See now a filthy mob of butchers standing
With bloodstained hand in hand around the King.
There took anew the oath
Of love—such love !—and loyalty !
Their oath 's a sham, their freedom 's a pretence,
Prussians they'll be no more—oh, happy we !

Black, red and gold now gleams amidst the sunshine,
Sinks the black eagle from our sight profaned ;
Here ends thy famous life, thou house of Zollern,
Here fell a King, but not in battle's strife.
No longer can our eyes endure
To look upon the fallen star ;
Prince, thou wilt rue what here thou hast accomplished,
Nor any loyal as thy Prussians find.

Thereupon he broke into a violent fit of weeping, such
as I only saw him give way to on one other occasion, when
I opposed him at Nikolsburg on the question of the continuation of the war.   (See vol. ii., chap. 9.)

Up to the time of my Frankfort appointment I was so

far in favour with the Princess, his wife, that I was summoned on occasion to Babelsberg in order to hear her political views and wishes, the exposition of which she generally ended with the words : ' I am glad to have heard your opinion,' though she had not given me the opportunity of expressing it. Prince Frederick, afterwards Emperor (then eighteen or nineteen years of age, but looking younger), used on these occasions to let me feel his political sympathy by warmly shaking hands with me in a friendly manner in the dusk of evening, as I was entering my carriage to take my departure, as if he were not allowed openly to express his feelings in the daylight.

In the last twenty years of Frederick William III's government the question of German unity had only appeared in the shape of student aspirations and the penal suppression thereof. Frederick William IV's ' Deutsch ' (or, as he used to write it, ' Teutsch ') national sentiment was heartier and livelier than that of his father, but was hindered in its practical realisation by a garnish of mediævalism and by a dislike of clear and firm decisions. This led to his neglecting the favourable opportunity of March 1848; and this was not to be the only opportunity he neglected. In the days between the South German revolution (including that at Vienna) and March 18, so long as it was obvious that of all the German states, Austria included, Prussia was the only one that remained on a firm footing, the German Princes were ready to come to Berlin and seek protection under conditions which went even further in the direction of union than has been realised nowadays. Even the self-confidence of Bavaria was shaken. If the congress of Princes summoned to Dresden for March 20 by a declaration dated March 10 of the Austrian and Prussian government had come about—then, judging by the disposition of the participating Courts, such readiness for self-sacrifice on the altar of the Fatherland as was evinced in France on August 4, 1789, might have been expected. This view of things corresponded to the actual circumstances of the time. Military Prussia was strong and intact enough to arrest the progress of the revolutionary wave, and to offer the remaining German states such guarantees for law and order in the future as then appeared acceptable to the other dynasties.

March 18 was an instance how mischievous the encroachment of crude force may be even to the objects which are to be attained thereby. Nevertheless, on the morning of the 19th nothing was yet lost. The insurrection was overthrown. Its leaders (amongst them my old university acquaintance, Assessor Rudolf Schramm) had fled to Dessau, took the first tidings of the retreat of the troops for a trap laid by the police, and only returned to Berlin after receiving the newspapers. I believe that had the victory (the only victory won over insurrection at that time by any government in Europe) been more resolutely and more wisely turned to account, German unity was attainable in a stricter form than ultimately came to pass at the time I had a share in the government. Whether it would have been more serviceable and durable I will not attempt to decide.

If the King had in March definitely crushed the Berlin rising, and had prevented its recrudescence, we should, after the collapse of Austria, have experienced no difficulty at the hands of the Emperor Nicholas in reforming Germany into a durable organisation. His sympathies were originally more in the direction of Berlin than of Vienna, although Frederick William IV did not personally possess them, and could not do so with the differences of character between the two men.

The procession through the streets in the colours of the *Burschenschaft* on March 21 was very little calculated to make up for what had been lost both at home and abroad. The result of it was to so completely reverse the situation that the King stood no longer at the head of his troops, but of the barricade-fighters—of those intractable masses before whose threats the Princes a few days before had sought his protection. The idea of treating the transference of the projected congress of Princes from Dresden to Potsdam as the one single outcome of the March days was untenable in the face of this undignified procession.

The softness of Frederick William IV, under the pressure of uninvited and perhaps treacherous advisers and the stress of women's tears, in attempting to terminate the bloody event in Berlin, after it had been victoriously carried through, by commanding his troops to renounce the victory they had won, exercised on the further development of our policy in the first instance all the mischief of a neglected opportunity. Whether the progress would have been lasting if the King had maintained the victory of his troops, and made the most of it, is another question. At any rate the King would not have been in the crushed mood in which I found him during the second United Diet, but in that soaring flight of eloquence, invigorated by victory, whch he had displayed on the occasion of the homage in 1840, at Cologne in 1842, and elsewhere. I venture upon no conjecture as to what effect upon the King's attitude, upon his romantic mediæval reminiscences of the Empire as regarded Austria and the Princes, and upon the previous and subsequent strong royalist sentiment in the country, would have been produced by a consciousness that he had definitely overcome the insurrection which elsewhere on the continent outside of Russia remained face to face with him as the sole victor.

A victory won on the pavement would have been of a different sort and of less range than that afterwards won on the battlefield. It has, perhaps, proved better for our future that we had to stray plodding through the wilderness of intestine conflicts from 1848 to 1866, like the Jews before they entered the Promised Land. We should hardly have been spared the wars of 1866 and 1870 even if our neighbours, who collapsed in 1848, had regained strength and courage by means of support from Paris, Vienna, and other quarters. It is a question whether the operation of historical events upon the Germans by the shorter and quicker path of a victory in March 1848 would have been the same as that which we see to-day, and which gives the impression that the dynasties, and more especially those which were formerly prominently ' particularistic,' are more friendly disposed towards the Empire than are the political groups and parties.

My first visit to Sans-Souci took place under unfavourable conditions. In the early part of June, a few days before the retirement of the Minister-President Ludolf Camphausen, I was at Potsdam, when a court messenger sought me out at the inn to tell me that the King wanted to speak to me. I said, being still under the impression of my critical mood, that I regretted I could not comply with his Majesty's commands as I was about to go home, and my wife, whose health was in a very delicate state, would be anxious if I stayed away longer than had been arranged. After some time Edwin von Manteuffel, aide-de-camp in waiting, appeared, repeated the command, in the form of an invitation to dinner, and added that the King put a special messenger at my disposal to inform my wife. I had no choice but to repair to Sans-Souci. The party at table was very small, comprising, if I remember aright, besides the ladies and gentlemen in attendance, only Camphausen and myself. After dinner the King took me on to the terrace, and asked me in a friendly sort of way: ' How are you getting on?' In the irritable state I had been in ever since the March days I replied: ' Badly.' The King said: ' I think the feeling is good in your parts.' Thereupon, under the impression made by some regulations, the contents of which I do not remember, I replied: ' The feeling was very good, but since we have been inoculated with the revolution by the King's officials under the royal sign-manual, it has become bad. What we lack is confidence in the support of the King.' At that moment the Queen stepped out from a shrubbery and said: ' How can you speak so to the King!' ' Let me alone, Elise,' replied the King, ' I shall soon settle his business'; and turning to me, he said: ' What do you really reproach me with, then?' ' The evacuation of Berlin.' ' I did not want it done,' replied the King; and the Queen, who had remained within hearing, added: ' Of that the King is quite innocent. He had not slept for three days.' ' A King ought to be able to sleep,' I replied. Unmoved by this blunt remark the King said:

' It is always easier to prophesy when you know. What would be gained if I admitted that I had behaved like a donkey? Something more than reproaches is wanted to set an overturned throne up again. To do that I need assistance and active devotion, not criticism.' The kindness with which he said all this, and much more to the same effect, overpowered me. I had come in the spirit of a *frondeur*, who would not have cared if he had been dismissed ungraciously; I went away completely disarmed and won over.

Upon my representing that he was master in the country parts, and possessed the power to restore the threatened order everywhere, he said he must be careful not to forsake the strictly legal path; if he must break with the Berlin Assembly—the 'day-labourer parliament,' as it was called in certain circles—he must have strict law on his side, otherwise his case would have a weak footing and the whole monarchy be in danger, not only of internal disturbances, but also from without. He possibly meant by that a French war, in partnership with insurrections in Germany. It seems to me more probable, however, that at the moment when he wanted my services he specially avoided expressing to me his fear of damaging his views for Prussia in Germany. I replied that strict legality and its limitations appeared to me obliterated in the actual situation, and would be as little respected by his opponents, when once they had the power, as on March 18; and that I saw the situation more in the light of war and self-defence than in that of legal argumentation. The King persisted, however, that his situation would be too weak if he quitted the legal footing, and I took away with me the impression that he was for the moment subordinating the possibility of the restoration of order in Prussia to the ideas that Radowitz used to instil into him, the ' black, red and gold theories,' as they were called at the time.

Among the numerous conversations that ensued upon this one, I remember these words of the King: ' I want to carry out the struggle against the tendencies of the National Assembly, but in the present state of the matter, while I may be fully convinced of my right, it is uncertain whether others, and ultimately the great masses of the people, will be also convinced. In order that I may be sure of this, the Assembly must put itself still farther in the wrong, especially in questions where my right to defend myself by force is plain not only to myself but to every one.'

I could not induce the King to share my conviction that his doubts as to his power were without foundation, and that therefore it only came to the question whether he could believe in his rights when he proposed to defend himself against the usurpations of the Assembly. That I was right was immediately proved by the fact that every military order given in view of risings both large and small was carried out zealously and without scruple, and even under circumstances in which a manifestation of military obedience was from the outset bound up with the overthrow of an actually existing armed resistance. On the other hand, a dissolution of the Assembly, as soon as its activity was recognised to be dangerous to the state, would not have touched the question of obedience to military commands in the rank and file. Even the marching of larger masses of troops into Berlin, after the storming of the arsenal and similar incidents, would have been regarded, not merely by the soldiers, but also by the majority of the population, as a praiseworthy exercise of an undoubted royal prerogative, although, perhaps, it might not be so regarded by the minority who had the conduct of affairs. Even if the civic guard had shown any disposition to resist, they could thereby only have intensified the troops' legitimate thirst for battle. I can scarcely fancy that the King in the summer could have had any doubts as to his material power to put an end to the revolution in Berlin. I rather suspect that his mind was exercised by *arrières pensées* as to whether the Berlin Assembly, and reconciliation with it and its legal footing, could be made use of directly or indirectly, under some constellation or other; either by means of a combination with or against the Frankfort parliament, or by the use of pressure on the German question from other quarters. He may have doubted, too, whether the formal breach with Prussian popular representation would compromise German prospects. In any case, I do not think the King's inclinations were responsible for the procession in German colours; he was at that time so much affected both in body and mind that he could offer but little resistance to any suggestions that were made to him with decision.

During my intercourse at Sans-Souci, I gained knowledge of the persons who possessed the confidence of the King, even in political matters, and sometimes met them in his cabinet. They were, in particular, Generals von Gerlach and von Rauch, and subsequently Niebuhr, the Private Secretary.

Rauch was the more practical of the two. Gerlach, in deciding upon actual events, had a weakness for clever aphorisms; he had a noble nature with high ideals, and was free from the fanaticism of his brother, President Ludwig von Gerlach; in private life modest and as help-

less as a child, courageous and highflying in politics, but
somewhat hindered by physical indolence. I recollect
that in the presence of both brothers, the President and
the General, I was led to express my opinion, as to the
charge of unpracticalness brought against them, in the following manner. ' If we three,' I said, ' saw an accident
in the street from where we are now standing at this window, the President would improve the occasion by a sen-
tentious remark on our want of faith, and the instability
of human affairs; the General would immediately tell us
the proper thing to do in order to help down below, but
would not stir a finger himself; I should be the only one
who would go down or call somebody to help.' Thus the
general was the most influential politician in the *camarilla*
of Frederick William IV, a noble and unselfish character,
and a loyal servant of the King, but hindered, intellectually as much as bodily, by his ponderous person from a
prompt execution of his excellent ideas. On days when
the King had behaved unjustly or ungraciously to him I
have no doubt the old church hymn

> Put not thy trust in Princes, who
> Like cradles rock from side to side ;
> They who to-day ' Hosanna ' cry,
> Say next : ' Let him be crucified!'—

would be sung at evening prayers at the general's house.

But his devotion to the King did not suffer the slightest diminution during this Christian outburst of temper.
Moreover, he was devoted body and soul to the King, even
when, in his opinion, the monarch erred. This was plain
from the fact that he may be said to have ultimately met
his death of his own free will by following behind the dead
body of his King bareheaded, helmet in hand, and that in

a high wind and very cold weather. This last act of an old servant's devotion to his master's body ruined an already much enfeebled health. He came home ill with erysipelas, and died in a few days. His end reminded one of the way in which the followers of the old Germanic princes used voluntarily to die with them.

Besides Gerlach, and perhaps in a still higher degree, Rauch had influence with the King after 1848. Highly gifted, the incarnation of common sense, brave and honest, without much schooling, with the tendencies of a Prussian general of the best type, Rauch was on many occasions actively employed in diplomacy at St. Petersburg as a military plenipotentiary. On one occasion he appeared at Sans-Souci from Berlin with a verbal message from the Minister-President, Count Brandenburg, to beg the King to decide an important question. As the King, who found a decision difficult, could not make up his mind, Rauch at last drew his watch from his pocket and said, with a look at the dial: 'My train starts in twenty minutes, so your Majesty will have to give your command as to whether I am to say 'yes' or 'no' to Count Brandenburg, or whether I am to tell him that your Majesty will say neither 'yes' nor 'no.' This remark came from him in a tone of irritability only tempered by military discipline, an expression of the ill-humour which the clear-sighted, resolute general, already wearied by a long fruitless discussion, naturally felt. The King said: 'Oh, well, "yes," if you like,' whereupon Rauch immediately withdrew, to hurry as fast as he could through the town to the railway station. The King stood in silence for some time, as if weighing the consequences of the decision to which he had unwillingly come, after which

BISMARCK

he turned towards Gerlach and me, and said, 'Oh! that
Rauch! He can't speak German correctly, but he has
more common sense than we all.' Then, as he left
the room, he turned to Gerlach and added: ' He has
always been cleverer than you.' Whether the King was
right on this point I will not decide; Gerlach was the
wittier, Rauch the more practical.

The development of events offered no opportunity of
utilising the Berlin Assembly for the German cause,
while its encroachments increased; and so the idea ma-
tured of transferring it to another place, in order to free
its members from the pressure of intimidation, and, if occasion arose, to dissolve it. Therewith the difficulty of
forming a ministry which would accept the task of carrying out these measures increased. At the very opening of the Assembly it was not easy for the King to find
ministers at all, especially such men as would enter pliably
into his not always consistent views—men, too, whose
fearless firmness would at the same time be a guarantee
that they would not be found wanting if affairs took
a decisive turn. I can call to mind many abortive attempts of that spring. George von Vincke, whom I
sounded, replied that he was a man ' from the Red Soil,'
more suited for criticism and opposition than for playing
the part of a minister. Beckerath would only undertake
the formation of a ministry if the Extreme Right surrendered to him unconditionally and assured him of the King's
support. Men who had influence in the National Assembly did not wish to spoil their prospect, when orderly
conditions had been re-established, of becoming in the
future and remaining constitutional parliamentary ministers. Among others, I noticed in Harkort, whom we had

54

thought of as Minister of Commerce, an opinion that to bring about the restoration of order we must have a specialist ministry of officials and soldiers, before really constitutional ministers could take over the business. After that, the ground would be prepared.

The aversion to becoming a minister was strengthened by the idea that such a position was not unaccompanied with personal danger, as the case of actual ill-treatment of Conservative deputies in the streets had already shown. In view of the habits which the population of the streets had adopted, and of the influence exercised over it by the deputies of the Extreme Left, it was necessary to be prepared for still greater excesses, if the government attempted to oppose democratic pressure and guide it into more settled channels.

Count Brandenburg, indifferent to such anxieties, declared himself ready to take the presidency of the Council, and then the difficulty was to find him fit and acceptable colleagues. A list presented to the King contained my name also: as General Gerlach told me, the King had written in the margin 'only to be employed when the bayonet governs unrestricted.' * Count Brandenburg himself said to me at Potsdam : 'I have taken the matter in hand, but have scarcely looked into the newspapers; I am unacquainted with political matters, and can only carry my head to market. I want a *mahout*, a man in whom I trust and who tells me what I can do. I go into the matter like a child into the dark, and except Otto Manteuffel [then at the head of the Ministry of the Interior], know nobody who pos-

* Gerlach is more trustworthy than the source whence Count Vitzthum von Echstädt must have drawn in *Berlin und Wien*, p. 247, where he makes the marginal note run : ' Red Reactionary, with a scent for blood, to be used *later*.'

sesses previous training as well as my personal confidence, but at the same time still has scruples. If he wishes it, I will enter the Assembly to-morrow; if he does not, we must wait and find some one else. Go over to Berlin and stir up Manteuffel.' This succeeded, after I had talked it into him from nine o'clock till midnight, had undertaken to inform his wife at Potsdam of it, and had explained to him the measures taken in the theatre and its neighbourhood for the personal security of the ministers.

Early in the morning of November 9, General von Strotha, who had been appointed War Minister, came to me, sent by Brandenburg, in order to have the situation made clear to him. I did that as well as I could, and asked: 'Are you ready?' He answered with the rejoinder: 'What dress has been decided upon?' 'Civilian dress,' I replied. 'That I don't possess,' said he. I provided him with a hired servant, and luckily, before the appointed hour, a suit was hunted up at a tailor's. Various measures had been taken for the security of the ministers. First of all, in the theatre itself, besides a strong posse of police, about thirty of the best shots in the light infantry battalions of the guard were so disposed that they could appear in the body of the house and the galleries at a given signal; they were unerring marksmen, and could cover the ministers with their muskets if they were actually threatened. It was assumed that at the first shot all who were present would speedily vacate the body of the house. Corresponding precautions were taken at the windows of the theatre, and at various buildings in the Gensdarmenmarkt, in order to protect the ministers from any possible hostile attack as they left the theatre; it was assumed that even large masses, meeting there, would scatter as soon as shots were fired from various directions.

Herr von Manteuffel, moreover, called my attention to the fact that the entrance of the theatre in the narrow Charlotten-Strasse was not covered. I undertook to manage that the house opposite, which was the residence of Count Kniephausen, the Hanoverian minister (then absent on leave), should be occupied by troops. I repaired the same night to Colonel von Griesheim, at the Ministry of War, who was entrusted with the military arrangements, but found that he had scruples as to whether a minister's house should be used for such purposes. I then went to see the Hanoverian *chargé d'affaires*, Count Platen, who resided in the house belonging to the King of Hanover, Unter den Linden. He was of opinion that the official domicile of the embassy for the time being was in his house, Unter den Linden, and authorised me to write to Colonel von Griesheim that he placed the residence of his 'absent friend,' Count Kniephausen, at my disposal for police purposes. Having gone late to bed, I was aroused at seven o'clock in the morning by a messenger from Platen, begging me to go and see him. I found him in a state of great excitement, owing to the fact that a division of about a hundred men had been marched into the courtyard of *his* house, and consequently in the very place which he had designated as the embassy. Griesheim had probably given the order based upon my information to an official who had been the cause of the misunderstanding. I went to him and obtained an order for the commander of the division to occupy the Kniephausen mansion, which was done after it was daylight; while the occupation of the remaining houses had been secretly car-

ried out during the night. Perhaps the impression of
open determination that was incidentally given was responsible for the fact that, when the ministers repaired
to the theatre, the Gensdarmenmarkt was quite empty.

On November 10, Wrangel, having marched in at
the head of his troops, negotiated with the civil guard,
and persuaded them to withdraw voluntarily. I considered that a political mistake. If there had only been the
slightest skirmish Berlin would have been captured, not
by capitulation, but by force, and then the political position of the government would have been quite different.
The fact that the King did not immediately dissolve the
National Assembly, but adjourned it for some time and
transferred it to Brandenburg, trying to find out whether
he could get a majority there, with which it would be
possible to come to a satisfactory arrangement, shows
that, in the political development which the King may
have had in his mind, the *rôle* of the Assembly was, even
then, not played out. I remember certain symptoms tend-
ing to show that in the domain of the German question
this *rôle* had been considered. In the private conversations of the leading politicians during the prorogation of
the Assembly, the German question took a more prominent place than previously; and within the ministry itself
great hopes, in this respect, were reposed in Carlowitz the
Saxon, whose recognised eloquence would operate in a
'German-National' sense. As to what Count Brandenburg thought of the German cause, I received no immediate information from him at that time. He only expressed his willingness to do with soldierly obedience
whatever the King might command. Later, at Erfurt,
he spoke more openly to me on the matter.

CHAPTER III

THE latent German ideas of Frederick William IV, more than his weakness, were responsible for the ill-success of our policy after 1848. The King hoped that what was desirable would happen without his being required to outrage his legitimist traditions. If Prussia and the King had had no wish whatever for anything which they did not possess before 1848, even though it were but an historical *mention honorable*, as the speeches of 1840 and 1842 gave reason to suppose; if the king had had no aims and inclinations for the prosecution of which a certain popularity was necessary, what would have prevented him, when once the Brandenburg ministry had found a firm footing, from offering a like opposition to all that the revolution had acquired in the interior of Prussia, as to the rising in Baden and to the resistance of individual Prussian provincial towns? The progress of these risings had shown, even to those ignorant of it, that the military forces were trustworthy; in Baden even the Landwehr, in districts where it had been considered uncertain, had done its duty to the best of its ability. There was undoubtedly the possibility of a military reaction—the possibility, when once a constitution had been granted, of amending in a monarchical sense (and that more rigorously than actually happened) the Belgian formulary which was adopted as a basis. Any tendency to make the most of this possibility must in the mind of the

King have given way before the anxiety of losing that measure of goodwill in a national and liberal direction on which reposed the hope that the hegemony in Germany would fall to Prussia without war, and in a manner compatible with legitimistic ideas.

This hope or expectation, which even as late as the ' New Era' found timid expression in phrases about the German vocation of Prussia and moral conquests, was founded upon a double error which was paramount both at Sans-Souci and in the Paulskirche* from March 1848 to the spring of the following year—namely, an under-estimate of the vital energy of the German dynasties and their states, and an over-estimate of the forces which can be summed up in the term ' barricade,' comprehending therein all the impulses which prepare the way to a barricade, agitation and threats with street-fighting. The danger of subversion lay not in the thing itself, but in the fear of it. The more or less Phæacian governments were beaten in March, before they had drawn the sword, partly through fear of the enemy, partly through the private sympathy of their officials with him. In any case, it would have been easier for the King of Prussia at the head of the princes, by making the most of the victory of the troops in Berlin, to restore a semblance of German unity, than it afterwards was for the Paulskirche to do so. Whether the idiosyncrasy of the King would not have hindered such a restoration, even when holding fast the fruits of victory, or would have endangered the safety of what had been restored (as Bodelschwingh feared in March),

* [In May 1848 a German parliament, elected by universal suffrage, met in St. Paul's Church at Frankfort. It was by this body that the imperial crown was offered to Frederick William IV of Prussia.]

is at any rate difficult to determine. In the moods of his later years, as may be seen from the memoirs of Leopold von Gerlach and other sources, his original aversion to constitutional methods, his persuasion of the necessity of a greater measure of freedom for the royal authority than was allowed by the Prussian constitution, comes prominently forward. The idea of substituting for the constitution a royal charter was vividly before him even in his last illness.

The Frankfort Assembly, enmeshed in the same double error, treated dynastic questions as a point already surmounted, and, with the energy for theorizing peculiar to Germans, took this for granted even in the case of Prussia and Austria. Those deputies at Frankfort who could give accurate information as to the opinion of the Prussian provinces and the German lands of Austria were partly interested in suppressing the truth; the Assembly, honestly or dishonestly, deceived itself as to the fact that, in the case of a conflict between a resolution of the Frankfort Diet and a Prussian royal decree, the former, so far as seven-eighths of the Prussian population was concerned, would be regarded as of little or no weight. Whoever lived in the eastern provinces of the kingdom in those days will still recollect that the proceedings of this Frankfort parliament, among all the elements in whose hands the actual power lay, and who in case of conflict would have had to command or bear arms, were not taken as seriously as might have been expected from the dignity of the scientific and parliamentary magnates there assembled. Not only in Prussia, but also in the great central states, a command from the King summoning brute force *en masse* to the assistance of the prince would at that time have had a sufficient effect, had it come to pass; not everywhere to the same degree as in Prussia, but nevertheless in a degree which would everywhere have supplied the need of a police force, if the princes had had the courage to appoint ministers who would have stood up for their cause firmly and openly. This was not the case in Prussia in the summer of 1848; but, in November, immediately upon the King's resolve to appoint ministers who were prepared to support the prerogative without regard to parliamentary decisions, the whole bugbear had vanished, and the only danger remaining was lest the return stroke should exceed the measure of reason. In the other North German states there were not even such conflicts as the Brandenburg ministry had to encounter in individual provincial towns. Even in Bavaria and Wurtemberg, despite anti-monarchical ministers, the monarchy proved ultimately stronger than the revolution.

When the King declined the imperial crown on April 3, 1849, but drew from the decree of the Frankfort Assembly a 'title' of whose value he was well aware, he was principally moved to do this because of the revolutionary, or at any rate parliamentary source of the offer, and because of the Frankfort parliament's lack of a legitimate mandate, owing to the want of acquiescence on the part of the ruling houses. But even if all these defects had been absent, at any rate in the King's view, nevertheless a continuation and invigoration of the institutions of the Empire, such as took place under the Emperor William, was scarcely to be expected during his reign. The wars which the latter sovereign waged would not have been avoided; only they would have come about *after* the constitution of the Empire as a consequence thereof, and not *before*, as a step to preparing and establishing the Empire. Whether Frederick William IV could have been moved to take the lead at the right time, I do not know; that was difficult even in the case of his brother, in whom the military vein and the feelings of a Prussian officer were paramount.

When I note the conditions both personal and material in the Prussia of those days as not ripe for the assumption of the leadership of Germany in war and peace, I do not mean to say that I then foresaw it with the same clearness as I see it to-day, when I look back upon a development of forty years since elapsed. My satisfaction in those days at the refusal of the imperial crown by the King was due, not to the judgment I had formed of his personal qualities, but rather to a keener sensitiveness for the prestige of the Prussian crown and its wearer, and still more to my instinctive distrust of the development of events since the barricades of 1848 and their parliamentary consequences. As regards the latter, I and my political friends were under the impression that the leading men in parliament and in the press, partly consciously but for the most part unconsciously, promoted and carried out the programme of ' making a clean sweep of everything,' and that the actual ministers were not the men to direct or check such a movement. My point of view with regard to the matter was not essentially different from that of a member of a parliamentary group to-day, based on attachment to friends and distrust or enmity towards opponents. The persuasion that an opponent, in everything he undertakes, is at best of limited intelligence, but more probably malicious and unscrupulous as well, and the aversion to dissent and break away from the members of one's own group, still dominates

the life of groups to-day; and at that time the convictions
on which these phenomena so dangerous to political life are
based were much livelier and much more honest than they
are to-day.

In those days opponents knew little of each other;
since then they have had forty years of opportunities to
do so, as the *personnel* of the more prominent party-men
for the most part changes only slowly and slightly. Then,
however, people mutually regarded each other as really
stupid or wicked; they really had the feeling and the
persuasion, which they nowadays *pretend* to have, in order
to produce an effect upon electors and monarchs, or because
such sentiments belong to the programme adopted by
those who have taken service in—'jumped into'—a particular group, from a belief in its justification and a confidence in its leaders. Nowadays political pushingness
plays a greater share in the existence and maintenance of
groups than was the case fifty years ago. Convictions
were then more straightforward and spontaneous, even if
the passions, the hatred, and the mutual distrust among
the groups and their leaders, the disposition to sacrifice
the interests of the country to the interest of the group,
are nowadays perhaps still more strongly developed. 'En
tout cas le diable n'y perd rien.' Byzantinism and in-
sincere speculation on the King's pet fancies went on,
indeed, in small upper coteries; but among the parliamentary groups the race for Court favour had not started.
Belief in the power of the monarchy was, erroneously, for
the most part slighter than belief in one's own importance; people dreaded nothing more than to be considered
servile or 'ministerial.' Some strove according to their
own convictions to strengthen and support the monarchy.

Others fancied they would find their own and their country's welfare in contending with, and weakening, the King; and this is a proof that, if not the power at least belief in the power of the Prussian monarchy was weaker then than it is now. The underestimate of the power of the Crown underwent no change even from the circumstance that the personal will of a not very strong-willed monarch like Frederick William IV sufficed to blunt the point of the whole German movement by the refusal of the imperial crown, and that the sporadic risings, which broke out immediately afterwards with the aim of realising the national wishes, were easily suppressed by the royal power.

The situation favourable for Prussia, which lasted during the short period elapsing between the fall of Prince Metternich in Vienna and the retreat of the troops from Berlin, was renewed, even if the outlines were fainter—thanks to the observation of the fact that the King and his army, after all their mistakes, were still strong enough to suppress the rising in Dresden and bring about the alliance of the three kings. A speedy utilisation of the situation in a national sense was possible, perhaps, but presupposed clear and practical aims and resolute action. Both were wanting. The favourable time was lost in considering the details of the future constitution, one of the widest spaces being occupied by the question as to the German Princes' right of embassy beside that of the German Empire.[1] In those days in the circles to which I had access at Court, and among the deputies, I advocated the view that this right of representation abroad did not

---

[1] Compare Bismarck's statement in his speech before the Reichstag on March 8, 1878 (*Politische Reden*, vii. p. 184).

possess the importance generally attached to it, but was subordinate to the question of the influence of the individual princes of the *Bund* in the Empire or abroad. If the influence of any such prince on politics was small, his embassies abroad would not weaken the impression of the unity of the Empire; but if his influence in peace and war, on the political and financial conduct of the affairs of the Empire, or on the decisions of foreign courts, was strong enough, there was no means of preventing princes' correspondents or any sort of more or less distinguished private people, down to the category of international dentists, from being the intermediaries of political negotiation.

It appeared to me more useful, instead of indulging in theoretical dissertations on the meaning of paragraphs of the constitution, to place the actually existing vigorous military power of Prussia in the foreground, as had happened on the occasion of the rebellion in Dresden, and might have happened in the extra-Prussian states. The events at Dresden had shown that among the Saxon troops discipline and fidelity were unshaken, as soon as the Prussian reinforcements had made the military situation tenable. Similarly the Hessian troops in the fighting at Frankfort, the Mecklenburg troops in Baden, had shown themselves trustworthy as soon as they had been convinced that they were led by men who knew what they were about, received orders that did not conflict one with another, and were not required to allow themselves to be attacked without defending themselves. If in those days we had sufficiently strengthened our army at the proper time, beginning at Berlin, and taken the lead with it in the military domain, without an afterthought, I cannot see how any doubt as to a successful issue could have been justified. The situation was not so clear in all questions of right and conscience as at the beginning of March 1848, but, politically at any rate, it was not unfavourable.

When I speak of afterthoughts, I mean the renunciation of approbation and popularity on the part of the related princely houses, parliaments, historians, and the daily press. The daily current which then roared its loudest in the press and in the parliaments imposed upon people as being the voice of public opinion; but it affords no measure of the people's mood, upon which depends the readiness of the masses to render obedience to the demands made upon them by the authorities in the regular way. The intellectual power of the upper ten thousand in the press and the tribune is sustained and directed by so great a multiplicity of conflicting efforts and forces that governments cannot adopt it as a clue for their conduct, so long as the gospels preached by orators and writers, by virtue of the credence they find in the masses, do not command the use of material forces close packed in a limited space. If this is the case, a *vis major* comes upon the scene, and politics have to reckon with it. So long as this effect (which as a rule is slow in coming) does not occur, so long as the noise is made only by the shrieking of the *rerum novarum cupidi* in the greater centres, and by the emotional needs of the press and parliamentary life, then, so far as the politician of realities is concerned, Coriolanus' opinion of popular manifestations holds good, although no mention of printer's ink is made in it. In those days, however, the leading circles in Prussia allowed themselves to be deafened by the noise of parliaments great and small, without measuring its importance by the barometer afforded them by the attitude of the

67

troops, whether in their ranks or in the presence of a summons to arms. The sympathies of the higher grades of officials, partly with the Liberal and partly with the National sides of the movement, contributed largely to the illusion which I was able to note as existing at that time at the Court and in the King as to the real relation of forces. It was an element which, but for an impulse received from the highest quarters, might have been given an obstructive though not actually decisive basis.

As regards the temptation which the situation offered, the King had a feeling which I would compare to the unpleasant sensation by which, though I am a great lover of swimming, I used to be seized whenever I took the first step into the water on a cold stormy day. His scruples as to whether matters were ripe were nourished among other things by the historical investigations which he carried on with Radowitz, not only on the subject of the Saxon and Hanoverian right of representation abroad, but also on the distribution of seats in the ' Diet ' between ruling and mediatised princes, sovereigns, and ' Personalists,' counts ' received ' and ' not-received,' among the various categories composing the bulk of the Diet—the case of *Freier Standes-herr* von Grote-Schauen demanding special investigation.

In those days I was not so intimately connected with military procedure as I was later, but I do not think I am mistaken in assuming that in the movements of the troops to suppress the risings in the Palatinate and in Baden more *cadres* and brigade-depôt staffs were employed than would have been advisable or expedient if mobile troops ready for campaigning had been marched in. It is a fact that the War Minister at the time of the Olmütz meeting alleged to me as one of the most urgent reasons for peace, or at least for a postponement of war, the impossibility of mobilising the army promptly, or indeed at all, seeing that, in Baden or elsewhere, the staffs were, outside their mobilisation districts, short of their full complement. If in the spring of 1849 we had kept clearly before our eyes the possibility of a warlike solution, and had preserved intact our capacity of mobilisation by the employment of none but troops on a war footing, then the military force at the disposal of Frederick William IV would not only have been sufficient to crush every insurrectionary movement in and outside of Prussia, but the forces set on foot would at the same time have provided us in 1850 with the means of preparing unsuspected for the solution of the chief questions in dispute, in case it had become acute enough for the question of military power to arise. Our clever King was not without political foresight, but lacked resolution; and his belief in his own absolute power, strong as a matter of principle, stood its ground in concrete cases against *political* counsellors, but not against the scruples of finance ministers.

Even then I was confident that the military strength of Prussia would suffice to suppress all insurrections, and that the results of the suppression would be all the more considerable in favour of the monarchy and of the national cause the greater obstacles there had been to overcome— and completely satisfactory, if all the forces from whom resistance was to be expected could be overcome in one and the same campaign. During the insurrections in Baden and the Palatinate, it was for a long time doubtful whither a part of the Bavarian army would gravitate. I remember that I said to the Bavarian ambassador, Count Lerchenfeld, just as he was taking leave of me at this

critical time in order to travel to Munich: ' God grant that
your army also, so far as it is untrustworthy, may revolt
openly; then there will be a big fight, but it will be decisive, and thus heal the sore.   If you make peace with the
untrustworthy part of your troops, the sore will remain
festering inwardly.'   Lerchenfeld, in anxiety and confusion, called me flippant.   I terminated the conversation
with the words, ' Be sure we shall tear through your job
and ours; the madder we are the better.'   He did not believe me, but nevertheless my confidence encouraged him;
and I believe to this day that the chances for a desirable
solution of the crisis of that time would have been still
better if the Baden revolution could have been previously
strengthened by the defection (so much feared in those
days) of a part of the Bavarian and Wurtemberg troops as
well.   No doubt, however, in that case they might have
remained unused.

I leave it undecided whether the half-heartedness and
timidity of the measures then taken to meet the serious
dangers were due only to finance-ministers' anxieties, or
to dynastic scruples of conscience and irresolution in the
highest places; or whether, in official circles, similar anxiety co-operated to that which in the March days, with
Bodelschwingh and others, stood in the way of the right
solution—namely, the fear lest the King, in proportion to
his renewed feeling of power and freedom from anxiety,
should also move in an autocratic direction.   I remember
to have noticed this anxiety among the higher officials and
in Liberal court circles.

The question still remains unanswered whether the
influence of General von Radowitz was actively exercised
upon the King from catholicising motives, in order to

prevent Protestant Prussia from observing the favourable opportunity, and to deceive the King till it was over. To this very day I do not know whether he was a catholicising opponent of Prussia, or only bent upon maintaining his position with the King.* It is certain that he made a skilful keeper of the mediæval wardrobe in which the King dressed up his fancies, and contributed thereby to make the King dawdle away the opportunities for practical intervention in the development of the present, over historical questions of form, and reminiscences of the annals of the Empire. The *tempus utile* for setting up the alliance of the three Kings was filled up in a dilatory manner with incidental questions of form, till Austria was once more strong enough to prevail upon Saxony and Hanover to withdraw, so that the two co-founders of this triple alliance fell away at Erfurt. During the Erfurt parliament, at a social gathering at General von Pfuel's house, the conversation turned on confidential reports received by certain deputies as to the strength of the Austrian army assembling in Bohemia to serve as a counterpoise and corrective to the parliament. Various figures

* General Gerlach wrote, in August 1850, as follows (*Denkwürdigkeiten*, i. p. 514): 'The King's respect for Radowitz depends upon two things. In the first place, his apparently acutely logical and mathematical mode of reasoning, by means of which his un-ideaed indifference enables him to avoid any possibility of contradicting the King. In this mode of thinking, so entirely opposed to his own current of ideas, the King sees a proof of the accuracy of his own calculations, and thus considers himself sure of his ground. Secondly, the King considers his ministers (and me also) as brute beasts, for the very reason that they have to settle with him practical current affairs, which never correspond with his own ideas. He does not believe that he has the capacity of making these ministers obedient to him, nor even the capacity of finding others; he therefore gives up the attempt, and fancies he has found in Radowitz a man able to restore Prussia, making Germany his starting-point, as Radowitz himself has confessed point-blank in his *Deutschland und Friedrich Wilhelm IV.*'

were given—80,000 men, 130,000 men. Radowitz quietly listened for a time, and then said in a decisive tone, his regular features wearing the expression peculiar to him of irrefutable certainty, 'Austria has in Bohemia 28,254 men and 7,132 horses.' The thousands he mentioned have remained in my memory *obiter;* the remaining figures I add arbitrarily in order to give a vivid image of the crushing precision of the general's statement. Naturally these figures, from the mouth of the official and competent representative of the Prussian government, for a time silenced every divergent opinion. How strong the Austrian army in Bohemia really was in the spring of 1850 is now of course known with certainty; that at the Olmütz period it consisted of considerably more than 100,000 men I was driven to assume from the confidential communications the Minister of War made to me in December of the same year.

The closer contact into which I came with Count Brandenburg at Erfurt enabled me to recognise that his Prussian patriotism was principally fed upon his reminiscences of 1812 and 1813, and was consequently, for that very reason, permeated by a German national feeling.

His dynastic, ' Borussian ' sentiment, however, and the notion of increasing the power of Prussia remained decisive with him. He had received from the King, who was then at work in his own way upon my political education, the commission to gain such influence as I might have in the group of the Extreme Right for the Erfurt policy, and attempted to do this by saying to me in the course of a solitary walk between the town and the Steigerwald, ' What danger can Prussia run in the whole affair? We calmly accept whatever is offered to us in the way of reinforcements, much or little, with the right provisionally to renounce what is not offered to us. Experience alone can show whether we can be satisfied in the long run with the constitutional provisions which the King has to make into the bargain. If it is no go, we can draw the sword, and drive the beggars to the devil!' I cannot deny that this military close to his exposition made a very favourable impression on me; but I had my doubts whether his Majesty's resolution at a critical moment would not depend on other influences than those of this chivalrous general. His tragic end confirmed my doubts.[1]

Herr von Manteuffel also was induced by the King to make the attempt to gain over the Prussian Extreme Right to support the policy of the government, and in this sense to bring about an understanding between us and the Gagern party. He did this by inviting Gagern and me alone to dinner, and leaving us to ourselves while we were still over our wine without a single explanatory or introductory remark. Gagern repeated to me, though in a less exact and intelligible form, what was known to us as the programme of his party, and, in a somewhat attenuated form, the proposal of the government. He spoke without looking at me, staring aside at the ceiling. Upon my remarking that what we Royalist Prussians feared most of all was that with this constitution the monarchical power would not remain strong enough, he sank, after a long and declamatory dissertation, into a contemptuous silence, which gave me an impression that may be translated by the words, ' Roma locuta est.' When Manteuffel came in

---

[1] According to Sybel (ii. 3) the story that Brandenburg died of a broken heart in consequence of the insolent treatment which fell to his lot at Warsaw, and of the pacific policy forced upon him, must, when compared with documentary facts, be regarded as legendary.

again, we had been sitting in silence for some minutes—I because I was awaiting Gagern's reply, he because, recollecting his position in the Diet of Frankfort, he considered it beneath his dignity to discuss with a Prussian squire otherwise than as laying down the law. He was more adapted to be a parliamentary orator and president than a political man of business, and had come to regard himself as a *Jupiter tonans*. After he had withdrawn, Manteuffel asked me what he had said. 'He harangued me as if I had been a public meeting,' I replied.

It is remarkable that in each of the families which then represented national Liberalism both in Germany and in Prussia—that is to say, Gagern and Auerswald—there were three brothers, and a general in each; moreover that the general in each case was the most practical politician of the brothers, and both were murdered as a result of revolutionary movements whose development had been promoted by each of them in his own sphere of activity in all patriotic good faith. General von Auerswald, who was murdered at Frankfort on September 18, 1848, because, as people said, he was taken for Radowitz, had boasted, on the occasion of the first United Diet, that he, as colonel of a cavalry regiment, had ridden hundreds of miles to support the opposition voters among the peasants.[1]

In November 1850 I was simultaneously summoned to my regiment as officer in the Landwehr, and as deputy to the impending session of the chamber.[2] On my way

[1] As is well known, General Frederick von Gagern was shot dead on April 20 near Kandern by the bullets of the Baden guerrillas as he was riding back to his troops after a fruitless interview with Hecker.

[2] According to a note on the margin of the MS., Prince Bismarck meant in this place to insert an experience which he repeatedly mentioned in his table-talk. I give the narrative as I remember it. As Bismarck happened to be on his way to Berlin with his writ of summons in his pocket, a Pomera-

via Berlin to join my regiment I reported myself to the
War Minister, von Stockhausen, who was a personal friend
of mine and grateful for some small personal services.
After I had overcome the resistance of the old porter and
been admitted, I gave expression to the martial sentiments
which had been excited by my summons to join my regiment and the tone of the Austrians. The minister, a
dashing old soldier of whose moral and physical courage
I was confident, spoke to me in substanceas follows :

'We must, for the moment, do all we can to avoid a
rupture. We have not sufficient power to stop the Austrians if they invade us even without the support of the
Saxons. We must abandon Berlin to them, and mobilise
at two centres outside the capital—in Dantzic, possibly, and
in Westphalia. It would be a fortnight before we could
bring perhaps 70,000 men in front of Berlin, and these
would not be sufficient against the forces which the Austrians already have in readiness against us.' It was necessary above all things, he continued, if we wanted to
fight, to gain time, and it was therefore to be wished that
the impending deliberations in the Chamber of Deputies
should not precipitate a rupture by discussions and decisions such as we might expect from the prevailing tone of
the press. He begged me to remain in Berlin, and confidentially to use a moderating influence upon my friends

---

nian mayor called Stranzke got into the stage-coach with him. The conversation of course immediately turned on political events. When Stranzke
heard of Bismarck's orders he naïvely asked : 'Where are the French ?' and
was visibly taken aback when Herr von Bismarck informed him that this
time he was not going against the French but the Austrians. 'I should
be very sorry,' said he, 'if we had to fire upon the "white collars," and not
upon those French blackguards,' so lively was the recollection that still
clung to him of the sufferings of Prussia after the defeat at Jena, and of the
brotherhood in arms of Prussians and Austrians in 1813 and 1814.

among the deputies who were already there or might arrive immediately afterwards. He complained of the dispersal of the permanent staff, which had been called out and employed on their peace footing, and was now scattered far from their recruiting districts and depots, partly in the interior of the country, but to a still greater extent in South-west Germany, and consequently in localities where a rapid mobilisation on a war footing could only be carried out with difficulty.[1]

The Baden troops had at that time been caused to enter Prussia by roads that were not easily passable, making use of the Weser district of Brunswick; a proof of the solicitude with which the frontiers of the confederated Princes were respected, whilst all the other attributes of their territorial sovereignty were lightly ignored or abolished in the constitution projected for the Empire and the alliance of the three kings. The projects were carried nearly to the point of mediatisation, but no one ventured to claim marching quarters outside the actual military routes provided for by treaty. It was only on the outbreak of the Danish war of 1864 that this timid tradition was broken through at Schwartau, and the lowered toll-bar of Oldenburg ignored by Prussian troops.

The reflections of a practical and honest general like Stockhausen I could not criticise, and cannot even now. From the military point of view our hands were tied as he said, and the blame for this was not his, but resulted from that want of system with which our policy was conducted, both in the military and the diplomatic depart-

---

[1] Cf. the speech of Bismarck in the Reichstag of Jan. 21, 1882 (*Politische Reden*, ix. 234); the above information gives the key to the proper understanding of the speech of Dec. 3, 1850.

ments during and subsequently to the March days—a mixture of levity and niggardliness. From a military point of view especially it was of such a kind that the measures taken could lead only to the supposition that a martial or even a military solution of the questions in suspense would in the last instance not be considered in Berlin at all. Men were too much preoccupied with public opinion, speeches, newspapers and constitution-mongering to arrive at decided views and practical aims in the domain of foreign, even if it were only extra-Prussian-German, policy. Stockhausen was not in a position to make good the sins of omission and the want of system in our policy by sudden military achievements, and had thus got into a situation which even the political leader of the ministry, Count Brandenburg, had not considered possible; for he succumbed to the disillusion which his lofty patriotic sense of honour experienced in the last days of his life.[1] It is unjust to accuse Stockhausen of pusillanimity; and I have reason to believe that even King William I, when I was his minister, shared my view with regard to the military situation in November 1850. However that may be, I had at the time no substantial foundation for such criticism as a Conservative deputy could exercise in regard to a minister, or, in the military domain, a lieutenant of Landwehr to a general.

Stockhausen undertook to inform my regiment, stationed in Lusatia, that he had ordered Lieut. von Bismarck to remain in Berlin. I next repaired to my colleague in the Diet, Justizrath Geppert, who was then the leader, not indeed of my group, but at any rate of that numerous body which might be called the Right Centre.

[1] See note on p. 73.

These were disposed to support the government, but considered that the energetic adoption of Prussia's national task was indicated, not only as a principle, but also as a motive for immediate military activity. When dealing with him I came in conflict at the outset with parliamentary views which did not coincide with the programme of the Minister of War, and had therefore to be at some pains to argue him out of a notion which, before my interview with Stockhausen, I myself had in the main shared, and which may be described as the natural product of wounded honour in the national or military Prussian party. I recollect that our conversations lasted a long time and had often to be repeated. Their effect on the groups of the Right may be gathered from the debate on the Address. I myself on December 3 expressed my then convictions in a speech from which the following sentences are extracted:[1]

'As we all are aware, the Prussian people has risen unanimously at the summons of its King. It has risen full of confiding obedience; it has risen to fight, like its forefathers, the battles of the King of Prussia, before it knew—mark this well, gentlemen—before it knew what was to be fought for in these battles; that perhaps no one who joined the Landwehr knew.

'I had hoped to find this feeling of unanimity and confidence repeated in the sphere of the representatives of the nation, in those narrower spheres in which the reins of government have their origin. A short residence at Berlin, a cursory glance at what is going on here, has shown me that I was mistaken. The draft of the Address calls this a great period; I have found nothing great here but personal ambition, nothing great but mistrust,

[1] *Politische Reden*, i. 261.

nothing great but party rancour. These are three great nesses that, in my opinion, stamp this age as petty, and afford the friend of his country a dismal glimpse into our future. Want of unity in the circles which I have indicated is in the draft Address flimsily concealed by big words, which every one interprets as he pleases. In the Address and in the amendments to it I have not been able to discover a trace of that confidence which inspires the country; of the devoted confidence that is based on attachment to his Majesty the King, on the experience which the country has had good opportunity of gaining of the ministry which has guided it for the last two years. I should have thought this all the more needed, owing to the necessity, as it appeared to me, that the impression which the unanimous rising of the country has had upon Europe should be heightened and strengthened by the unity of those who do not belong to our armed force, at the moment when we are confronting our neighbours in arms, when we are hurrying armed to our frontier; at a moment when a spirit of confidence animates even those in whom it has not seemed at other times to exist; at a moment when every question of the Address which touches upon foreign policy is pregnant with peace or war—and, gentlemen, what a war! No campaign of single regiments towards Schleswig or Baden, no military promenade through disturbed provinces, but a war on a large scale against two of the three great continental Powers, while the third, eager for booty, is arming upon our frontiers, and knows full well that in the cathedral of Cologne is to be found the jewel which can close the French revolution and make secure those who hold power there—I mean the imperial crown of France. . . .

BISMARCK

'It is easy for a statesman, whether he be in the cabinet or the chamber, to blow a blast with the wind of popularity on the trumpet of war, warming himself the while at his own fireside; or to thunder orations from this tribune and then to leave it to the musketeer who is bleeding to death in the snow, whether his system win fame and victory or no. There is nothing easier than that; but woe to the statesman who in these days does not look around him for a reason for war, which will hold water when the war is over. . . .

'According to my conviction, Prussian honour does not consist in Prussia's playing the Don Quixote all over Germany for the benefit of mortified parliament celebrities who consider their local constitution in danger. I look for Prussian honour in Prussia's abstinence before all things from every shameful union with democracy; in Prussia's refusal to allow, in the present and all other questions, anything to happen in Germany without her consent; and in the joint execution by the two protecting Powers of Germany, with equal authority, of whatsoever they, Prussia and Austria, after joint independent deliberation, consider reasonable and politically justifiable.

' The main question, in which peace and war are wrapped up, the shaping of Germany, the regulation of the relations between Prussia and Austria, and the relations of these two to the lesser states, is in a few days to be the object of the deliberations of the free conferences, and consequently cannot *now* be the object of a war. If any one wishes for war at any price, I would console that man by telling him that it is to be found *at any time* in the free conferences—in four or six weeks, in fact, if it is wanted. Far be it from me, at so important a moment as the present, to wish to hamper the action of the government by giving it advice. If I wanted to express a wish to the ministry, it would be this: that we do *not disarm before* the free conferences have yielded some positive result; there will be always time then to wage a war if we really do not wish to avoid it or cannot do so with honour.

' How German unity is to be found in the union I am unable to understand. It is an odd sort of unity that requires us at the outset from time to time to shoot down and run through our German fellow-countrymen in the south in the interests of this secession league; that finds German honour in the necessary gravitation of all German questions to Warsaw and Paris. Picture to yourselves two parts of Germany standing face to face in arms, the difference between their respective strengths being so slight that the advocacy of one of the two by another Power, even by one much feebler than Russia or France, would turn the scale decisively. It is beyond my comprehension what right any one who wishes to bring about such a state of things would have to complain that the decision under such circumstances should gravitate to the foreigner.'

My leading idea in this speech was to work for the postponement of the war, according to the views of the War Minister, until we were equipped. I could not publicly express this idea in perfect clearness; I could only hint at it. It would not have been demanding too much dexterity of our diplomacy to call upon it to postpone, avoid, or bring about the war as necessity might require.

At that time (November 1850) the Russian conception of the revolutionary movement in Germany was already much calmer than it had been at the first outbreak in March 1848. I was acquainted with the Russian military attaché, Count Benckendorf; and, from a confidential conversation with him in 1850, took away the impression that the German, inclusive of the Polish, movement no longer disquieted the St. Petersburg cabinet to the same degree as on the occasion of its outbreak, nor was regarded as a military danger in case of war. In March 1848 the development of the revolution in Germany and Poland appeared to the Russians incalculable and dangerous. The first Russian diplomatist to support another view in St. Petersburg by his dispatches was the then *chargé d'affaires* in Frankfort-on-Maine, Baron von Budberg, who was subsequently ambassador to Berlin. His dispatches on the subject of the proceedings and the significance of the Paulskirche meeting had from the outset a satirical colouring; and the contempt with which this young diplomatist spoke in them of the speeches of the German professors and of the authority of the National Assembly had so comforted the Emperor Nicholas that Budberg's career was made thereby, and he was very speedily promoted to the dignity of minister and ambassador. In these dispatches he had expressed from the anti-German point of view a political appreciation of events analogous to that which, with more of the concern natural to natives of the country, had prevailed in old-Prussian circles in Berlin, among which he had formerly lived; and one may say that the view, as the first adopter of which he made his mark at St. Petersburg, originated in the club at Berlin. Since then the Russians had not only materially strengthened their military position on the Vistula, but also had acquired a feebler impression of the military capacity of the revolution, as well as of the German governments of those days; and the language which, in November 1850, I heard from my friend the Russian ambassador, Baron Meyendorff, and his compatriots was that of complete confidence from the Russian point of view, permeated with an interest in the future of their friend Prussia, which was personally benevolent, but hurt me a good deal. It gave me the impression that Austria was regarded as the stronger member, and more to be relied on, and Russia herself as powerful enough to hold the balance between the two.

Although I was not so intimate as subsequently with the methods and usages of the foreign service, yet even as a layman I had no doubt that the occasion for war, whenever it was offered to us or appeared acceptable, even after Olmütz, might always be found in the Dresden negotiations and in breaking them off. Stockhausen had incidentally named to me six weeks as the interval he needed in order to be ready to fight; and in my opinion it would not have been difficult to gain double as much time by skilful conduct of the deliberations at Dresden, if the only cause for refusing a martial solution of the question had been the momentary unreadiness of our military material. The Dresden negotiations were not utilised in order to gain, in Prussian interests, either a greater result or an apparently justifiable pretext for war; but it has never been clear to me whether the remarkable limitation of our aims at Dresden proceeded from the King or from Herr von Manteuffel, the newly appointed Minister of Foreign Affairs. At the time I had only the impression that the latter, after his previous career as *Landrath*,

President of the Government, and head of the Ministry of the Interior, had not felt quite at his ease in presence of Prince Schwarzenberg's swaggering quality manners. Even the appearance of their respective establishments in Dresden—Prince Schwarzenberg on the first-floor with his liveries, silver plate, and champagne—the Prussian minister with his clerks and his water-bottles one pair higher—was adapted to produce an impression prejudicial to us, both in the self-consciousness of these representatives of the two Great Powers, and in the appreciation of them by the other German representatives. The old Prussian simplicity which Frederick the Great had recommended to his representative in London with the words, ' When you go a-foot, tell 'em there are a hundred thousand men behind you,' testifies to a spirit of brag which one can only credit the witty King with in one of his fits of exaggerated thriftiness. Nowadays every one has a hundred thousand men behind him; only we, it would appear, had not got them available at the Dresden period. The fundamental error of the Prussian policy of those days was that people fancied they could attain through publicist, parliamentary, or diplomatic hypocrisies results which could be had only by war or readiness for it, by fighting or by readiness to fight; in such shape that they seemed forced upon our virtuous moderation as a reward for the oratorical demonstration of our ' German sentiment.' At a later day these were known as ' moral conquests ; ' it was the hope that others would do for us what we dared not do for ourselves.

CHAPTER IV

DIPLOMATIST

Upon the resolve of the Prussian government to send to the Federal Diet, as restored to activity by Austria, and thereby to complete its numbers, General von Rochow, who had been accredited to St. Petersburg and remained so, was provisionally appointed envoy to the Diet. At the same time two Secretaries of Legation—myself and Herr von Gruner—were put upon the staff. Before my appointment as *Legationsrath*, the prospect was held out to me by his Majesty and his minister, von Manteuffel, of an early promotion to the post of envoy. Rochow was to introduce and coach me; but he himself could not do the work that the business required, and employed me to put it into shape without keeping me posted up in the policy.

The conversation (briefly[1] given in a letter of my late friend, J. L. Motley, to his wife) which I had with the King previous to my appointment had the following tenor. On my replying to a sudden question from the minister Manteuffel as to whether I would take the post of envoy to the *Bund* with a simple ' Yes,' the King sent for me and said, ' You have a good pluck to undertake straight off an office to which you are a stranger.' ' The pluck is on your Majesty's part in entrusting me with such a post. However, your Majesty is of course not

[1] See Motley's letter of July 27, 1855 ; *Correspondence of J. L. Motley*, vol. i. p. 173.

bound to maintain the appointment, as soon as it ceases to justify itself. I myself cannot be sure whether or not the task is beyond my capacity until I have had closer acquaintance with it. If I find that I am not equal to it I shall be the first to demand my recall. I have the pluck to obey if your Majesty has the pluck to command.' Whereupon the King rejoined, ' Then we will try the thing.'

On May 11, 1851, I arrived at Frankfort. Herr von Rochow, with less ambition than love of ease, weary of the climate and the exhausting Court life of St. Petersburg, would have preferred to keep permanently the Frankfort post, which satisfied all his wishes. He therefore intrigued in Berlin to have me appointed envoy to Darmstadt, and accredited simultaneously to the Duke of Nassau and the city of Frankfort; and perhaps would further not have been indisposed to let me have the St. Petersburg post in exchange. He loved life on the Rhine, and intercourse with the German courts. Nevertheless, his exertions met with no success. On July 11 Herr von Manteuffel wrote to me that the King had approved of my appointment as envoy to the Federal Diet. ' Of course it goes without saying,' wrote the minister, ' that we cannot send away Herr von Rochow brusquely; I therefore intend to write him a few lines about it to-day. I feel certain of your acquiescence if I proceed in this matter with all respect to the wishes of Herr von Rochow, to whom I cannot but be thankful for undertaking this difficult and thankless mission, in contrast to many other people who are always ready to criticise, but draw back when it comes to action. I need not assure you that I do not refer to you: for you at any rate have mounted into the breach with us, and will, I fancy, also defend it alone.'

On July 15 followed my appointment to the Diet. Despite the respect with which he was treated, Herr von Rochow was cross, and requited me for disappointing his wish by leaving Frankfort early one morning, without telling me of his departure or handing over to me the business and the documents. Informed of the matter from another quarter, I arrived at the station in time to thank him for the kindness he had shown me. So much has been [1] published, both private and official, as to my activity and my observations at the Diet, that there are only gleanings left for me.

I found at Frankfort two Prussian commissaries from the days of the interim, Oberpräsident von Boetticher—whose son was afterwards, as State Secretary and minister, to be my assistant—and General von Peucker, who gave me my first opportunity of studying the nature and properties of decorations. He was a skilful, brave officer, of high scientific culture, which he subsequently turned to account as inspector-general of the military education and training system. In the year 1812, while serving in York's corps, his cloak was stolen from him, and he was obliged to take part in the retreat in his close-fitting uniform, lost his toes from frostbite, and suffered other damage from the cold. Despite his physical ugliness, this clever and valiant officer won the hand of a beautiful countess Schulenburg, through whom subsequently the

[1] *Preussen im Bundestage*, 1851–59. *Documente des K. Preuss Bundestags Gesandtschaft*. Edited by Dr. v. Poschinger. 4 vols. Leipzig, 1882–84.—*Bismarck's Briefe an den General Leopold v. Gerlach*. Edited by H. Kohl. Berlin, 1896. *Bismarckbriefe*. Edited by H. Kohi (Bielefeld, 1897), p. 59, &c.

rich inheritance of the house of Schenk Flechtingen in the Altmark came to his son. In remarkable contrast to his intellectual qualities stood his weakness for externals, which made the slang of Berlin richer by one expression. Any one who wore too many decorations at once was said to ' Peucker.'

On the occasion of a morning visit, I found him standing before a table on which lay spread out his well-earned decorations, first won upon the battlefield. Their traditional sequence on his breast had been disturbed by a new star with which he had just succeeded in getting invested. After the first greeting he spoke to me, not a word about Austria and Prussia, but desired my opinion from the point of view of artistic taste as to the place where the new star ought to be inserted. The feeling of affectionate respect which I had received from my childish years for this highly meritorious general determined me to enter into the subject with perfect gravity, and to help him to settle the point before we proceeded to talk business.

I confess that when I received my first decoration in 1842, a medal for saving life, I felt happy and elated, because I was then a young squire not *blasé* in that respect. In the service of the state I speedily lost this unsophisticated sentiment. I do not remember to have experienced an objective satisfaction on late occasions when I received decorations, only a subjective pleasure at the outward translation into act of the kindness with which my King requited my attachment, or other monarchs confirmed to me the success of my political efforts to gain their confidence and goodwill. Our ambassador von Jordan, at Dresden, made the reply to a jocose proposal that he should part with one of his numerous decorations : ' Je vous les cède toutes, pourvu que vous m'en laissiez une pour couvrir mes nudités diplomatiques.' Indeed, a *grand cordon* is part of an ambassador's toilette; and if it is not that of his own court, the possibility of being able to have a change is just as much desired by elegant diplomats as it is by ladies in regard to their clothes. In Paris I have seen senseless acts of violence against crowds cease abruptly when ' un monsieur décoré' came in the way of them. I have never found it necessary to wear decorations except at St. Petersburg and Paris; in both those places, when walking in the streets, you must show a ribbon on your coat if you want to be treated with the requisite politeness by the police and the public. Elsewhere I have in every case only put on the decorations actually demanded by the occasion; it has always appeared to me a bit of *chinoiserie* when I have observed the morbid extent to which the collector's mania has developed in regard to decorations among my colleagues and fellow-workers in the bureaucracy—how, for instance, *Geheimraths*, although the cascade of orders spouting over their breasts was already beyond their control, would pave the way to the conclusion of some small treaty, because they wanted the order of the other contracting state to complete their collection.

The members of the chambers who in 1849–50 had to revise the constitution granted, developed a very exhausting activity; there were sittings of committees from eight to ten o'clock, sittings of the whole House from ten to four, which were sometimes even repeated at a later hour of the evening, and alternated with protracted sittings of groups. I could therefore satisfy my need for active

movement only at night; and I recollect many a night
walking up and down between the opera house and the
Brandenburg gate in the lime avenue. By accident my
attention was at this time drawn to the hygienic value of
dancing, which I had given up in my twenty-seventh year,
feeling that it was an amusement only for young people.
At a court ball a lady who was a friend of mine sent me
off to seek her absent partner for a cotillon, and when I
could not find him, begged me to take his place. After
I had got over my first fear of giddiness on the smooth
floor of the White Hall, I danced with pleasure, and got
a sounder sleep after it than I had done for some time.
At Frankfort everybody danced, foremost of all, for all
his sixty-five years, the French ambassador, M. Marquis
of Tallenay, who, after the proclamation of the Empire
in France, became 'Monsieur le Marquis de Tallenay;'
and I easily fell into the habit, although at the *Bund* I
had plenty of time for walking and riding. In Berlin,
too, when I had become minister, I did not refuse to
dance when called up by ladies of my acquaintance or
commanded by princesses; but I always had to hear sar-
castic remarks from the King for doing so. He would
say to me, for instance: 'I am reproached with having
selected a frivolous minister. You should not confirm
that impression by dancing.' The princesses were then
forbidden to choose me for a partner. Indeed, Herr von
Keudell's persistent capacity for dancing threw difficulties
in my way with his Majesty when the question of his promotion arose. This was of a piece with the simple nature
of the Emperor, who was wont to preserve his dignity by
avoiding unnecessary demonstrations which might challenge criticism. In his notion a dancing statesman was

in place only in the formal quadrilles of princes; in the rapid waltz one lost all credit, in his eyes, for wisdom in council.

After I had made myself at home on Frankfort ground —not without severe collisions with the representative of Austria, in the first instance in the matter of the fleet, wherein he attempted to curtail Prussia in authority and in finance, and to cripple her for the future—the King sent for me to Potsdam, and told me, on May 28, 1852, that he had now resolved to send me to the diplomatic high school at Vienna. I was to go there first as substitute and subsequently as successor to Count Arnim,[1] who was seriously ill. With that object he gave me the following letter of introduction to his Majesty the Emperor Francis Joseph on June 5:

' Your Imperial Majesty will permit me to introduce the bearer of this letter to your court in a few lines in my own handwriting. He is Herr von Bismarck-Schön-hausen. He belongs to a family of knightly rank which, settled in our Marches for a longer time than my own house, has ever, and singularly in him, preserved its ancient virtues. The maintenance and confirmation of the gratifying condition of our rural districts are largely due to his fearless and energetic labours in the evil days of recent years. Your Majesty is aware that Herr von Bismarck fills the post of my envoy to the *Bund*. Now, inasmuch as the state of health of my ambassador at your Majesty's imperial court, Count von Arnim, has made his temporary absence necessary, and the relations between our courts do not admit, according to my idea, of his replacement by

[1] Henry Frederick Count von Arnim-Heinrichsdorf-Werbelow, born 1791, died 1859.

a subordinate, I have selected Herr von Bismarck to provide a deputy for Count Arnim during his absence. It
is satisfactory to me to think that your Majesty will thus
make the acquaintance of a man who with us is honoured
by many, and hated by some, because of his frank and
chivalrous obedience and his irreconcilable attitude towards
the revolution down to its roots. He is my friend and
loyal servant, and comes to Vienna with a fresh, lively,
and sympathetic impress of my principles, my mode of
action, my will, and, I may add, of my love towards Austria and your Majesty. He can, if it be considered worth
the trouble, do what very few are in a position to do—
give your Majesty and your highest councillors full information on many subjects; for if monstrous misunderstandings of old date are not too deeply rooted (which God in
His mercy forbid!), the short period of his official functions at Vienna may be truly fraught with blessing. Herr
von Bismarck comes from Frankfort, where what the middle states, big with their Rhine confederation, rapturously
call the differences between Austria and Prussia have always found their loudest reverberation and often their
source; and he has observed these events and their ways
with keenness and impartiality. I have commanded him
to reply to every question addressed to him on the subject
by your Majesty and your ministers as if they proceeded
from myself. Should it please your Majesty to require
of him any explanation as to my view and treatment of
the Zollverein affair, I am sure that my attitude in these
matters will succeed in obtaining, if not the good fortune
of your approbation, at least your attention. The presence of the dear and noble Emperor Nicholas has really
done my heart good. The sure confirmation of my old

DIPLOMATIST

and fervent hope that your Majesty and I are genuinely united in the conviction that our threefold union—immovable, religious, and energetic—*alone* can deliver Europe and our wayward but so beloved German Fatherland from the present crisis, fills me with thankfulness towards God and increases my old and loyal love for your Majesty. I trust you will preserve your love for me, my dearest friend, as in those wonderful days on the Tegernsee, and strengthen your confidence in me, and your friendship, so powerful, so weighty, so indispensable to me and to our common Fatherland.

'From the bottom of my heart then, dearest friend, I commend myself to your friendship, as your imperial Majesty's loyal and most faithful and devoted uncle, brother, and friend.'

I found in Vienna the 'monosyllabic' ministry—Buol, Bach, Bruck, &c.—no friends of Prussia, but amiable to me from their belief in my susceptibility to the Emperor's goodwill, and in the services I could render in return in the domain of business. Externally I was received with more honour that I could have expected; but in the way of business—that is, in reference to the customs affair—my mission bore no fruit. Austria already had in view a customs-union with us, and neither then nor later did I consider it advisable to meet their efforts in that direction.

A certain degree of similarity in the matter of consumption is a necessary basis for community of interest in customs; even the difference of interests within the German Zollverein, between North and South, East and West, is productive of difficulties, only to be overcome by that goodwill which springs from national cohesion.

BISMARCK

Between Hungary and Galicia on the one side, and the Zollverein on the other, the difference in consumption of dutiable goods is too great for a community of tariffs to appear practicable. The standard of distribution of the customs revenue always puts Germany at a disadvantage, even though figures made it appear that Austria was in that position. In Cis- and still more in Trans-Leithania Austria chiefly lives upon its own, and not upon imported, products. Besides this, I had not then in general, and even now I only have in scattered instances, the necessary confidence in the non-German subordinate officials in the East.

Our only Secretary of Legation at Vienna received me with some ill-temper at not being *chargé d'affaires*, and applied to Berlin for leave of absence. This was refused by the minister, but immediately granted by myself. Thus it came about that I was obliged to apply to the Hanoverian ambassador, Count Adolf Platen, an old friend of mine, to present me to the ministers and introduce me to diplomatic society. He asked me one day in a confidential conversation whether I too thought that I was destined to be Manteuffel's successor. I replied that I had no desire that way, at least at present. Still I believed that the King meant to make me his minister some time later on, wished to train me for the post, and with this object in view had sent me on an extraordinary mission to Austria. It was my wish, however, for ten years more or so, to see the world as envoy at Frankfort or at various Courts, and then for some ten years more to be minister of state, if possible with distinction; finally to settle down in the country and reflect on my past experiences, and, like my old uncle at Templin near Potsdam, to graft fruit-

trees.[1] This jocose conversation was reported by Platen to
Hanover, and brought to the knowledge of Klenze, the
Director-General of the Taxes, who transacted customs
business with Manteuffel, and in me hated the squire as a
Liberal bureaucrat would. He had nothing better to do
than to send garbled information out of Platen's report to
Manteuffel, making out that I was labouring to bring
about his fall. On my return from Vienna to Berlin on
July 8, I experienced the outward effects of this tattling.
It took the form of a coolness in my relations with my
chief, and I was no longer invited as formerly to live
at his house when I came to Berlin. My friendly relations with General von Gerlach also came in for suspicion.

The recovery of Count Arnim allowed me to terminate
my residence at Vienna, and brought to nought for the
time being the King's former design of appointing me as
Arnim's successor. Even, however, if his recovery had
not taken place, I should not have cared to take up his
post, as I already had the feeling that the way I had come
forward at Frankfort had made me *persona ingrata* in
Vienna. I was afraid that they would continue to treat me
as a hostile element there, make my service difficult, and
discredit me at the Court of Berlin, which it would be
easier to do by means of Court correspondence if I was
employed at Vienna than by way of Frankfort.

I remember conversations on the subject of Vienna
at a later period during long railway journeys when I
was alone with the King. At those times I took the line
of saying: ' If your Majesty commands, I will go thither,

---

[1] Cf. Bismarck's letter written to Manteuffel in Prussia, July 23, 1852,
in the *Proceedings of the Federal Diet*, iv. 99 &c.

but not willingly. I incurred the dislike of the Austrian Court in the service of your Majesty at Frankfort, and shall have the feeling of being delivered over to my adversaries if I have to be ambassador at Vienna. Any government can injure any ambassador accredited to it, and his position may be ruined by such means as are employed by the Austrian policy in Germany.'

The King's reply used to be: 'I will not command you; you must go of your own free will, and beg me to let you go; it is a finishing school of diplomatic education, and you ought to thank me for taking charge of your education in this direction, for it is worth your while.' Even the position of a minister of state was beyond my desires at this time. I was persuaded that, the King being what he was, I could not attain any position as minister that I should find tenable. He looked upon me as an egg which he had laid and hatched out himself; and in cases of difference of opinion would have always had the feeling that the egg wanted to be cleverer than the hen. That the aims of Prussia's foreign policy, as they floated before me, did not altogether coincide with his was clear to me, as were also the difficulties which a responsible minister of that master would have to overcome during his fits of autocracy, with his often abrupt changes of view, his irregularity in matters of business, and his accessibility to uninvited back-stairs influences on the part of political intriguers, such as have found entrance to the royal house from the time of our Electors' adepts down to later days—even in the days of the austere and homely Frederick William I—' pharmacopolæ, balatrones, hoc genus omne.' [1] The difficulty of being at the same time an

---

[1] Horace, Sat. ii. 1, 2.

obedient and a responsible minister was greater in those days than it was under William I.

In September 1853 the prospect was open to me of becoming a minister of state in Hanover. Just after I had gone through a cure at the baths at Norderney, I was sounded by Bacmeister, who had just retired from Schele's ministry, as to whether I would be a minister of King George. I expressed myself to the effect that I could only serve in the foreign policy of Hanover if the King was willing to go completely hand in hand with Prussia. I could not take off my ' Prussianity ' like a coat. On the way to my own people at Villeneuve, on the Lake of Geneva, whither I went from Norderney *via* Hanover, I had several conferences with the King. One of them took place in a closet situated on the ground-floor of the palace between his bedroom and the Queen's. The King wished the fact of our conversation not to be known, but had commanded me to come to dinner at five o'clock. He did not recur to the question of my becoming his minister, but merely asked me as an expert in Federal Diet affairs for a statement on the manner and fashion in which the Constitution of 1848 might be revised with the help of resolutions of the *Bund*. After I had developed my views, he asked me to reduce them to writing on the spot. I consequently wrote down the chief features of my plan of action, with the impatient King sitting close to me at the same table, under the aggravating difficulties caused by seldom-used writing materials, ink thick, pens bad, writing-paper rough, and no blotting-paper: the state-paper, four pages long, and all covered with ink-blots, which I finally presented to him, could not be regarded as a fair copy up to Chancery mark. The King added nothing but his signature, and even that with difficulty, in the room in which he had received me for the sake of secrecy. The secrecy indeed was interrupted by the fact that it was now six o'clcck, and that the dinner party which had been invited for five could not remain ignorant of the cause of the delay. When the clock standing behind the King struck the hour, he sprang up, and, without saying a word, with a rapidity and certainty astonishing when one considered his blindness, made his way through the over-furnished apartment into the adjacent bedroom or dressing-room. I remained alone, without directions, with no knowledge of the geography of the palace, and without anything to guide me but a remark of the King's, that one of the three doors in the room led into the bedroom of the Queen, who was ill with measles. Being at length compelled to tell myself that no one was coming to conduct me, I stepped through the third door and found myself face to face with a footman who did not know me, and was terrified and agitated at my appearance in that part of the palace. He was, however, immediately pacified when, suiting my answer to the accent of his suspicious question, I replied in English, and requested him to conduct me to the royal table.

In the evening—I do not remember whether it was the same day or the next—I had another long audience without witnesses. In the course of it I observed with astonishment how remissly the blind monarch was served. The only light in the big room consisted of a double candlestick, with two wax tapers to which heavy metal shades were fastened. One of these, as the wax burnt down to the socket, fell to the ground with a crash like the sound of a gong. Nobody appeared, however; there was no one in the adjoining room; and I had to ask his Majesty where the bell-rope was that I had to pull. This neglect of the King struck me all the more, as the table at which we were sitting was so littered with every imaginable sort of public and private papers, that as the King moved about several of them fell to the ground and I had to pick them up. No less remarkable was it that the blind King should transact business for hours at a time with a strange diplomatist like myself, without any minister to take cognisance.

The mention of my residence in Hanover at that time reminds me of an incident which I have never clearly understood. A consul named Spiegelthal had been sent from Berlin to assist the Prussian commissary who had to negotiate in Hanover on the customs matters then pending. When I alluded to him in a conversation with my friend the Minister von Schele as a Prussian official, von Schele laughingly expressed his astonishment. ' Judging by his action, he would have taken the man for an Austrian agent.' I telegraphed in cipher to Minister von Manteuffel, and advised that the luggage of Spiegelthal, who was returning next day to Berlin, should be overhauled at the frontier custom house and his papers impounded. My expectation of hearing or reading something of the matter during the next few days was not fulfilled. While I was spending the last days of October in Berlin and Potsdam, General von Gerlach said to me, among other things: ' Manteuffel has sometimes very curious ideas; he lately wanted Consul Spiegelthal to be invited to the royal table, and had his way by making a cabinet question of it.'

CHAPTER V

THE 'WOCHENBLATT' PARTY—THE CRIMEAN WAR

In the circles opposed to the monarchy some little hope
was retained on behalf of the German cause by means of
leverage according to the views of the Duke of Coburg, of
English and French assistance, but primarily of Liberal
sympathies among the German people. The active and
practical realisation of these hopes was confined to the
little circle of the Court opposition, which, under the name
of the Bethmann-Hollweg group, tried to win over the
Prince of Prussia to themselves and their efforts. This
was a group which had no hold at all upon the people,
and very little upon the National Liberal tendency indicated by the name of 'Gotha.' I never exactly regarded
these gentlemen as German national enthusiasts, far from
it. Count Charles von der Goltz, who is still alive (1891),
and was for many years the influential aide-de-camp of the
Emperor William, to whom he kept access always open
for his brother and his brother's friends, was originally a
polished and sensible officer of the Guards, an out-and-out
Prussian courtier, who only took so much interest in extra-
Prussian Germany as his position at Court necessitated.
He was a man of the world and a sportsman; good-looking,
a favourite with the ladies, and cut a good figure in Court
ballrooms. Politics, however, were not his first thought,
but only became of value to him when he had need of
them at Court. That the remembrance of Olmütz was the

means to gain the Prince as a confederate in the struggle against Manteuffel, nobody could know better than he; and he had plenty of opportunities, both on journeys and indoors, to keep the smart operating on the susceptibilities of the Prince.

The party, or more correctly coterie, subsequently named after Bethmann-Hollweg, found its original mainstay in Count Robert von der Goltz, a man of unusual competence and energy. Herr von Manteuffel had been clumsy enough to treat this ambitious and capable man badly. The Count, who had lost his post in consequence, became the manager to the company which first appeared upon the stage as the Court group, and subsequently as the ministry of the Regent. It began to make itself felt in the press, especially through the ' Preussische Wochenblatt,' which it founded, and through personal intrigues in political and court circles. The ' financing ' of the business (to use a stock-exchange expression) was provided for by the vast wealth of Bethmann-Hollweg, Count Fürstenberg-Stammheim, and Count Albert Pourtalès; and its political task, the immediate aim of which was the overthrow of Manteuffel, was entrusted to the skilful hands of Counts Goltz and Pourtalès. Both wrote French elegantly and fluently, whilst Herr von Manteuffel, in the composition of his diplomatic documents, depended mainly upon the homely traditions of his officials, who were recruited from the French colony in Berlin. Count Pourtalès also had experienced unpleasantness at the hands of the Minister-President while working under him, and had been encouraged by the King as Manteuffel's rival.

Goltz, without doubt, wished to be a minister of state sooner or later, if not Manteuffel's immediate successor.

He had the stuff for it too, much more so indeed than Harry von Arnim, because he had less vanity and more patriotism and character. It is true he had also, by virtue of his innate energy, more bitterness and temper in his disposition, which might be held to detract from his practical achievement. I contributed to his appointment to St. Petersburg, and subsequently to Paris; and rapidly promoted Harry von Arnim from the unimportant position in which I found him, not without opposition in the cabinet. But I experienced at the hands of these, the most capable of my diplomatic colleagues, what Yglano experiences from Anselmo in Chamisso's poem.[1]

Rudolf von Auerswald also had reluctantly attached himself to the group, but came to me at Frankfort in June 1854 to tell me that he considered his campaign of the last four years as lost, wished to get out of it, and promised, if he obtained the post of envoy to Brazil, to concern himself no further with internal politics.[2] Although I recommended Manteuffel, in his own interests, to close with the bargain, and in this honourable manner to neutralise the hostility of so subtle an intelligence, of so experienced and honourable a man, who was at the same time a friend of the Prince of Prussia, yet both his and General von Gerlach's distrust of or aversion to Auerswald was so strong that the minister refused to appoint him. In general, Manteuffel and Gerlach, although not agreeing very well among themselves, were united against the Bethmann-Hollweg party. Auerswald remained in the country and took a prominent part in the negotiations between these anti-Manteuffel elements and the Prince.

[1] *Vetter Anselmo.*

[2] See letters to Leopold von Gerlach, June 6, 1854, edited by H. Kohl, p. 156.

Count Robert Goltz, who had been my friend from my youth, attempted at Frankfort to win me also over to the group. I declined to accede to it if I was expected to co-operate in bringing about the fall of Manteuffel; alleging as my motive that, as was the case, I had accepted the post at Frankfort with Manteuffel's full confidence, and did not consider it honourable to utilise my position with regard to the King to bring about Manteuffel's fall, so long as he did not put me in the necessity of breaking with him; and that in that case I would notify the feud to him openly and tell him the reason. Count Goltz was just then about to be married, and told me that the wish next his heart was the post of envoy at Athens. He added bitterly: ' They have got to give me a post anyhow, and a good one; I am not anxious about that.'

Sharp criticism of the Olmütz policy—which indeed was not so much the fault of the Prussian negotiator as of the unskilful management, to say the least of it, of Prussian policy up to the time of his meeting with Prince Schwarzenberg—and the picture of its consequences formed the first weapon with which Manteuffel was attacked by Goltz, and the sympathy of the Prince of Prussia gained. In the soldierly feelings of the latter, Olmütz was a sore point, with respect to which nothing but military discipline and loyalty to the King could overcome the sense of mortification and grief. In spite of his great love for his Russian relations, which finally took the shape of an intimate friendship with Alexander II, he could not get rid of the feeling of a humiliation suffered by Prussia at the hands of the Emperor Nicholas—a feeling which became the more intensified as his disapproval of Manteuffel's policy and Austrian influences brought him nearer to the

German mission of Prussia which at an earlier period had lain farther from him.

It appeared in the summer of 1853 as if Goltz were drawing near his aim—not indeed of ousting Manteuffel, but of becoming minister. General Gerlach wrote to me on July 6:

'As I hear from Manteuffel, Goltz has declared to him that he could only enter the ministry if the *entourage* of the King was changed, i.e. if I were dismissed. Moreover, I believe—nay, I can say I know for a fact—that Manteuffel wanted to have Goltz at the Foreign Office, in order to have a counterpoise against other persons there, such as Le Coq and so on [rather no doubt against Gerlach himself and his friends at court]; this now, thank God, has come to nothing, owing to Goltz's refractoriness. I fancy a plot is being hatched—whether consciously or unconsciously, half or wholly, to all the persons concerned therein, I will not take upon me to decide—to form a ministry under the auspices of the Prince of Prussia, in which (after the removal of Raumer, Westphalen, and Bodelschwingh) Manteuffel is to perform as President, Latenberg as Public Worship, Goltz as Foreign Affairs, and which can be sure of commanding a majority in the Chamber, a thing I do not consider very difficult. Thus the poor King sits between a majority in the Chamber and his successor, and cannot stir. All that Westphalen and Raumer have brought to pass, and they are the only men who have done anything, would be lost again, to say nothing of further consequences. Manteuffel, being twice over a November-man, would be as *inevitable* as he now is.'

The opposition between the various elements which sought to determine the resolutions of the King increased,

and the attack of the Bethmann-Hollweg group on Manteuffel grew lively during the Crimean war. On all
occasions critical for our friendship with Austria, the Minister-President gave most emphatic effect to his dislike of
a breach with Austria, and of such a policy as led to the
Bohemian battlefields. In Prince Schwarzenberg's time,
subsequently in that of the Crimean war and the utilisation
of Prussia for the benefit of Austria's Eastern policy, our
relations with her reminded one of those between Lepo-
rello and Don Giovanni. At Frankfort, where, at the
time of the Crimean war, all the states of the *Bund*, with
the exception of Austria, tentatively demanded that Prussia should represent them in presence of the coercion of
Austria and the Western Powers, I could not as the
spokesman of Prussian policy avoid a feeling of shame, of
bitterness, when I saw how, in face of the demands of
Austria, not even presented in courteous form, we sacrificed all our own policy and every independent view; how
we fell back from one position to another, and, under the
pressure of our own inferiority, sought protection on Austria's towing-line, in fear of France and in humility towards
England. The King was not insusceptible to this impression of mine, but at the same time was not disposed to shake
it off by adopting a policy conceived in the grand style.

After the declaration of war against Russia by England
and France, on March 28, 1854, we entered into the offensive and defensive alliance of April 20 with Austria, whereby Prussia pledged herself, if circumstances required, within thirty-six days to concentrate 100,000 men: one-third
in East Prussia and two-thirds at Posen or Breslau; and,
again, if circumstances demanded it, to augment her army
to 200,000 men, and to come to an understanding with

Austria on all these points. On May 3 Manteuffel wrote to me the following letter, showing some pique :—

'General von Gerlach has just informed me of his Majesty the King's command to you to present yourself here for the purpose of conferring upon the negotiation of the Austro-Prussian alliance at the *Bund*, also that he, the General, has already written to you to this effect.' In conformity with this royal command, concerning which, I may state, I had no previous knowledge, I do not hesitate to suggest to you with all deference that you should proceed hither without delay. Considering the negotiations pending at the Federal Diet, your stay here should not be of long duration.'

During the discussion of the treaty of April 20 I proposed to the King to utilise this occasion for raising Prussian policy out of a secondary, and in my opinion unworthy, position; and for assuming an attitude which would have won for us the sympathy of and the lead among those German states which desired, with and through us, to preserve an independent neutrality. I considered this practicable if, when Austria should call upon us to bring up our troops, we should at once acquiesce in a friendly and willing manner; but should station 66,000, and in point of fact more men, and not at Lissa, but in Upper Silesia, so that our troops should be in a position whence they could with equal facility step over the frontier of either Russia or Austria, especially if we did not trouble ourselves about overstepping, without saying anything about it, the figure of 100,000. With 200,000 men his Majesty would instantly become the master of the entire

---

[1] This letter is published in the correspondence of General Leopold von Gerlach with Otto von Bismarck, envoy to the Federal Diet, p. 166.

European situation, would be able to dictate peace, and to gain in Germany a place worthy of Prussia.[1] France, owing to her absorption in the Crimean conflict, was not in a position seriously to threaten our western frontier. Austria had her available forces stationed in East Galicia, where they were losing more men through illness than they would have done on the battlefield. They were nailed fast there by the Russian army in Poland, on paper at least 200,000 strong, whose march into the Crimea would have decided the situation there had the dispositions on the Austrian frontier allowed it to appear feasible. There even were diplomatists at that time who made the restoration of Poland under Austrian patronage one of the items of their programme. Both those armies stood fixed opposite to one another; and it lay in the power of Prussia, by her assistance, to secure supremacy to one of them.

The effect of an English blockade, which might have affected our coasts, would not have been more dangerous than those of the Danes, which we had several times undergone, and which had no less effectually in former years closed our ports; it would be counterbalanced by the establishment of Prussian and German independence of the pressure and menace of a Franco-Austrian alliance and overpowering of the intervening middle states. During the Crimean war old King William of Wurtemberg said to me in confidential audience in the chimney corner at Stuttgart: ' We South German states cannot simultaneously risk the enmity of Austria and France. We are too near to that sallyport, Strasburg, and could undoubtedly be occupied

---

[1] Compare Bismarck's remarks in his speech in the Reichstag of February 6, 1888. *Political Speeches*, xii. 45.9.

from the west before help could reach us from Berlin.
Wurtemberg would be invaded; and even if I could with
honour retreat into the Prussian camp, the laments of my
subjects under the oppressive rule of the enemy would in-
evitably call me back; the Wurtemberg shirt is nearer to
me than the coat of the Confederation.'[1]

The not unfounded hopelessness which underlay these
utterances of that discreet old gentleman, and the more or
less angry feelings of the other confederated states—not
only in Darmstadt where Herr von Dalwigk-Coehorn certainly relied on France—these moods would soon have
changed had an energetic Prussian attitude in Upper
Silesia demonstrated that neither France nor Austria
was at that time capable of offering us resistance in
superior force if we determined to avail ourselves of their
denuded and compromised situation. The King was not
insensible to the mood of conviction in which I represented to him the facts and the eventualities of the case.
He smiled, well pleased, but said in the Berlin dialect:
'My dear boy, that is all very fine, but it is too expensive
for me. A man of Napoleon's kind can afford to make
such master-strokes, but not I.'

The dilatory adherence of the middle states to the
treaty of April 20, upon which they deliberated at Bamberg; the efforts of Count Buol to create a *casus belli*
which were frustrated by Russia's evacuation of Wallachia
and Moldavia; the alliance of December 2, concluded with
the Western Powers without the knowledge of Prussia; the

[1] Compare the expression of Bismarck in the speeches of January 22,
1864, and May 2, 1871. *Political Speeches*, ii. 276, v. 52.

four points of the Vienna conference, and further course of events until the peace of Paris on March 30, 1856, have been related by Sybel from the archives : my official attitude on these questions is to be found in the work *Preussen im Bundestage*. Upon the proceedings in the cabinet concerning the considerations and influences which determined the King amid the shifting phases, I received constant communications from General von Gerlach, from which I introduce those of greatest interest. From the autumn of 1855 we had agreed upon a form of cipher for this correspondence, in which States were indicated by the names of villages familiar to us, and persons denoted—and not without humour—by suitable characters from Shakespeare.[1]

'Berlin : April 24, 1854.

' Manteuffel has concluded his treaty with General Hess, and that in a manner that I can describe only as a lost battle. All my military calculations, all your letters, proving decisively that Austria would never venture, without us, to conclude a definite treaty with the Western Powers, have availed nothing. We must allow ourselves to be made timorous by the timid, though I must do Manteuffel justice so far, that it is not impossible that out of sheer fear Austria might have made the bold spring towards the west.

' Be it as it may, this decision is a *fait accompli,* and we must now, as after a lost battle, gather together the scattered forces in order again to be in a position to withstand the ad-

[1] Consult the key to the letters of Bismarck to General L. von Gerlach, edited by H. Kohl, p. 35, l. 7 (but on p. 352, l. 4, read Fortinbras ; at l. 8, Trinculo). Bismarck uses the cipher for the first time in the letter of December 21, 1855 ; Gerlach, in the letter of January 15, 1856 (*Bismarck-Jahrbuch*, ii. 212 ff.).

versary; and the first thing to that end is that in the treaty everything is made a matter of mutual agreement. But, for this very reason, the next and very mischievous consequence will be that as soon as we have stated what seems to us the justifiable interpretation, we shall be charged with double dealing and breach of faith. We must therefore make ourselves hide-proof against this, and anticipate anything of the sort by a definite interpretation of the treaty at Vienna as well as at Frankfort, and that too before danger of a collision can occur. For the matter so stands that the hands of a powerful, courageous foreign minister remain still unbound. At St. Petersburg we make every step independently; we can therefore remain consistent, can attain to unity, and by its means avail ourselves of reciprocity and all that is lacking in the treaty. I have endeavoured to silence Budberg to the best of my power; Niebuhr is very active and zealous in this field, and, as usual, his conduct is excellent and skilful. Of what use, however, is this cobbling, that at best can be only a thankless task? It lies in the nature of man, and so in that of our master, that if he, in company with a servant, has shot a buck, or rather a doe, he keeps him in the first instance and maltreats his discreet and faithful friends. That is the position in which I am at present, and truly it is not an enviable one.' [1]

'Sans-Souci: July 1, 1854.

' Matters have once more become frightfully complicated, but are again in such a position that, if everything comes off, we may regard a good ending as possible. . . . If we do not hold Austria fast as long as practicable, we burden ourself with a serious tax. We call to life the

[1] Cf. the *Gerlach-Bismarck Correspondence*, p. 163 f.

Triad, which is the beginning of the Rhine Confederation,
and bring French influences up to the very gates of Berlin.
The Bamberg lot have now endeavoured to constitute themselves into a Triad under the protectorate of Russia, knowing well it is easy to change a protectorate, the more so
as the Franco-Russian alliance will certainly be the end of
the song if England's eyes are not soon opened to the folly
of the war, and of her alliance with France.'[1]

'Sans-Souci: July 22, 1854.

' For German diplomacy, in so far as it emanates from
Prussia, a brilliant battlefield opens, for it seems, alas,
that Prokesch does not miscalculate when he blows the war
trumpet for his Emperor. The reports from Vienna are
nothing particular, though I do not in the least abandon
the possibility that, at the eleventh hour, Buol and the
Emperor will fall asunder. It would be the greatest error
that could be made if what to me is the not quite comprehensible anti-French enthusiasm of Bavaria, Wurtemberg,
Saxony, and Hanover, is allowed to pass so wholly unutil-
ised. As soon as there is daylight concerning Austria—
that is to say, as soon as her sympathy with the Western
Powers is definitely known, the most active negotiations
with the German states must begin, and we must form a
league of princes wholly different from, and more secure
than, that of Frederick II.'[2]

'Charlottenburg: August 9, 1854.

' Manteuffel, so far, is quite reasonable; but, as you
know, untrustworthy. I believe your problem is, how to
work for the right road from two sides. First, that *you* carry

[1] Cf. *op. cit.* p. 174 f.   [2] *Ibid.* p. 178 f.

off the right policy over the head of your friend Prokesch, and give him to understand that now every pretext has vanished for encouraging Austria in her lust for war against Russia; and then that you point out to the German Powers the way in which they must go. . . . It is a misfortune that the stay [of King Frederick William] in Munich has again in certain places stirred up a " Germanomaniac" enthusiasm. A German army of reserve with him at the head is the confused idea, and one that has no good · influence on politics. Louis XIV said, " L'État c'est moi ; " with far greater truth can his Majesty say, " L'Allemagne c'est moi." '

The following letter to me from the Private Secretary Niebuhr affords a further glimpse into the mood of the Court :

'Putbus : August 22, 1854.

' I certainly do not fail to recognise good intentions even when, according to my conviction, they are not in the right place, and still less rightly carried out; and as little do I overlook the right of interests, even if it is diametrically opposed to what I hold to be right. But I ask for truth and sincerity of thought, and the lack of these qualities nearly drives me to despair. I cannot indeed reproach our policy with lack of outward truth, but I do charge it with insincerity toward ourselves. We should hold a very different position, and should have forborne a great deal if only we had confessed to ourselves our real motive instead of keeping up the illusion that the individual acts of our policy followed as consequences from its correct fundamental idea.

' Our continued participation in the Vienna conferences after the entry of the English and French fleets into the Dardanelles, and now our recent support of the claim of the Western Powers and of Austria at St. Petersburg, have their real basis in the childish fear "of being forced out of the European concert," and "of losing our position of a Great Power;" the height of silliness. For to speak of a European concert when two Powers are at war with a third is like speaking of wooden iron; neither do we owe our position as a Great Power to the goodwill of London, Paris, or Vienna, but solely to our own good sword. Over and above this, however, there is everywhere a touchiness against Russia that I well comprehend and share; but that we cannot afford to indulge in without at the same time bringing trouble on ourselves.

'A man who is not sincere towards himself always fails to be lucid also. We certainly do not live and do our business in such an absence of lucidity as prevails in Vienna, where business is done every moment in a dead sleepy fashion as though they were already at war with Russia. But how one can be neutral and a peacemaker and at the same time recommend such proposals as this last of the Maritime Powers wholly passes my feeble comprehension.'

The following fragments of letters are also from Gerlach:

'Sans-Souci : October 13, 1854.

' After reading everything, and balancing one thing against another to the best of my power, I consider it very probable that Austria will not fail to get the two-thirds. Hanover is playing a false game, Brunswick's sympathies are with the Western Powers, the Thuringians equally so, Bavaria is in all frames of mind, and his Majesty the King is a wavering reed. There are even doubtful reports about Beust; and in addition to all this we have Vienna apparently decided on war. It is evident that the attitude of armed expectancy is no longer tenable, not even financially, and retreat is considered more dangerous than an advance. Moreover, to face about would be in no sense easy, and I fail to see where the Emperor is going to get the necessary determination from. At first, and on the surface, Austria can come to an understanding with the revolutionary plans of the Western Powers more easily than Prussia—for example, the restoration of Poland, ruthless procedure against Russia, and so forth, while there is as little doubt that France and England could put her into a difficulty on the other side even more easily than we could, whether in Hungary or in Italy. The Emperor is in the hands of his police—and during the last years I have learnt what that means*—and has allowed himself to be deceived by lies how Russia incited Kossuth, and so forth. He has stifled his conscience therewith, and what the police cannot compass is achieved by Ultramontanism and rage against the Orthodox Church and Protestant Prussia. On this account there is even now talk of a kingdom of Poland under an Austrian archduke.

'. . . It follows from all this that we must be well on the lookout for any eventuality, even be prepared for a war against the Western Powers allied with Austria, that it will not do to depend upon any of the German Princes, and

---

* Gerlach no doubt was here thinking of Ohm and Hantge, also the news which the imaginative and well-paid Austrian Tausenau reported from London concerning dangerous plots on the part of the German refugees. The King must have had his doubts about the trustworthiness of this information. He sent instructions directly from the cabinet to Bunsen the ambassador to make inquiries through the English police, whereby it transpired that the German refugees in London had too much to do to earn a livelihood to trouble themselves about any outrage.

so on. May the Lord grant that we be not found weak!
but it would be an untruth were I to say I place implicit
trust in those who guide our destinies. Let us therefore
hold fast together. In the year 1850 Radowitz brought
us to a point much the same as that to which Buol over
there has brought us by letting things drift.'

'Sans-Souci: November 15, 1854.

'As regards Austria, their policy has at length become
clear to me through their last proceedings. At my age
one is slow of comprehension. Austrian policy is not
Ultramontane in the main, in the sense his Majesty takes it
to be, although it makes use of Ultramontanism when circumstances require: it has no great plans of conquest in
the East, although it does a little that way too; neither
does it think about the German imperial crown. All that is
much too exalted, but is made use of now and again merely as a dodge to gain its end. Austrian policy is a policy
of fear, based on the difficult position it is in from a domestic and foreign point of view in Italy and Hungary,
in finance, in the smash-up of justice, in the fear of Bonaparte, in the dread of Russian revenge, also in the fear of
Prussia, whom they credit with far more power of mischief
than any one here has ever supposed. Meyendorff says:
" My brother-in-law, Buol, is a political dastard; he fears
every war, but, of course, a war with France more than a
war with Russia." This verdict is accurate, and it is
this fear that determines Austria.

' In my belief, if one reflects that it is always dangerous
to stand alone, that matters are in such a condition here,
at home, that it is also dangerous to force them to a head,
also that neither Manteuffel nor ——— is to be relied

upon, it seems conformable with prudence to concur with
Austria as far as possible. Over and above this possibility, however, lies that alliance with France which we
neither morally, financially, nor from a military point of
view can suffer. It would be our death; we should lose
our renown of 1813–1815, on which we live; we should
be obliged to concede fortresses to the justly mistrustful
allies, we should have to maintain them. Bonaparte,
" l'élu de sept millions," would soon find a king for Poland
who would stand upon a similar title, and for whom voters
could easily be found in any required number.' [1]

'Potsdam : January 4, 1855.

' I think we should be of one mind, if you were here,
as to what should be done—that is, even if not in principle. For I hold by the word of Holy Scripture that evil
must not be done that good may result therefrom ; because
of those who do this, the damnation is just. To court
Bonaparte and the Liberals is wicked; but also, in the present case, according to my opinion, equally unwise. You
forget (a mistake into which every one falls who has been
absent from here for any length of time) the personages
who are the determining quantity. How can you finesse
in such indirect ways with a wholly unprincipled and untrustworthy minister who will be drawn involuntarily into
the wrong road, and with a master, to say nothing further,
untrustworthy and eccentric? Reflect, I beg, that Manteuffel is before all things a Bonapartist, reflect on his behaviour at the *coup d'état*, or on Quehl's writings at that
time patronised by him; and, if you need anything more
recent, I can tell you that he has just written to Werther
[at that time ambassador to St. Petersburg] the foolish

[1] *Briefwechsel*, s. 203, 79.

opinion that, if one wishes to make use of Russia, one must accede to the arrangement of December 2 in order to have a voice in the negotiations.

' If the negotiations at Vienna assume such a character that one can calculate on some result, we shall at once gain adherents, and we and our 300,000 men will not be ignored. As yet it would not be possible to do so had we not, by halting—not, as often happens, between two directions, but between three—a much rarer occurrence—lost all confidence and all power of inspiring fear.

' I wish very much that you could come here, if only for a few days, in order to see the lie of things for yourself. I know, from my own experience, how easily one loses one's bearings by a prolonged absence. For it is mainly on account of the highly personal elements in our circumstances that it is so difficult to make them intelligible in writing, especially when there are unreliable, unprincipled characters in the game. It is to me very uncanny when his Majesty has secrets with Manteuffel; for when the King is certain of his case before God and his conscience, he is more open towards many others, not only towards me, than he is towards Manteuffel. With these secret doings, however, arises a blend of weakness and finesse upon the one side, and of servile animosity upon the other, that as a rule brings much unhappiness upon the world.' [1]

' Berlin : January 23, 1855.

'. . . . What quite beats me is the universal and widespread Bonapartism and the indifference and levity with which the approach of this greatest of all dangers is regarded. Is it so difficult then to recognise whither

---

[1] Compare *Briefwechsel*, 216 sqq.

this man wants to go? . . . And how do matters stand here? " The king can do no wrong." As to him I am silent. Manteuffel is wholly Bonapartist. Bunsen and Usedom are no Prussians, either of them. Hatzfeldt, in Paris, has a Bonapartist wife, and has been so tarred with it that his brother-in-law here considers the old Bonaparte an ass in comparison with the present. What can come out of it all, and how can the King be reproached when he is so served—to say nothing of irregular advisers?'

' L. v. G.'[1]

An active and enterprising anti-Austrian policy had less prospect of sympathy from Manteuffel than from the King. My former chief gave me indeed the strong impression, during a *tête-à-tête* discussion with him of these questions, that he shared my ' Borussian' indignation at the contemptuous and insulting kind of treatment we experienced during the Buol-Prokesch policy. If, however, the situation grew ripe for treatment, if it became necessary to take an effective diplomatic step in an anti-Austrian direction, or to maintain our sympathy with Russia so far as not to come forward in a way directly hostile toward our hitherto friendly neighbour, then as a rule matters would come to such a head, that a cabinet crisis between the King and the Minister-President would arise, and the former would threaten, on occasion, to replace the latter by me or by Count Alvensleben; in one case, in the winter of 1854, by Count Albert Pourtalès of the Bethmann-Hollweg coterie, although his view of foreign politics was the very

---

[1] *Briefwechsel*, 222 sqq. The remainder of Gerlach's letters from the years 1855-1860 have been published in the *Bismarck-Jahrbuch*, ii. 191; iv. 158 ; vi. 83.

opposite of mine, and also hardly compatible with that of Count Alvensleben.

The end of the crisis always was that the King and the minister came together again. One of the three counter-candidates, Count Alvensleben, had declared quite publicly that he would not accept office under this monarch. The King wanted to send me to him at Erxleben; but I backed out of this because, a short time previously in Frankfort, Alvensleben had repeated the above declaration to me in bitter tones. When we saw each other later, his resentment had increased; he was inclined to disregard a summons from the King, and wished that I might find it possible to intervene in the matter. But the King did not approach me again on the subject of Alvensleben, perhaps because at the time after my visit to Paris (August 1855) a coldness, especially on the part of her Majesty the Queen, had arisen against me at Court. Count Pourtalès was too independent for the King by reason of his wealth. The King was of opinion that poor ministers, with an eye to their salaries, were more amenable. I myself evaded the responsible post under this master the best way I could, and reconciled him once more with Manteuffel, whom I visited for this purpose at his estate (Drahns-dorf).[1]

In this situation the party of the ' Wochenblatt,' as it was called, played a curious double game. I recollect the comprehensive memoranda which these gentlemen inter-

---

[1] Compare the expression in the Reichstag Speeches of February 6, 1888; *Political Speeches*, xii. 448–9.

changed among themselves, and how, by imparting them to me, they even sought now and then to win me over to their side. The aim specified in these as that which Prussia should strive as the champion of Europe to attain, was the partition of Russia by the forfeiture of the Baltic provinces, including St. Petersburg, to Prussia and Sweden, the loss of the entire territory of the Republic of Poland in its widest extent, and the disintegration of the remainder by a division between Great and Little Russians, regardless of the fact that the greater part of Little Russia had once formed a part of the Polish territory when at its largest. In justification of this programme the theory of Baron von Haxthausen-Abbenburg ('Studies of the Internal Economy of Russia, the Life of the People, and, in particular, the Agrarian Institutions') was made use of; namely, that the three zones with their mutually supplementing products could not fail to secure predominance in Europe to the hundred millions of Russians provided they remained united.

From this theory grew the corollary that the natural bond between us and England should be developed, together with dark insinuations that if Prussia with her army served England against Russia, England on her side would further Prussian policy in the sense of what was then called the 'Gotha' policy. It was positively predicted that, aided by the alleged public opinion of the English people, in union now with Prince Albert, who gave the King and the Prince of Prussia uninvited lectures, now with Lord Palmerston, who in November 1851, in a speech to a deputation of suburban radicals, had described England as the 'judicious bottle-holder' of every nation that was fighting for its freedom, and later had Prince Albert denounced in a pamphlet as the most dangerous opponent to his efforts in the direction of freedom, Germany and her affairs would attain the form which in after days was won in fight on the battlefield by the army of King William.

Upon the question whether Palmerston or another English minister would be inclined, arm in arm with the 'Gothaizing' Liberals and the *Fronde* at the Prussian Court, to challenge Europe to an unequal war, and sacrifice English interests on the altar of the German efforts for unity—or the further question as to whether England would be in a condition to side with Prussian politics without any other continental support than that of Prussian policy guided in the Coburg direction—no one felt a call to think things out to their conclusion, least of all the advocates of the very ingenious experiment. Phrases and the readiness to take part in any folly in the interests of the party covered all gaps in the airy structure of the then bye-policy of the Court in sympathy with the Western Powers. With these childish Utopias the heads clever enough, no doubt, of the Bethmann-Hollweg party played at being statesmen, believing it possible to treat a body of sixty-six million Great-Russians as if it were a *caput mortuum* in the future of Europe which they could misuse as they pleased without making it a certain ally of every future enemy of Prussia, and without forcing Prussia in every war with France to guard her rear in the direction of Poland, seeing that any arrangement likely to satisfy Poland in the provinces of Prussia and Posen and even in Silesia is impossible without breaking up and decomposing of Prussia. Not only did these politicians consider themselves wise, but they were honoured as such by the Liberal press.

In connection with the achievements of the Prussian Wochenblatt another recollection occurs to me, namely, of a memorandum alleged to have been drawn up under the Emperor Nicholas in the Foreign Office at St. Petersburg for the instruction of the heir to the throne; applying to present circumstances the basis of Russian policy as laid down in that apocryphal will of Peter the Great which appeared at Paris somewhere about the year 1810, making it appear that Russia was occupied in undermining all other states with a view to universal sovereignty. I was told later that this lucubration, which made its way into the foreign, especially the English, press, was furnished by Constantine Frantz.

While Goltz and his colleagues at Berlin were conducting their affairs with a certain dexterity, of which the article just mentioned is a sample, Bunsen, our ambassador in London, was imprudent enough in April 1854 to send to the minister Manteuffel a lengthy memorandum calling for the restoration of Poland, the extension of Austria as far as the Crimea, the deposition of the Ernestine line from the throne of Saxony, and more of the same kind; and recommending the co-operation of Prussia in this programme. Simultaneously he sent word to Berlin that the English government would agree to the acquisition of the Elbe Duchies by Prussia, if she would join with the Western Powers; and in London he had given it to be understood that the Prussian government was ready for this, subject to the *quid pro quo* indicated.[1] He had no authority to make either declaration. It was too much at any rate for the King, when he discovered it, much as he loved Bunsen. The King told Manteuffel

[1] See von Sybel, *Die Begründung des Deutschen Reichs*, ii. 181.

to instruct him to take a long leave of absence, which ultimately became retirement.   In the biography of Bunsen, edited by his family, this memorandum is printed with the most mischievous portions omitted, though without indication of the omission, and the official correspondence which ended in the leave of absence is reproduced with a partial colouring.   A letter that the press got hold of in 1882—from Prince Albert to Baron von Stockmar, in which ' Bunsen's fall ' was declared to be the result of Russian intrigue, and the conduct of the King was criticised with much disapproval—gave occasion for the publication of the complete text of the memorandum, and also, though they were put in a favourable light, of the true circumstances of the case from the documents.

Into the plans for the dismemberment of Russia the Prince of Prussia had not been initiated.   How it came about that he was successfully won over to an anti-Russian view—how he, who prior to 1848 had given currency to his apprehensions of the King's national and liberal politics only within the strict limits of brotherly regard and subordination, was moved to a pretty active opposition to the politics of the government—transpired in a conversation which I had with him during one of the crises in which the King had summoned me to Berlin to aid him against Manteuffel.   Immediately on my arrival I was commanded to the Prince, who, in a state of agitation brought about by his environment, expressed the wish that I should speak to the King in the sense of support to the Western Powers and opposition to Russia.   He said: ' You see here two conflicting systems—one represented by Manteuffel, the other, friendly to Russia, by Gerlach and by Count Münster at St. Petersburg.   You come here fresh, and are called to the King somewhat as an arbitrator. Your opinion will therefore turn the scale; and I conjure you to express yourself as not only the European situation, but a really friendly interest for Russia demands. Russia is challenging all Europe, and she will succumb in the end. All these splendid troops'—this occurred after the battles before Sebastopol, disadvantageous to the Russians—'all our friends who have fallen there'—he named several—' would still be alive if we had rightly exerted our influence and had constrained Russia to peace.' The end would be that Russia, our old friend and ally, would be annihilated or dangerously crippled. The task allotted to us by Providence was to bring about peace with a high hand, and to save our friend, albeit against his will.

In some such form as this Goltz, Albert Pourtalès, and Usedom—in their policy calculated on Manteuffel's fall— had got the Prince to accept the part destined for Prussia as ·the opponent of Russia; and in this the aversion of the Princess his wife to Russia served them in good stead.

In order to deliver him from this sphere of ideas I represented to him that we had absolutely no real cause for a war with Russia, and no interest in the Eastern question that could possibly justify a war with Russia, or even the sacrifice of our prolonged good relations with Russia. On the contrary, every victorious war against Russia, considering our mutual interests as neighbours, would burden us not only with a lasting feeling of revenge on Russia's part, which we should have drawn on ourselves without any real cause for war, but also with a very redoubtable problem, namely, the solution of the Polish question in a form that would be tolerable to Prussia. If our own interests spoke in no way for, but rather against, a breach with Russia, we should without provocation be attacking our hitherto friend and perpetual neighbour either out of fear of France or for the *beaux yeux* of England and Austria. We should be assuming the part of an Indian vassal-prince, who has to conduct English wars under English patronage, or of York's corps at the commencement of the campaign of 1812, in which we were constrained, through a then justifiable fear of France, to take part as her obedient allies.

My speech offended the Prince. Colouring angrily, he interrupted me with the words: ' There is here no question at all of vassals or of fear.'

He did not, however, break off the conversation. If you had once gained the Prince's confidence, and stood well in his favour, you might speak straight out to him— even be violent. I inferred that I had not succeeded in shaking the frame of mind to which the Prince under domestic and English influences, besides those of Bethmann-Hollweg & Co., had in all honesty resigned himself. I should, no doubt have prevailed with him against the influence of the last-named party, but against that of the Princess I was powerless.

During the Crimean war, and if I recollect rightly in connexion therewith, a prolonged theft of despatches was notorious. An impoverished police-agent,[1] who long ago, when Count Bresson was French ambassador to Berlin, had proved his dexterity by swimming across the Spree at nights, getting into the Count's villa at Moabit and transcribing his papers, was instigated by Manteuffel to gain access, through bribed servants, to the wallets in which the incoming despatches and the correspondence arising

[1] Tächen.

out of their perusal passed to and fro between the King, Gerlach, and Niebuhr, and to copy the contents. Paid with Prussian frugality he sought a wider market for his labours, and found it first through the mediation of the agent Hassenkrug with the French ambassador, Moustier, and afterwards with other people.[1]

Among the agent's customers was von Hinckeldey, the First Commissioner of Police. He came one day to General von Gerlach with the copy of a letter in which he—the general—had written to some one, probably to Niebuhr: ' Now that the King is at Stolzenfels with high company, so and so, among them Hinckeldey, have repaired there also. The Bible says, " Wheresoever the carcass is, there will the eagles be gathered together;" now it may be said that where the eagle is, there the carrion collects.' Hinckeldey took the general to task, and in answer to his question how he came by this letter said, ' This letter cost me thirty thalers.' ' How extravagant!' returned the general. ' I would have written you ten such letters for thirty thalers.'

My official statements concerning Prussia's share in the peace negotiations at Paris (*Preussen im Bundestage*, Part ii., pp. 312–317, 337–339, 350) will be supplemented by the following letter to Gerlach :

' Frankfort: Feb. 11, 1856.

' I had always hoped that we should adopt a firmer attitude, until it was decided to invite us to the conference, and that we should continue in the same if no invitation were sent. It was, in my judgment, the only means of

[1] Compare Gerlach's *Denkwürdigkeiten*, ii. 346 sqq.

bringing about our assistance at it. According to my yesterday's instructions we are ready all at once to enter,
with more or fewer reservations, upon an attitude which
will pledge us and the *Bund* to the support of the preliminaries. When they have once obtained that, after
even the Western Powers and Austria have so far subscribed only to a *projet* of preliminaries, why should they
trouble themselves any more about us at the conference?
They would much rather utilise our adhesion and that of
the middle states in our absence, as they require and
please, in the consciousness that they need only demand
and we surrender. We are too good for this world! It
does not become me to criticise the decision of his Majesty and of my chief after it is made; but criticism grows
in me without any assistance on my part. During the first
twenty-four hours after the reception of that flourish I suffered severe correction from a continuous attack of bilious
sickness, and a slight fever does not quit me for a moment. I can recollect an analogous condition of body and
mind only during the events of the spring of 1848, and
the more I explain the situation to myself the less can I
discover anything whereon my Prussian sense of honour
can erect itself. A week ago everything seemed to me
riveted and nailed; and I myself asked Manteuffel to let
Austria choose between two proposals, either of which
would be agreeable to us, but I never let myself dream that
Count Buol would reject both, and that he would prescribe
for us the answer we were to give to his own proposal. I
had hoped that, whatever our answer might ultimately prove
to be, we should not let ourselves be captured before our
presence at the conference was assured. But how does our
position now stand?

' Four times in two years Austria has successfully played against us the game of claiming the whole ground on which we stood, and we, after a little sparring, have had to resign the half or so. Now, however, it is a matter of the last square foot on which it was still possible for Prussia to take up a position. Made arrogant by her successes, Austria not only demands that we, who call ourselves a Great Power, and claim equality in our dual rights, should sacrifice to her this last remnant of independent position, but prescribes to us the forms in which we are to make our abdication, imposes upon us an indecent haste measured by hours, and denies us every equivalent that might have offered a plaster for our wounds. Not even an amendment in the declaration which Prussia and Germany are to make do we dare resolutely to propose. Pfordten settles matters with Austria because he believes he may assume the acquiescence of Prussia; and if Bavaria has spoken, then it is *res judicata* for Prussia. On similar occasions during the last two years we, at least at the outset, laid a Prussian programme before the German courts, but not one of them would come to a decision till we had come to an explanation with Austria. Bavaria now comes to an explanation with Vienna, and we fit into the ruck with Darmstadt and Oldenburg. Therewith we surrender the last thing they want of us for the time, and when they have got the decision of the *Bund*, inclusive of the Prussian vote, in their pocket, we shall soon see Buol shrugging his shoulders, and regretting the impossibility of overcoming the opposition of the Western Powers to admitting us to the conference. In my feeling we cannot calculate on Russia's support; for the Russians would very well like the loss of temper which would ensue among us if we relinquished the last shreds of our policy for an entrance-ticket to the conference. Moreover, the Russians obviously are more afraid of our "mediating" support of their opponents' policy than expectant of any assistance from us at the conference. My talks with Brunnow, and the St. Petersburg letters which I have seen, in spite of all the diplomatic cunning of the former, leave me in no doubt on this point.

'Our own method of securing participation in the conference is and remains to withhold here our declaration upon the Austrian proposals. What need would there be of a Prussian grumbler at the conference if they have the decision of the *Bund*, and us with it, in their pocket? Austria will be able to explain it nicely if we are not present. From the Austrian government press and from Rechberg's demeanour it is evident that even at this moment they are limiting the inadequate reservations of the Austro-Bavarian draft expressly to Article V.*

'With regard to the *conditions particulières* which have been set up by the belligerent Powers, a free verdict is reserved to us and to the *Bund;* but not with regard to those to be set up by Austria. And as regards the interpretation of the four points, the assumption that Russia and Germany consent beforehand to the interpretation of them held by the representative protecting power, Austria, has been justified by the fact that reservation thereto previously desired by us is declined by Bavaria and Austria, and we have set our minds at rest about it.

'We tear up all these calculations if we here and now

---

* 'Les puissances belligérantes réservent le droit qui leur appartient de produire dans un intérêt européen des conditions particulières en sus des quatre conditions.'

decline to express ourselves until in our view the right
moment for it has come. So long as we take up this attitude we are wanted, and shall have court paid to us.
Here, too, the attempt will hardly be made to outvote us.
Even Saxony and Bavaria stand only on the "presumption"
of our agreement with the present Austrian programme;
they have accustomed themselves to our giving way in
the long run, and therefore they permit themselves such
presumptions. If, however, we have the courage of our
opinions, it will be found worth while to await Prussia's
declaration when decisions are being taken on German
politics. If we firmly persist in deferring our resolution
and declare as much to the German courts, we have even
to-day a good majority on our side; even if—as can
scarcely be the case—Saxony and Bavaria had sold themselves neck and crop to Buol.

'If we wish to run no risks we must be prepared for
independent consultations by Sardinia and the Turks in
Paris upon the current value of German interests in the
two points appropriated by the *Bund*, we being represented
thereat by Austria. And we shall not even be the first
in Austria's train, for, in pursuance of this presumptive
mandate for Germany, Count Buol will get advice from
Pfordten and Beust rather than from Manteuffel, whom he
hates personally; and if he has Saxony and Bavaria on his
side he will calculate on Prussia's opposition less after the
resolution of the *Bund* than before.

'Would it not be infinitely preferable to such eventualities that we, as a European Power, should have
negotiated direct with England and France concerning
our admittance, rather than that we should do so as one
who is not *sui juris*, under the guardianship of Austria,

130

and go to the conference as merely an arrow in Buol's quiver? [1]

'v. B.'

The impression expressed in the foregoing letter, that we were being contemptuously treated by Austria in form as well as in fact, and that we ought not tamely to submit to this contemptuous treatment, did not remain without results on the shape taken later by the relations between Prussia and Austria.

[1] For continuation see Horst Kohl, *Bismarck's Letters to General Leopold v. Gerlach*, p. 281 f.

CHAPTER VI

AN argument with the Prince of Prussia upon Haxthausen's theory of the three zones gave me, among other things, the means of realising that the memoranda which the Goltz group had turned to account as a party weapon against Manteuffel with the King and the Prince, and then had caused to be utilised by the press and through foreign diplomatists, had not failed to make an impression on him.

The Prince was even more effectively influenced in the direction of the Western Powers by his wife than by the political arguments of the Bethmann-Hollweg coterie, and was led into a sort of opposition—very much alien to his military instincts—against his brother. Princess Augusta preserved from her youthful days at Weimar to her life's end the impression that French, and still more English, authorities and persons were superior to those of her own country. She was of true German blood in one way; in her was verified that national fashion of ours most sharply expressed in the phrase, ' That does not come from far, so it is good for nothing.' In spite of Goethe, Schiller, and all the other great men in the Elysian Fields of Weimar, that intellectually eminent capital was not free from the nightmare that until the present time has weighed upon our national sentiment, namely, that a Frenchman, and in the fullest degree an

Englishman, by reason of his nationality and birth is a superior being to a German; and that the approbation of public opinion in Paris and in London constitutes a more authentic proof of our own worth than does our own consciousness. Her own intellectual endowments, and the recognition which the practical proof of her sense of duty in various departments gained from us, never wholly liberated the Princess Augusta from the oppression of that nightmare. A cocksure Frenchman with a voluble French tongue imposed upon her,* an Englishman had always the presumption on his side, till the contrary was proved, that he was to be treated in Germany as a superior person. This idea prevailed in Weimar seventy years ago, and its aftertaste was frequently enough perceptible to me during my activity in office. In all likelihood at the time of which I speak the efforts made by the Princess of Prussia towards securing an English marriage for her son strengthened her in the direction in which Goltz and his friends were seeking to influence her husband.

The Crimean war brought into view the aversion of the Princess to everything Russian, rooted in her from childhood upwards, but hitherto not conspicuous. At balls, in the time of Frederick William III, where I first saw her as a young and beautiful woman, she was wont, in her choice of partners, to favour diplomats, Russian as well as others, and would select among them, to tempt to the smooth surface of the parquet, those who had more talent for conversation than for dancing. Her aversion to Russia, visible later, and in time operative, is difficult to explain psychologically. The remembrance of the murder of her grandfather, the Emperor Paul, can

* Her reader (Gérard) passed for a French spy.

scarcely have had so enduring an effect. A more likely conjecture is to be found in the after effects of an early lack of sympathy between the Russian mother, the Grand Duchess of Weimar, a person of high political and social gifts, with her Russian visitors, and the lively temperament of a grown-up daughter, inclined to take up the leading place in their circle; perhaps also, one may guess, some private dislike to the domineering personality of the Emperor Nicholas. Certain it is that the anti-Russian influence of this exalted lady, both as queen and as empress, frequently rendered the carrying out of the policy I recognised as necessary very difficult in my dealings with his Majesty.

Essential help was furnished to the Bethmann-Hollweg group by Herr von Schleinitz, the Princess's special politician; who, for his part, was drawn into the fight against Manteuffel owing to his removal, on grounds connected with the service, from the well-situated, but not very industriously-managed, post at Hanover, the circumstances being such that the arrears of his salary as envoy out of office were not paid to him till after he had become a minister. As the son of a Brunswick minister, as a competent diplomatist accustomed to Court-life, and to the social advantages of the foreign service, without fortune, out of tune with the service, but standing in the good graces of the Princess, he was naturally sought after by Manteuffel's opponents, and readily attached himself to them. He was the first Foreign Minister of the new era, and died Minister of the Household to the Empress Augusta.

During breakfast—and this habit of the Prince was retained in the Emperor William—the Princess discoursed to her husband, laying before him letters and newspaper articles which at times had been concocted *ad hoc*. Hints which I took leave on occasion to give that certain letters might, by the Queen's management, have been procured and placed there through Herr von Schleinitz, brought upon me a very sharp snub. The King with his chivalrous feeling entered the lists absolutely on his wife's side, even when the appearances were clearly against her. He emphatically refused to believe such a thing even if it were true.

I have never held it to be the duty of an envoy at a friendly court to notify in his dispatches home every inharmonious detail; especially as at St. Petersburg I was honoured with a confidence which I should have thought it hazardous to give to foreign diplomatists in Berlin. Every piece of information calculated to excite ill-feeling between ourselves and Russia would have been used by the policy of the Queen, at that time as a rule anti-Russian, to the loosening of our relations with Russia; whether from aversion to Russia, or from transitory considerations of popularity, or from goodwill towards England, and in the presumption that goodwill towards England, and even towards France, was a sign of a higher grade of civilisation and culture than goodwill towards Russia.

In 1849, after the Prince of Prussia, as governor of the Rhine Province, had permanently transferred his residence to Coblenz, the antagonistic attitude of the two Courts of Sans-Souci and Coblenz gradually settled down into a smothered opposition, in which the female element played a part on the side of the King, though in a less degree than on that of the Prince. The influence of Queen Elizabeth in favour of Austria, Bavaria, and Saxony was, as a result of the bond naturally proceeding from community of view and kindred family sympathies, less prejudiced and less concealed. No personal sympathy existed between the Queen and the Minister von Manteuffel, nor, indeed, looking to their difference of temperament, could it have done so; but all the same their influence on the King not infrequently coincided, and especially at critical moments, in the direction of the Austrian interest; although on the Queen's side it was exerted as decisive only within certain limits, such as were drawn for her by wifely and princely sensitiveness in the interest of her husband's crown. Care for the King's reputation swayed her, especially in critical moments, even though it showed itself less in the form of stimulus to action than in that of a feminine shrinking from the consequences of her own views, and in the resulting abstinence from carrying influence further.

In the Princess a prejudice developed itself during her residence in Coblenz, which biassed her political activity and continued to the end of her life.

Catholicism, an exotic for North Germans, and especially in the sphere of thought of a little town in the midst of a purely Protestant population, had a definite attraction for a Princess who was in general more interested in everything foreign than in the familiar, the everyday, the homely. A Catholic bishop seemed a more distinguished person than a general-superintendent. A certain goodwill towards the Catholic cause which had been peculiar to her even in earlier days, for example, in the choice of her male attendants and servants, was developed to the full during her stay in Coblenz. She got into the way of looking upon the local interests of the old Land of the Crozier as assigned to her charge, and defending

136

them and its clergy. That modern denominational consciousness based on historical tradition, which often made
the Prince's Protestant sympathies stand out sharply, was
alien to his wife. What success her bid for popularity in
the Rhine country had was shown *inter alia* by what Count
von der Recke-Volmerstein wrote to me on October 9,
1863; that perfectly loyal people on the Rhine were advising that the King should not attend the festival of the
building of the cathedral, but that he should rather send
her Majesty, ' who would be received with enthusiasm.'
An example of the effective energy with which she supported the wishes of their clergy was furnished by the
modification which had to be made in the building of the
so-called Metz railway because the clergy had taken up
the case of a churchyard which would be disturbed by it.
They were so successfully supported by the Empress in the
matter that the direction of the line was changed, and
difficult engineering had to be carried out *ad hoc*.

On October 27, 1877, von Bülow, the State Secretary,
wrote to me that the Empress had applied to Minister
Falk for a travelling subvention to an ultramontane
painter, who not only had no wish for it himself, but was
occupied upon the glorification of Marpingen with paint-
ings. On January 25, 1878, he (von Bülow) informed me:
' Before his departure [for Italy] the Crown Prince had a
very stormy scene with the Empress, who desired that as
the future sovereign of eight million Catholics, he should
visit the venerable old Pope. When the Crown Prince,
upon his return, presented himself to the Emperor, the
Empress had also come down (from her own apartments).
The conversation taking a turn that did not please her
concerning the attitude of King Humbert, and then com-

ing to a stop, she rose up, with the words: " Il paraît que
je suis de trop ici," whereupon the Emperor said in quite
a melancholy tone to the Crown Prince, " On these matters
nowadays your mother is as unaccountable as ever." '

Among the bye-influences whereby these court dissensions were complicated was the antipathy taken by the
Princess towards the Oberpräsident von Kleist-Retzow,
who occupied the ground floor of the palace below the apartments of the Prince. He was an annoyance to the Princess by his personal appearance, as an orator on the
Extreme Right, and because of his countrified habit of
conducting domestic worship with hymns every day with
the members of his household. More at home in official
than in courtly relations, the Oberpräsident regarded his
existence in the palace and in the palace grounds as a
kind of championship of the royal prerogative, in counterpoise to alleged encroachments of the Prince's household; and honestly believed that he would be somewhat
remiss towards the King, his master, if he did not ener-
getically uphold, toward the wife of the heir to the throne,
the claims of the Oberpräsident to the use of domestic
premises for household purposes against the claims of the
Prince's Court.

The chief of the headquarter staff at Sans-Souci, after
the death of General von Rauch, was Leopold von Gerlach,
and his supporters, though not always—sometimes even
rivals, were the Private Secretary Niebuhr and Edwin von
Manteuffel; during the Crimean war Count Münster also.
In the Camarilla were also to be numbered Count Anthony
Stolberg, Count Frederic zu Dohna, and Count von der
Gröben.

At the Court of the Prince the interest of the state in

averting mischief due to petticoat influence had a steady
and clever champion in Gustav von Alvensleben, who
worked hard for making peace between the two Courts
without agreeing with the political measures of the government. He shared my opinion as to the necessity of
settling the question of rivalry between Prussia and Austria on the field of battle, because it was not soluble otherwise. He, the future leader of the fourth Corps at Beau-
mont and Sedan, and his brother Constantine whose
spontaneously-taken resolution at Vionville and Mars-la-
Tour stopped the French army of the Rhine before Metz,
were model generals. When I incidentally asked him his
opinion as to the issue of a first pitched battle between us
and the Austrians, he answered: ' We walk over them
till they stand on their heads!' And his confidence contributed to strengthen my courage in the difficult decisions
of 1864 and 1866. The antagonism in which his influence on the Prince, determined by considerations of state
and patriotism only, stood towards that of the Princess, put
him at times into a state of excitement to which he gave
vent in words that I do not want to repeat, but that expressed all the indignation of a patriotic soldier over ladies
playing at politics in language that very nearly came
within the penal statutes. That the Prince kept him as
his aide-de-camp considering the attitude he took towards
the Queen was the result of a characteristic which he
showed both as King and as Emperor: that he was a faithful master to a faithful servant.

CHAPTER VII

ONE result of the estrangement which arose between the minister Manteuffel and me, after my mission to Vienna, consequent upon the tale-bearing tattle of Klenze and others, was that, as I have said, the King frequently sent for me to frighten the minister when he would not agree with him. In one year I did 2,000 German miles in journeys between Frankfort and Berlin, *via* Guntershausen, continually lighting a new cigar at the stump of its predecessor, or else sleeping soundly. The King demanded not only my views upon questions of German and foreign policy, but commissioned me occasionally, when drafts from the Foreign Office were laid before him, to draw up counter-schemes. I then conferred with Manteuffel concerning these commissions and my papers in connexion therewith. As a rule, he declined to undertake to alter them, even though our political opinions were at variance. He was more inclined to meet the Western Powers and the wishes of Austria; while I, without representing Russian policy, saw no reason for risking our long-continued peace with Russia for other than Prussian interests; and I considered any steps taken by Prussia against Russia, for interests that were remote from us, to be the result of our fear of the Western Powers and of our discreet respect for England. Manteuffel avoided irritating the King further by a keener advocacy of his own notions, or making Austria and the

Western Powers angry by championing my alleged Russian ideas: he preferred to efface himself. Marquis Moustier was aware of this situation, and my chief took the opportunity of handing over to him the task of converting me to the policy of the Western Powers and to the advocacy of it with the King. During one visit that I made to Moustier, his quick temper led him to make the menacing remark: 'The line of policy you are on will take you to Jena,' whereupon I answered: 'Why not to Leipzig or Rossbach?' Moustier was not accustomed to such independent speech in Berlin, and was dumb and pale with anger. After a pause I added: 'Well, I suppose every nation has won and lost battles. I did not come to study history with you.' The conversation did not recover its flow. Moustier complained of me to Manteuffel, who carried the complaint to the King. He, however, praised me before Manteuffel, and later directly to myself, for giving the Frenchman the right answer.

The practically efficient forces of the Bethmann-Hollweg party—Goltz, Pourtalès, and sometimes Usedom—were also brought into a certain degree of currency with the King by means of the Prince of Prussia. It would happen that important dispatches were drafted, not by Manteuffel, but by Count Albert Pourtalès; that the King gave me the draft to revise, that I again took counsel with Manteuffel concerning the amending of them, that Manteuffel called in Le Coq, the under-secretary, who tested the composition, but solely from the point of view of French literary style, and justified a whole day's delay by averring that he had not been able to find the exact French equivalent to express something between obscure, indistinct, doubtful, hazardous—just as though the question at that time depended on such trifles.

I sought adroitly to withdraw from the part which the King wished me to play, and to pave the way to the best of my powers for an understanding between him and Manteuffel. A case arose in the serious discords which broke out concerning Rhino Quehl. After Prussia's separate efforts after national unity had been temporarily hindered by the restoration of the Federal Diet, an advance was made in Berlin towards a reform in domestic affairs, over which the King had loitered so long as he was considering how not to estrange the Liberals in the other German states. Concerning the aim and method of this reform, there arose between the Minister Manteuffel and the ' small but powerful party' a difference of opinion which came to a head curiously enough in a quarrel about the retention or dismissal of a comparatively subordinate personage, leading to a sharp public rupture. In the letter of July 11, 1851, wherein Manteuffel informed me of my appointment as envoy to the Federal Diet, he wrote: ' With regard to our internal conditions, especially the business of the estates, the affair would go quite tolerably if people would only proceed in it with a little more moderation and dexterity. Westphalen is excellent in the matter; I value him very highly and we are substantially of one opinion; Klützow's[1] feud does not seem to me to be very prosperous, and a number of unnecessary blun-

---

[1] The matter was one of differences of opinion on the question of the formation of the first Chamber.

ders of form have certainly turned up. Far worse, however, is the attitude which the "Kreuzzeitung" takes up in the matter. Not only does it triumph in a clumsy and irritating manner, but it wants also to press on to extremes which in all probability would not be agreeable to itself. If it were possible, for example, to set up the United Diet again with all its consequences *purè*, and if this came off, what would be gained thereby? I consider the position of the government much more favourable if they keep the matter to a certain extent floating until a fundamental organic transformation has proved itself to be necessary. I hope and wish that we may then revert, starting from the provincial Estates, right down, it may be, to the communal Estates, upon the old historical delimitations, which are not yet obliterated in the Rhine province, and are quite recognisable in all the old provinces, and that national representation may be made to proceed from these. But these are things that cannot be accomplished at a jump, at least not without great shocks, which for obvious reasons must be avoided. The "Kreuzzeitung" has now had a feud formally declared with me, and as the price and sign of submission has demanded the dismissal of the etc. Quehl, without reflecting that even if I wished to surrender a diligent and self-sacrificing man, which is not my intention, I could certainly not do so under such conditions.'

Rhino Quehl was a journalist, through whom Manteuffel had got his policy represented in the press as long ago as the Erfurt parliament; a man full of ideas and suggestions, correct and erroneous, who wielded a very adroit pen, but was burdened with too heavy a mortgage of vanity. The further development of the conflict between

BISMARCK

Manteuffel and Quehl on the one side, the ' Kreuzzeitung'
and the Camarilla on the other, and of the whole internal
situation, will be made intelligible by the following epistolary deliverances of Gerlach:

'Potsdam: May 17, 1852.

' I consider Manteuffel to be a good fellow; but what
a singular political life is his! He subscribed to the December Constitution, proclaimed himself for the Union
policy, ruthlessly put through the Local Government
Ordinance and the law for redemption of debt, amnestied
Bonapartism, and so on. That he has not been consistent
in these matters redounds to his glory; but, even though
his Majesty once said consistency is the most miserable of
all virtues, Manteuffel's inconsistency is a trifle strong.
People talk against the Chambers and Constitutionalism.
But since the middle of the eighteenth century all governments have been revolutionary, except England until the
Reform Bill, and Prussia during slight intermissions, in
1823 and 1847. The "Kreuzzeitung" was in truth not
in the wrong with its little apology for the Chambers;
and now our Premier yearns after Bonapartism, which un-
deniably has no future.

' Manteuffel said yesterday, moreover, that he would
summon you here, if only you could arrive at the right
time, to make acquaintance with the Emperor and Count
Nesselrode. But most important of all it is that you
deliver Manteuffel from Quehl, for he is still indispensable, and with Quehl there is no holding him. It would
cost him nothing to assert that he knows nothing about
the article in the "Zeit," indeed that this paper is no concern of his; but people may not let themselves be put off

with that, as the editor, Thile, was installed by Quehl and Manteuffel.

'I fear also the absolutist inclinations of Manteuffel junior.'[1]

'May 19, 1852.[2]

'In consequence of the newspaper article you touched upon in your last letter to me, Manteuffel is again being talked to from various quarters, to get him to separate from Quehl. I had not taken any part in the matter because I had once already had it out with him about the man, and we then in a certain way concluded a compact never to touch upon this theme again. Yesterday, however, Manteuffel himself began upon it to me; he defended Quehl in the most decided way, declared he would rather resign than separate from him; expressed unreservedly his hatred of the "Kreuzzeitung," and made some hazardous remarks concerning the management of the Ministry of the Interior, and certain personages of no consequence to us.'

'Sans-Souci: July 21, 1852.

'I have just received your letter, dated Ofen-Frankfort, of June 25 and July 19,[3] the beginning of which is as interesting as the ending. But you demand from me what is impossible. You ask me to explain to you the state of matters here, which is so confused and intricate that those on the spot do not understand it. Wagener's coming forward against Manteuffel cannot be justified unless he intends completely to isolate himself from the party. A paper like the "Kreuzzeitung" cannot be allowed to take

[1] Compare *Briefwechsel* 32 and 99 (with wrong date).
[2] *Bismarck's Letters to L. v. Gerlach*, pp. 30, 31.
[3] *Bismarck's Letters*, p. 32 sqq.

the field against a Prime Minister unless the whole party
is thrown into opposition, as was the case under Radowitz. . . . . Such a *bellum omnium contra omnes* cannot
continue. Wagener will be compelled *nolens volens* to
chime in with the " Preussische Wochenblatt," which is a
great misfortune; Hinckeldey and little Manteuffel, otherwise pronounced enemies, have allied themselves over
the " Kreuzzeitung," like Herod and Pilate. The most
distressing of all to me is the Minister Manteuffel, who is
difficult to support, but who must be supported because
his presumptive successors are terrible. Every one clam-
ours for him to dismiss Quehl. I believe little would
be gained thereby; Quehl's probable successor Fr.[1] is perhaps still worse. If Manteuffel does not make up his
mind to an alliance with honest folk there is no help for
him. . . . .'[2]

' Sans-Souci : October 8, 1852.

' I made use of Manteuffel's extraordinary behaviour
with his creatures, I made use of Radowitz's appointment to speak openly to Manteuffel, but nothing came of
it. I told him I did not belong to those who wished to
send Quehl into destitution, but that he surely might com-
bine with more decent people, and strengthen himself in
association with them. But in vain. Now he is again at
work with that Bonapartist Frantz. I do not want to
justify Wagener's doings, especially his obstinate opposition to all advice and warning that reaches him; but he is
right in this, that Manteuffel is completely destroying the
Conservative party and is irritating him, Wagener, to the

[1] Constantine Frantz.
[2] Compare *Briefwechsel* &c., p. 37 (date wrong and disfiguring errors
of reading).

146

utmost. It is, after all, a remarkable phenomenon that the "Kreuzzeitung" is the only newspaper in Germany that is prosecuted and confiscated. Of that which affects me most in all this, of the effect of this state of affairs upon his Majesty, I will say nothing. Think, anyhow, of means to attract men who will strengthen the ministry. And do come here once more, and see for yourself the state of affairs. . . .'[1]

'Charlottenburg : February 25, 1853.

' I have lately drawn his Majesty's attention to the fact that it would not be well for Wagener, who risked every-thing for the good cause, shortly to be sitting in prison, while his adversary, Quehl, became a *geheimer Rath* by mere *vis inertiæ*. Niebuhr has also succeeded in reconciling the King with Wagener, although the latter still persists in his intention of resigning the editorship of the "Kreuz-zeitung." . . . Manteuffel has a downward tendency, *via* Quehl, Lewinstein, &c., because he doubts the truths that come from above instead of believing them. He says with Pilate, "What is truth?" and looks for it in Quehl and company. Even now at every opportunity he lets himself be influenced by Quehl into a very nasty secret and pas-sive opposition to Westphalen and his measures, which after all contain the most courageous and best acts of our administration since 1848. He allows Quehl to use the press in the most shameless manner against Westphalen, Raumer, &c., and, as I am assured, to be paid for doing so. So it can scarcely be avoided that Quehl and com-pany bring about Manteuffel's fall at last, which I consider

[1] Compare *Briefwechsel* &c., p. 43.

147

would be a misfortune for the simple reason that I do not know any possible successor.'[1]

'Potsdam : February 28, 1853.

'I am doing my utmost to keep up the " Kreuzzeitung," or rather first of all to keep Wagener for the " Kreuzzeitung." He says he cannot carry on this cause in opposition to Quehl's intrigues. This fellow uses the King's money, which, through Manteuffel's confidence, he has at command to give considerable remuneration to Wagener's contributors and withdraw them from the " Kreuzzeitung." It is said that he even requests the ambassadors to find out the names of the foreign correspondents of the " Kreuzzeitung," in order to alienate them.'[2]

'June 20, 1853.

' I don't like the look of domestic affairs at all. I fear that Quehl will get the better of Westphalen and Raumer, simply because Manteuffel supports his influence with the King on the ground that he is indispensable—an opinion which his Majesty recognises for right reasons and wrong.'

'Charlottenburg : June 30, 1853.

' If I compare one with another the various statements concerning the Quehl intrigues; if I attribute any importance to the notice that Quehl has made a sort of compact with the Hollweg party, according to which Manteuffel is to be let off, and the other unpopular ministers, Raumer, Westphalen, Bodelschwingh, ruthlessly attacked;

---

[1] Compare *Briefwechsel* &c., p. 72 sqq. (inexact in the rendering of the text).

[2] Cf. *Briefwechsel* &c., p. 74 &c. (Here also the text has been arbitrarily altered.)

when I further consider that Manteuffel has a bad conscience towards me concerning his relations to the Prince of Prussia, that he now holds Niebuhr closer to his heart than he does me, while formerly he often complained about Niebuhr to me; when, finally, I reflect that Quehl represents the Prince of Prussia and his son as agreeing with himself and Manteuffel, and expresses himself accordingly, as I know from the most trustworthy sources—if all this looks to Radowitz (*sic*) I feel the ground shaking under my feet; although it will scarcely be possible to win the King over to this business, and it is all, thank God, pretty indifferent to me personally. But you, my respected friend, who are still young, you must arm and strengthen yourself at the right moment to tear asunder this web of lies and save the country.' [1]

'Sans-Souci : July 17, 1853.

' Q.'s Court is now made up; he has Excellencies in his anteroom and on his sofa. On the other hand I consider it not impossible that Manteuffel one day throws over Quehl, for gratitude is not a characteristic attribute of this irresolute and therefore often desperate statesman. But what will happen if Manteuffel goes? A ministry could be found, but scarcely one that would get on with his Majesty for even four weeks. For these reasons, and because of my genuine love and esteem for Manteuffel, I should not like to take it on my conscience that I had brought about his fall. Think over these things and write to me. . . .' [2]

Soon after the date of this last letter the disagreement between the King and Manteuffel became so acute that the latter retired in the sulks to his estate of Drahnsdorf.

[1] Compare *Briefwechsel*, p. 91 sqq.   [2] *Ibid.*

BISMARCK

In order to make him an ' obedient minister ' the King
this time did not use my ministerial candidature as a scarecrow, but commissioned me to go and see Count Albrecht
von Alvensleben, the ' old lark-eater ' as he called him, at
Erxleben, and ask him if he would take the presidency in
a ministry in which I should have the Foreign Office.
The Count had shortly before, with extremely contemptuous expressions concerning the King, explained to me
that during the government of his Majesty he would not
under any circumstances enter any cabinet.[1]   I told the
King this, and my journey did not take place.   Later,
however, when the same combination again was suggested,
he expressed his readiness to accept it, but the King was
then on good terms with Manteuffel, who in the meantime
had taken the vow of ' obedience.'   Instead of the expedition to Erxleben I travelled of my own accord to Manteuffel in the country, and advised him to separate from
Quehl, and quietly and without any explanation to his
Majesty to resume his official functions.   He replied to
the effect of his letter of July 11, 1851, that he could not
drop an able man who served him with devotion.   I thought
I gathered from what he said that Manteuffel had other
reasons for sparing Quehl, so I said: ' Entrust me with
full powers to free you from Quehl without causing a breach
between you.   If I succeed, then take the news of Quehl's
departure to the King, and put the business along as
though no dissension had occurred between you and
his Majesty.'   He acted upon this suggestion, and we
agreed that he should cause Quehl, who just then was
travelling in France, to come and see me at Frankfort on
his return: this was done.   I made use of the King's plans

[1] Cf. *supra*, p. 119.

150

about Alvensleben in order to convince Quehl that, if he did not depart, he would be to blame for his patron's fall, and recommended him, as long as there was time, to make use of the latter's power. I said to him: ' Cut your pipes while you still sit among the reeds; it will not last much longer,' and I got him so far as to specify his wishes; they were, the consulate-general at Copenhagen with a largely increased stipend. I informed Manteuffel and the matter seemed settled, but dragged on some time before it was finally concluded, because at Berlin they had been so clumsy as to divulge the security of Manteuffel's position before Quehl had taken his departure. At Berlin he had found that his position and Manteuffel's were not so insecure as I had pictured them to be, and thereupon he made some difficulties which served to better his position in Copenhagen.[1]

I had to transact similar negotiations with agents who were employed in connexion with the theft of dispatches from the French Embassy, among others with Hassenkrug, who, during the time of the proceedings concerning that theft, was put under arrest by the police in France, apparently by his own consent, and was sequestered for a year and a day until the matter was forgotten.

The King in those days hated Manteuffel; he did not treat him with his natural politeness, and used biting expressions about him. In what light he considered the position of minister is shown by a remark about Count Albert Pourtalès, whom he also occasionally used as scarecrow to Manteuffel.[2] ' He would be the minister for me

---

[1] Cf. *Bismarck's Letters to L. v. Gerlach* of August 6 and 13, 1853 (edition by H. Kohl, pp. 96, 97).
[2] Cf. *supra*, p. 118.

if he had not too much income by 30,000 reichsthalers; therein lies the source of disobedience.' Had I become his minister, I should have been more exposed to this conception than any one, because he looked upon me as his foster-son, and looked on unconditional ' obedience' as the most essential element in my royalism. Every independent opinion from me would have estranged him; even my objection to definitely undertaking the post at Vienna had seemed to him as a sort of felony. Two years later I had to make an experience of the kind, the effects of which lasted long.

My frequent summonses to Berlin were not always caused by foreign politics, but from time to time by occurrences in the Diet to which I had been elected on Oct. 13, 1851, at the fresh election which had been rendered necessary by my appointment as envoy.

When the question of the alteration of the first Chamber into the House of Lords was under discussion, I received the following communication from Manteuffel dated April 20, 1852: ' Bunsen is always urging the King towards the peerage. He asserts that it is the belief of the greatest statesmen in England that the continent will in a few years fall into two divisions: (*a*) Protestant states with a constitutional system upborne by the pillar of the peerage; (*b*) Catholic-jesuitic-democratic-absolutist states. In the last category he places Austria, France, and Russia. I consider this quite erroneous. No such categories exist. Every state has its own particular course of development. Frederick William I was neither Catholic nor democratic, only absolutist. But such statements

make a great impression on his Majesty. The constitutional system which proclaims the rule of the majority is,
in my opinion, anything but Protestant.'

On the following day, April 21, the King wrote to me:

'Charlottenburg: April 21, 1852.

' I wish to remind you, dearest Bismarck, that *I count
on you and on your help* in the approaching discussion in
the second Chamber about the formation of the first. I
do this the more urgently, as I unfortunately know from
the most trustworthy sources all about the dirty intrigues
which are arranged in a conscious (?) or unconscious (?)
union of scabby sheep from the Right and stinking goats
from the Left, in order to destroy my designs. This is a
melancholy outlook under any circumstances, but enough
to make one "tear one's hair out," in the sphere of the
dearly purchased lying-machine of French constitutionalism. May God better it! Amen.

' FREDERICK WILLIAM.'

I wrote to General Gerlach[1] that I was one of the
youngest members among these people. If I had known
his Majesty's wishes earlier, I could perhaps have succeeded in winning some influence; but the command of
the King, if carried out by me in Berlin, and represented
in the Conservative party in both Houses, would simply
destroy my parliamentary position, which might be of
service to the King on other questions—if, that is to say,
simply as the commissioner of the King, without representing my own ideas, I were to use up my influence in the

---

[1] On April 23, 1852. Hitherto the text of this letter has not been
published ; compare, however, the remarks in the letter to Manteuffel of
April 23 (*Preussen im Bundestage* iv. 72).

short space of two days. I asked, therefore, whether I could not make the commission given me by the King, to negotiate with the Prince of Augustenburg, a reason for my keeping away from the Diet. I received by telegram the reply not to appeal to the Augustenburg business, but to come at once to Berlin, and so I started on April 26.

Meanwhile, in Berlin, a decision was taken at the instance of the Conservative party which ran counter to the King's views, and the campaign undertaken by his Majesty seemed thereby to be lost. When on the 27th I reported myself to General von Gerlach in the wing of the palace at Charlottenburg, near the guard-house, I learnt that the King was angry with me because I had not started at once, for he held that, had I appeared at once, I could have prevented the decision. Gerlach went to the King to report my arrival, and came back, after a fairly long delay, with the answer: his Majesty would not see me, but I was to wait. This contradictory message is characteristic of the King; he was angry with me and wished to make me understand that by the refusal of an audience; but, at the same time, to assure me of a renewal of his favour after a short lapse of time. It was a kind of educational method, just as at school one was occasionally turned out of the class to be allowed to join it again. I was, in a sort of way, interned in the Charlottenburg palace, a state of affairs that was alleviated for me by a good and well-served luncheon. The appointment of the King's household outside Berlin, especially at Potsdam and Charlottenburg, was that of a *Grand Seigneur* in his country house. Whenever one was there, one had all that one could require at the usual times, and also between times if one wanted anything. The management of the household was certainly not conducted on a Russian footing, but it was in thoroughly good style, and was lavish according to our ideas, without degenerating into extravagance.

After about an hour's waiting I was summoned to the King by the adjutant on duty, and was received somewhat more coolly than usual, but not so ungraciously as I had feared. His Majesty had expected that I would appear at the first call, and had calculated upon my being in a position, within the twenty-four hours preceding the division, to make the Conservative party turn right-about face, as by a military command, and wheel into line with the King's design. I explained that he was overestimating my influence on the party and underestimating its independence. I said that I had no personal convictions in this question which were opposed to those of the King; and that I was ready to represent the latter to my comrades in the group if he would give me time, and was disposed to bring forward his wishes once more in a new form. The King, obviously appeased, agreed to this, and at last dismissed me with the commission to start a propaganda for his plans. This was accomplished with more success than I had myself anticipated; the opposition to the reconstruction of the corporation was supported only by the leaders of the group; and its adherence to it did not depend so much upon the convictions of the whole as upon the authority which the acknowledged leaders in each group generally hold—and not unjustly, for, as a rule, they are the best speakers, and usually the only hard-working men of business, who save the others from the trouble of studying the questions which come up. One of the less regarded

BISMARCK

members of the group, if he attempts opposition, is easily
put down by the leader of the group, who is generally a
readier speaker, in such a way as for the future to take
from him all desire for revolt, unless he is endowed with
a lack of modesty, such as is not common with us in just
those classes to which Conservatives generally belong.

I found our group, which at that time was numerous,
containing, I believe, over one hundred members, under
the ban of certain political tenets imposed upon them by
their leader. For my own part I had to some extent eman-
cipated myself from the party leaders since that time at
Frankfort when I had found myself on the defensive
against Austria, and therefore on a road of which they
disapproved; and although in this question our relation
to Austria was not at stake, nevertheless the difference of
opinion concerning these relations had shattered my belief
in party control altogether. Meanwhile the immediate
result of my pleading surprised me greatly, not so much
with regard to the immediate notion of the King, but
with regard to adherence to himself. When it was put
to the vote, the leaders remained isolated; almost the
whole group was prepared to follow in the path of the
King.

When I now look back at these proceedings it seems
to me that the three or six leaders against whom I stirred
up the Conservative group were at bottom in the right in
their opposition to the King. The first Chamber was
more competent in the solution of such problems as come
before a body of this kind in constitutional life than the
present House of Lords. It enjoyed among the people
a confidence which the House of Lords hitherto has not
gained. The latter has had no opportunity for any prom-

inent political achievement except during the conflict period at that time; through the fearless loyalty with which it stood by the monarchy it had proved itself on the defensive side quite equal to the duties of an Upper House. It is probable that in the future it will show the same firm courage if the monarchy is in a critical situation. It is, however, doubtful to me whether it will exercise the same influence as the old first Chamber did in averting similar crises during the apparently peaceful times in which it is possible to prepare for them. It shows a flaw in the constitution if in the estimate of public opinion an Upper House becomes an organ of government policy or even of the King's policy. According to the Prussian constitution, the King with his government has in and for himself a share in legislation equal to that of each of the two Houses; he has not only his full veto, but the complete executive power in virtue of which the initiative in legislation practically, and the execution of the laws legally, pertains to the crown. The royal authority, if it is conscious of its own strength and has the courage to apply it, is powerful enough to form a constitutional monarchy without requiring the aid of an obedient House of Lords as a crutch.

Even during the Conflict if, when the budget law was sent up to it, the House of Lords had adopted the resolutions of the Chamber of Deputies, the consent of the third factor, the King, would still by Art. 99 have been indispensable in order to give the force of law to the budget. In my opinion King William would still have refused his consent even if the decision of the House of Lords had coincided with that of the House of Deputies. I certainly do not believe that the first Chamber would have acted in

BISMARCK

this way; on the contrary, I suspect that their debates,
by greater attention to the practical and technical points
and freedom from party passion, would at an earlier
stage have had a moderating effect upon the Chamber of
Deputies, and thereby have in part prevented the latter's
tendency to excess. . The House of Lords never had the
same weight in public opinion, which inclined to see in it
a *doublure* of the administration, and a parallel form of
expressing the will of the King.

Even in those days I was not inaccessible to such considerations; on the contrary, repeatedly when the King
discussed his plans with me, I urged him strongly, side by
side with a certain number of hereditary members, to make
the greater portion of the House of Lords derive from
electoral corporations, the foundation of which would be
the 12,000 to 13,000 manors, supplemented by property of
equal value, by the magistrates of important towns, and by
those who, though without landed estate, paid the highest
taxes upon a high assessment, and that the non-heredi-
tary portion of the members should be chosen for a fixed
period, and subject to dissolution, just as the Chamber of
Deputies is. The King rejected this suggestion so totally
and contemptuously that I had to relinquish every hope of
his consent to a discussion on the subject.

Upon what was to me the new ground of legislation I
had at that time not that certainty of belief in the wisdom
of my own ideas that would have been desirable in order to
encourage me under the equally new direct relations with
the King, and in consideration of my official position, to
hold with tenacity opinions of my own which differed from
his.

To have felt myself entitled and bound to do that,
158

if circumstances arose, I should have needed a longer experience in state affairs than I then possessed. If twenty years later there had arisen a question concerning the retention of the First Chamber or its transformation into the Upper House, I would have made a cabinet question of the first alternative.

The attitude I had taken up in the Conservative group exercised a disturbing influence upon the plans which the King entertained or professed to entertain for me. When at the beginning of the year 1854 he began to face more directly the aim of making me a minister, his intentions were opposed not only by Manteuffel, but also by the 'Camarilla,' the chief persons of which were General Gerlach and Niebuhr. These, like Manteuffel, were not inclined to share with me their influence over the King and imagined that they would not agree with me so well in daily intercourse as at a distance. Gerlach was strengthened in this presumption by his brother, the president, who was accustomed to describe me as a Pilate-like character taking for his text ' What is truth?' thus holding me unreliable as a member of a group. This opinion concerning me was also very sharply expressed in the conflicts within the Conservative group and its more private committees when, by reason of my post as envoy to the Federal Diet, and because I was in charge of the report to the King concerning German affairs, I desired to have a greater influence upon the attitude of the group in German and foreign policy, while President Gerlach and Stahl claimed the absolute general leadership in all directions. I found myself opposed to both, more, however, to Gerlach than to Stahl, and the former even at that time declared that he foresaw our ways lay separate and that we should end as adversaries. And agreeably to this I have always sided with Below of Hohendorf and Alvensleben of Erxleben in the changing phases of the Conservative group.

In the winter of 1853 to 1854 the King repeatedly sent for me and often held me fast for some time; in this way, to outside observers, I fell into the category of the pushing set who strove to bring about Manteuffel's fall, sought to prepossess the Prince of Prussia against his brother, and to secure places, or at least commissions for themselves, and who were occasionally treated by the King as rivals of Manteuffel *cum spe succedendi.* After I had on several occasions been played off against Manteuffel by the King to such an extent that I had to write out counter-drafts of dispatches, I begged Gerlach, whom I found in a small anteroom adjoining the King's cabinet in the wing of the palace lying next the Spree, to get me permission to return to Frankfort. Gerlach entered the cabinet and spoke, whereupon the King cried out, 'Let him wait in the devil's name till I tell him to go!' When Gerlach came out, I told him laughingly that I had got my orders already. I therefore remained in Berlin for some time longer. When at length the time came to depart, I left behind me the draft of an autograph letter which the King was to write to the Emperor Francis Joseph; this I had elaborated by command of his Majesty, and Manteuffel had undertaken to lay it before the King after having agreed with me concerning the contents. The centre of gravity lay in the concluding sentence, but even without this the draft formed a well-rounded document, essentially modified, to be sure, in its range. I handed the aide-de-camp in waiting then on duty a copy of the draft with the request to draw the King's attention to the fact that the concluding sentence was the important part of the document. This precautionary measure was not known of at the Foreign Office; collation in the palace showed, as I feared, that its purport had been altered and brought more in accordance with Austrian policy. During the Crimean war and the negotiations that preceded it, the conflicts in government circles frequently turned upon a phrase seeming to favour either the Western Powers and Austria or Russia, which was no sooner written than it lost all practical importance.

A more serious question of editing in a way to interfere with the course of events cropped up in August 1854. The King was in Rügen; I was on the way from Frankfort to Reinfeld, where my wife lay ill, when on August 29 a superior postal official who had been ordered to hunt me down handed me at Stettin an invitation from the King to proceed to Putbus. I would gladly have suppressed myself, but the postal official did not understand how a man of the old Prussian stamp could wish to evade such a summons. I went to Rügen, not without some anxiety of being again urged to become a minister and so entering into untenable relations with the King. The King received me graciously on August 30, and acquainted me with a difference of opinion concerning the situation brought about by the retreat of the Russians from the Danube principalities. The matter referred to Count Buol's dispatch of August 10, and the draft of an answer submitted by Manteuffel, but thought by the King to be too Austrian. By command I made out another draft in opposition to the Prime Minister, which was approved by his Majesty and sent to Berlin, to be forwarded in the first place to Count Arnim, and then to be communicated to the

German governments.[1] The temper of the King, indicated by the acceptance of my draft, was also shown in the
reception of Count Benckendorf who arrived at Putbus with
letters and verbal commissions, and whom I was able to
meet with the news that the English and French had landed
in the Crimea. ' Pleased to hear it,' he returned, ' we are
very stròng there.' The Russian current was flowing strong.
I considered that I had done my political duty; I had received bad news of my wife and begged for permission to
set out. This was indirectly refused by my being transferred to the suite—a token of high favour. Gerlach
warned me not to overrate it. ' Do not imagine for a
moment,' said he, ' that you have been politically smarter
than we. You are for the moment in favour, and the
King presents you with this dispatch as he would present
a lady with a bouquet.'

How true this was I learnt at once, but to its full
extent only later and by degrees. When I persisted in
my desire to depart, and in reality set out on September
1, I brought myself into serious disfavour with the King;
my domestic life was worth more to me than the whole
kingdom, he had told Gerlach. But how deep the displeasure had been was only made clear to me during and
after my journey to Paris. My draft dispatch accepted
with such approval was stopped by telegraph and then
altered.

[1] Cf. Sybel, ii. 204.

CHAPTER VIII

IN the summer of 1855 Count Hatzfeldt, our ambassador in Paris, invited me to visit the Industrial Exhibition;[1] he still shared the belief then existent in diplomatic circles that I was very soon to be Manteuffel's successor at the Foreign Office. Although the King had entertained such an idea on and off, it was already then known in the innermost Court circles that a change had taken place. Count William Redern, whom I met in Paris, told me that the ambassadors continued to believe I was destined to be made a minister and that he himself had also believed this; but that the King had changed his mind—of further details he was ignorant. Doubtless since Rügen.

August 15, Napoleon's day, was celebrated among other ways by a procession of Russian prisoners through the streets. On the 19th the Queen of England made her entry, and on August 25 a state ball was given in her honour at Versailles at which I was presented to her and to Prince Albert.

The Prince, handsome and cool in his black uniform, conversed with me courteously, but in his manner there was a kind of malevolent curiosity from which I concluded that my anti-occidental influence upon the King was not unknown to him. In accordance with the mode of thought

---

[1] See *Bismarck-Jahrbuch*, iii. 86.

peculiar to him, he sought for the motives of my conduct not where they really lay, that is, in the anxiety to
keep my country independent of foreign influences—influences which found a fertile soil in our narrow-minded
reverence for England and fear of France—and in the desire to hold ourselves aloof from a war which we should
not have carried on in our own interests but in dependence upon Austrian and English policy.

In the eyes of the Prince—though I of course did not
gather this from the momentary impression made during
my presentation, but from ulterior acquaintance with
facts and documents—I was a reactionary party man who
took up sides for Russia in order to further an Absolutist
and 'Junker' policy. It was not to be wondered at that
this view of the Prince's and of the then partisans of the
Duke of Coburg had descended to the Prince's daughter,
who shortly after became our Crown Princess.

Even soon after her arrival in Germany, in February
1858, I became convinced, through members of the royal
house and from my own observations, that the Princess
was prejudiced against me personally. The fact itself did
not surprise me so much as the form in which her prejudice against me had been expressed in the narrow family
circle—'she did not trust me.' I was prepared for antipathy on account of my alleged anti-English feelings and
by reason of my refusal to obey English influences; but
from a conversation which I had with the Princess after
the war of 1866 while sitting next to her at table I was
obliged to conclude that she had subsequently allowed
herself to be influenced in her judgment of my character
by further-reaching calumnies. I was ambitious, she said,
in a half-jesting tone, to be a king or at least president of

a republic. I replied in the same semi-jocular tone that I was personally spoilt for a republican; that I had grown up in the royalist traditions of the family and had need of a monarchical institution for my earthly well-being : I thanked God, however, I was not destined to live like a king, constantly on show, but to be until death the king's faithful subject. I added that no guarantee could however be given that this conviction of mine would be universally inherited, and this not because royalists would give out, but because perhaps kings might. 'Pour faire un civet, il faut un lièvre, et pour faire une monarchie, il faut un roi.' I could not answer for it that for want of such the next generation might not be republican. I further remarked that in thus expressing myself I was not free from anxiety at the idea of a change in the occupancy of the throne without a transference of the monarchical traditions to the successor. But the Princess avoided every serious turn and kept up the jocular tone, as amiable and entertaining as ever; she rather gave me the impression that she wished to tease a political opponent.

During the first years of my ministry I frequently remarked in the course of similar conversation that the Princess took pleasure in provoking my patriotic susceptibility by playful criticism of persons and matters.

At that ball at Versailles Queen Victoria spoke to me in German. She gave me the impression of beholding in me a noteworthy but unsympathetic personality, but still her tone of voice was without that touch of ironical superiority that I thought I detected in Prince Albert's. She continued to be amiable and courteous, like one unwilling to treat an eccentric fellow in an unfriendly way.

In comparison with Berlin it seemed a curious arrange-

ment to me that at supper the company ate in three classes,
with gradations in the menu, and that such guests as
were to sup at all were assured of this by having a ticket
bearing a number handed to them as they entered. The
tickets of the first class also bore the name of the lady pre-
siding at the table to which they referred. These tables
were arranged to accommodate fifteen or twenty. On entering I received one of these tickets for Countess Walewska's table and later on in the ball-room two more from two
other lady patronesses of diplomacy and of the Court. No
exact plan for placing the guests had therefore been made
out. I chose the table of Countess Walewska, to whose
department I belonged as a foreign diplomatist. On the
way to the room in question I came across a Prussian officer in the uniform of an infantry regiment of the guard,
accompanied by a French lady; he was engaged in an animated dispute with one of the imperial household stewards
who would not allow either of them to pass, not being provided with tickets. After the officer, in answer to my
inquiries, had explained the matter and indicated the lady
as a duchess bearing an Italian title of the First Empire,
I told the court official that I had the gentleman's ticket,
and gave him one of mine. Now, however, the official
would not allow the lady to pass, and I therefore gave
the officer my second ticket for his duchess. The official
then said significantly to me: ' Mais vous ne passerez pas
sans carte.' On my showing him the third, he made a
face of astonishment and allowed all three of us to pass.
I recommended my two *protégés* not to sit down at the
tables indicated on the tickets, but to try and find seats
elsewhere; nor did any complaints concerning my distribution of tickets ever come to my ears. The want of

organisation was so great that our table was not fully occupied, a fact due to the absence of any understanding among the *dames patronesses.* Old Prince Pückler had either received no ticket or had been unable to find his table; after he had turned to me, whom he knew by sight, he was invited by Countess Walewska to take one of the seats that had remained empty. The supper, in spite of the triple division, was neither materially nor as regards its preparation upon a level with what is done in Berlin at similar crowded festivities; the waiting only was efficient and prompt.

What struck me most was the difference in the regulations for the free circulation of the throng. In this respect the palace of Versailles offers much greater facilities than that of Berlin on account of the larger number and, if we except the White Hall, the greater spaciousness of the apartments. Here those who had supped in class 1 were ordered to make their exit by the same way as the hungry ones of class 2 entered, their impetuous charge betraying certainly less acquaintance with the customs of Court society. Personal collisions occurred among the belaced and beribboned gentlemen and super-elegant ladies, giving rise to scuffles and abusive language, such as would be impossible in our palace. I retired with the satisfactory impression that in spite of all the splendour of the imperial Court the Court service, the breeding and manners of Court society were on a higher level with us, as well as in St. Petersburg and Vienna, than in Paris, and that the times were past when one could go to France and to the Court of Paris to receive a schooling in courtesy and good manners. Even the etiquette of small German Courts, antiquated as it was, especially in

comparison with St. Petersburg, was more dignified than
the practice of the imperial Court. It is true that I had
already received this impression in Louis Philippe's time,
during whose reign it became quite the fashion in France
to distinguish oneself in the direction of excessively free
and easy manners, and of abstention from courtesy, especially towards ladies. Although it had become better in
this respect during the Second Empire, the tone in official and Court society and the demeanour of the Court
itself still remained below the standard of the three great
eastern Courts. Only in the Legitimist circles aloof from
the official world were things different both in the time
of Louis Philippe and in that of Louis Napoleon; there
the tone was faultless, courteous, and hospitable, with occasional exceptions of the younger gentlemen spoilt by
their contact with Paris, who borrowed their habits not
from the family but from the club.

The Emperor, whom I saw for the first time during
this visit to Paris, gave me to understand in several interviews, but at that time only in general phrases, his desire and intentions respecting a Franco-Prussian alliance.
His words were to the effect that these two neighbouring
states, which by reason of their culture and their institutions stood at the head of civilisation, were naturally thrown
upon each other's assistance. Any inclination to express
before me such grievance as might arise from our refusal
to join the Western Powers was kept out of the foreground.
I had the feeling that the pressure which England and
Austria exercised in Berlin and Frankfort to compel us to
render assistance in the western camp was much stronger,
one might say more passionate and rude, than the desires
and promises expressed to me in an amicable form, with

which the Emperor supported his plea for our understanding with France in particular. He was much more indulgent than England and Austria respecting our sins against occidental policy. He never spoke German to me, either then or later.

That my visit to Paris had caused displeasure at the court at home, and had intensified, especially in the case of Queen Elizabeth, the ill-feelings already entertained towards me, I was able to perceive at the end of September of the same year. While the King was proceeding down the Rhine to Cologne to attend the cathedral building festival, I reported myself at Coblentz and was, with my wife, invited by his Majesty to perform the journey to Cologne on the steamer; my wife, however, was ignored by the Queen on board and at Remagen.[1] The Prince of Prussia, who had observed this, gave my wife his arm and led her to table. At the conclusion of the meal I begged for permission to return to Frankfort, which was granted me.

It was not until the following winter, during which the King had again approached me, that he asked me once at dinner, straight across the table, my opinion concerning Louis Napoleon; his tone was ironical. I replied: ' It is my impression that the Emperor Napoleon is a discreet and amiable man, but that he is not so clever as the world esteems him. The world places to his account everything that happens, and if it rains in eastern Asia at an unseasonable moment chooses to attribute it to some malevolent machination of the Emperor. Here especially we have become accustomed to regard him as a kind of *génie du mal* who is for ever only meditating how to do mis-

[1] Cf. Bismarck's letter to Gerlach of October 7, 1855.

chief in the world.' I believe he is happy when he is able to enjoy anything good at his ease; his understanding is overrated at the expense of his heart; he is at bottom good-natured, and has an unusual measure of gratitude for every service rendered him.'

The King laughed at this in a manner that vexed me and led me to ask whether I might be permitted to guess his Majesty's present thoughts. The King consented, and I said: ' General von Canitz used to lecture to the young officers in the military school on the campaigns of Napoleon. An assiduous listener asked him how Napoleon could have omitted to make this or that movement. Canitz replied: "Well, you see just what this Napoleon was—a real good-hearted fellow, but so stupid!" which naturally excited great mirth among the military scholars. I fear that your Majesty is thinking of me much as General von Canitz thought of his pupils.'

The King laughed and said: ' You may be right; but I am not sufficiently acquainted with the present Napoleon to be able to impugn your impression that his heart is better than his head.' That the Queen was dissatisfied with my view, I was enabled to gather from the external trifles by which impressions are made known at court.

The displeasure felt at my intercourse with Napoleon sprang from the idea of 'Legitimacy,' or, more strictly speaking, from the word itself, which was stamped with its modern sense by Talleyrand, and used in 1814 and 1815 with great success, and to the advantage of the Bourbons as a deluding spell.

I insert here, from my correspondence with Gerlach,

---

¹ Cf. Bismarck's utterance in the Imperial Diet on January 8, 1885. *Politische Reden*, x. 373.

a few pieces of somewhat later date; my motive for intro-
ducing them will, however, be evident from the specimens
of his letters given above.

'Frankfort: May 2, 1857.[1]

'. . . Much as I agree with you in regard to internal
policy, I can enter but little into your conception of foreign
policy, with which I find fault in general, because it
ignores the reality of things. You start from the notion
that I sacrifice principle to an individual man who imposes upon me. I object to both the premises and the
conclusion. The man does not impose upon me at all.
The faculty to admire individuals is only moderately developed in me, and it is rather a defect in my vision
that it is sharper to detect weaknesses than merits. If
my last letter have perchance a livelier colouring, I beg
that you will regard this more as a rhetorical expedient
for influencing you. So far, however, as regards the
principle sacrificed by me, I cannot exactly formulate
concretely what you mean by that, and beg that you will
return to that point in your answer, since I feel that I
cannot afford to part company with you on a question of
principle. If by it you mean a principle to be applied
to France and its Legitimacy, then I fully admit that I
completely subordinate this to my specifically Prussian
patriotism; France interests me only in so far as she reacts
upon the condition of my country, and we can only deal
politically with the France which exists, and this France
we cannot exclude from the combinations. A legitimate
monarch like Louis XIV is just as hostile an element
as Napoleon I, and if the present successor of the latter
conceived to-day the idea of abdicating in order to enjoy

[1] *Letters from Bismarck to Gerlach*, p. 314.

the ease of private life, he would not be doing us at all a favour, nor would Henry V be his successor; even if he were placed upon the vacant and uncontested throne he would not maintain his position there. As a romanticist I may shed a tear over his fate, and as a diplomatist I would be his servant if I were a Frenchman; but as I am, France counts for me, without regard to the person at its head for the time being, merely as a piece, though an unavoidable one, in the game of political chess—a game in which I am called upon to serve only my own king and my own country. I cannot feel it right, either in myself or in others, that sympathies and antipathies with regard to foreign Powers and persons should take precedence over my sense of duty in the foreign service of my country; such an idea contains the embryo of disloyalty to the ruler or to the country which we serve. But especially if any one wants to cut his standing diplomatic relations and the maintenance of our understanding in time of peace, after this pattern, he immediately ceases to be a politician, and acts according to his personal caprice. In my opinion, not even the king has the right to subordinate the interests of the country to his own feelings of love or hate towards foreigners, but if he does so he is responsible to God and not to me, and therefore I am silent on that point.

'Or do you find the principle which I have sacrificed in the formula that a Prussian must always be an opponent of France? From what I have said above it may be seen that I do not borrow the standard for my conduct towards foreign governments from stagnating antipathies, but only from the harm or good that I judge them capable of doing to Prussia. In the policy of sentiment there is no reciprocity of any kind—it is an exclusively Prussian peculi-

arity; every other government takes solely its own interests
as the standard of its actions, however it may drape them
with deductions of justice or sentiment. Our own sentiments people accept, and make capital of them, on the calculation that they do not permit us to withdraw from the
process; and we are treated accordingly, that is, we are not
even thanked and are respected only as serviceable dupes.

' I think you will allow that I am right in maintaining
that our authority in Europe is not the same to-day as it
was prior to 1848; I even think it was greater at any time
between 1763 and 1848, with the exception, of course, of
the period from 1807 to 1813. I admit that our strength in
comparison with other great Powers, especially for aggres-
sion, was greater before 1806 than now, but not from 1815
to 1848; at that time all the Powers were pretty well what
they are now, and yet we must say like the shepherd in
Goethe's poem : " I am fallen but know myself not how."
Nor do I wish to pretend that *I* know how; but there is
no doubt much in this : we have no alliances and carry
out no foreign policy—that is, not actively—but content
ourselves with picking up the stones that fall into our
garden and brushing off, as well as we can, the mud that
is flung at us. When I speak of alliances, I do not mean
alliances offensive and defensive, for peace is not yet im-
perilled; all the shades, however, of possibility, probability, or purpose, in the event of war, of concluding this or
that alliance, or belonging to this or that group, still form
the basis of such influence as a state can at the present
day wield in time of peace. Whichever finds itself in
the combination that is weaker in the event of war is inclined to be more yielding; whichever completely isolates
itself renounces influence, especially if it be the weakest

among the Great Powers. Alliances are the expression
of common interests and purposes. Whether we have any
purposes or conscious aims at all in our policy at this
moment, I do not know; but that we have interests others
will remind us fast enough. Yet up to the present we
have the probability of an alliance only with those whose
interests most traverse and contradict ours—that is, with
the German states and Austria. If we desire to regard our
foreign policy as being limited to that, then we must also
become accustomed to the idea of seeing our European
influence reduced in time of peace to a seventeenth part
of the voices of the smaller council in the *Bund*, and in
the event of war of remaining behind by ourselves in the
Taxis Palace, with the Federal Constitution in our hand.
I ask you whether there is a cabinet in Europe which has
a more innate and natural interest than that of Vienna in
preventing Prussia from growing stronger and in lessen-
ing her influence in Germany; whether there is a cabinet
which pursues this design more zealously and cleverly,
which on the whole takes more coolly and cynically its own
interests alone as a guide for its policy, and which has
given us, the Russians, and the Western Powers more
numerous and striking proofs of perfidy and untrustwor-
thiness as a member of the same federation? Does Austria in any way stick at entering into any foreign alliance
that is to her advantage and openly threatening even
members of the German Federation on the strength of
such relations? Do you consider the Emperor Francis
Joseph to be in general of a nature to make sacrifices or
to yield, and with regard to non-Austrian interests in particular? Do you perceive any difference from the standpoint of "principle" between his Buol-Bach style of gov-

ernment and the Napoleonic? The present supporter of the latter system told me in Paris that for him "who am making every effort to get out of this over-tense system of centralisation, which ultimately pivots on a gendarme-secretary and which I consider one of the principal causes of the misfortunes of France," it was curious to see how Austria was making the most strenuous efforts to work herself into it. I continue my questions, and beg that you will not put me off with an evasive reply. Are there, besides the Austrian, any governments which feel less call to do something for Prussia than the German middle states? In times of peace they feel the necessity of playing some part in the *Bund* and in the Zollverein, of making their sovereignty a perceptible force on our frontiers, and of quarrelling with von der Heydt; while in war their conduct towards us is regulated by fear or distrust, and no angel can talk the distrust out of them so long as there exist maps at which they can cast a glance. And now another question. Do you then believe, and does his Majesty the King still really believe in the German *Bund* and its army in the event of war? I do not mean in the event of a French revolutionary war against Germany in league with Russia, but in a war of interests, in which Germany, Prussia, and Austria would have to stand on their own legs. If you believe in it, I cannot of course go on with the discussion, for our premises would be too divergent. What, however, could justify you in the belief that the Grand Dukes of Baden and Darmstadt, the King of Wurtemberg, or Bavaria, would play Leonidas for Prussia and Austria when the superiority of forces is not on the side of these Powers, and no one has the slightest ground for believing in unity and confidence

between them? King Max will scarcely tell Napoleon at
Fontainebleau that he will only pass the frontiers of Germany or Austria over his dead body.

'I am quite astonished to read in your letter that the
Austrians contend they had procured more for us at Neuchâtel than the French. Such shameless lying can only
come from Austria; even if they had wished they could
not have managed it, and would certainly not have picked
a quarrel with France and England for our sake. On the
contrary, they caused us as much difficulty in the "marching through" question as they could, calumniated us,
estranged Baden from us, and have now, together with
England, been our opponents in Paris. I know from the
French and from Kisseleff that in all the conferences
which Hübner attended without Hatzfeldt—and those
were just the decisive ones—he was always the first to
join in the English opposition against us; then followed
France, and afterwards Russia. But why should any
one do anything for us at Neuchâtel and take up the cud-
gels for our interests? Had any one anything to hope
for or to fear from us whether he did us that favour or
not? That any one should act in politics out of complaisance or from a sentiment of justice others may expect
from us, but not we from them.

' If we desire to go on living in such isolation, un-
heeded and occasionally bullied, I have of course no
power to change it; if, however, we desire to come once
more into consideration we cannot possibly attain that
aim by building our foundation solely on the sand of the
German *Bund* and calmly awaiting its collapse. As long
as each of us is convinced that a portion of the European
chess-board will remain closed against us by our own

choice, or that we must tie up one arm on principle while every one else employs both his to our disadvantage, this sentimentality of ours will be turned to account without fear and without thanks. I do not at all desire that we should conclude an alliance with France and con-spire against Germany; but is it not more sensible to be on friendly than on indifferent terms with the French so long as they leave us in peace? All I want to do is to rid other people of the belief that *they* may adopt whomsoever they wish as brothers, but that *we* would rather have our skin cut into strips than defend it with French aid. Courtesy is a cheap coin, and if it does no further service than that of ridding the others of the be-lief that they are always sure of France against us and we at all times in want of help against France, that is a great thing gained for the diplomacy of peace; if we de-spise this resource, and even act contrarily, then I do not know why we do not rather save or reduce the expenses of our diplomacy, for, do what that class will, it cannot bring to pass what the King can do with little trou-ble, namely, restore Prussia to a position of authority in peace by a display of friendly relations and possible alli-ances. With just as much ease can his Majesty cripple all the labours of the diplomatists by making a show of coolness in relations; for what can I here or any other of our envoys effect if we create an impression of being friendless or of relying upon Austria's friendship? If we wish not to hear laughter when we speak of Aus-tria's help in any matter of importance to ourselves, we must go to Berlin. And even in Berlin I know only a proportionately very small circle in which a feeling of bitterness will not betray itself as soon as our foreign

policy is mentioned. Our prescription for every evil is
to throw ourselves upon the neck of Count Buol and to
pour out our brotherly heart to him. When I was in
Paris a certain count sued for a divorce after having
caught his wife, formerly a circus-rider, *in flagrante de-
licto* for the twenty-fourth time; he was held up to the
admiration of the court by his lawyer as an example of a
gallant and indulgent husband, but his magnanimity is
nought compared with ours in regard to Austria.

'Our domestic relations suffer scarcely more from
their own defects than they do from the painful and universal feeling of our loss of reputation abroad and the
totally passive part played by our policy. We are a vain
nation; we feel hurt directly we cannot swagger, and
much, even in regard to our pockets, is forgiven and permitted a government which gives us importance abroad.
But while we are compelled to say with regard to home
matters that we rather expel by our own healthy humours
the diseases with which our ministerial physicians inoculate
us than are healed and guided to a wholesome *régime* by
them, we seek in vain for some consolation in foreign
affairs. You, my most respected friend, are well acquainted
with our policy; can you name a single aim that our politicians have set themselves or even a plan followed for a
few months? Even granted a position of affairs, do they
know what they really want? Is there any one in Berlin
with that knowledge, and do you think that a like void of
positive aims and ideas is to be found in the leaders of
any one other state? Can you moreover name a single
ally upon whom Prussia could count if war came this
very day or who would speak in our behalf in matters
that touch us nearly, like the Neuchâtel business, or who

would do anything whatever for us either because he reckons upon our support or fears our hostility? We are the best-natured and most harmless of politicians, and yet no one in reality trusts us; we are regarded as unsafe allies and harmless foes, precisely as if we behaved like Austria in foreign affairs and were as rotten at home. I do not speak of the present; but can you name to me one positive plan (precautionary ones in plenty) or a purpose which we have had in foreign politics since the triple alliance formed by Radowitz? Yes, one—the Jahde harbour; but up to the present that has remained a stagnant pool, and we shall amicably allow ourselves to be stripped of the Zollverein by Austria, because we have not the resolution to say simply No. I am surprised that we still possess diplomatists in whom the courage to hold an idea or the ambition to achieve something is not dead already, and I shall be just as content as the rest of my colleagues with simply executing my instructions, attending the sittings, and divesting myself of any interest in the general progress of our policy; this is better for one's health and one wastes less ink.

'You will probably say that because I am vexed that you are not of my opinion, I see things black and scold like a gutter-sparrow; but really and truly I would just as willingly labour to carry out another's ideas as my own, if I could only find any. To go on vegetating in this way we really do not require the whole apparatus of our diplomacy. Any way, the pigeons which come flying to us already roasted cannot escape us; I do not know, though, for we shall hardly open our mouths for them unless we happen to yawn. All I strive for is that we should accept and not reject whatever is likely to impress the cabinets in

time of peace with the notion that we are not on a bad
footing with France, that they cannot rely on our want of
aid against France and squeeze us accordingly, and that, if
we are unhandsomely treated, any alliance is open to us.
If then I announce that these advantages are to be had for
courtesy and for a show of reciprocity, I expect to have it
proved either that they are not advantages and that it is, on
the contrary, more expedient for our interests that foreign
and German Courts should be justified in starting from the
assumption that we must under all circumstances be armed
as foes against the West, and for that purpose require alliances and eventually assistance, even if they turn this
assumption to advantage as the basis of their political
operations directed against us; or that there are other
plans and aims with the combination of which the show
of a good understanding with France does not fit in. I
do not know whether the government has a plan (with
which I am unacquainted)—I do not think so; if, however,
we repel the diplomatic advances of a great Power only on
account of antipathies or sympathies for conditions and
persons which we cannot and would not alter, and if we regu-
late our political relations with two other great Powers
on the same basis, then I am within the mark if I say
that as a diplomatist I do not comprehend this, and consider that with the adoption of such a system in foreign
relations the whole profession of diplomacy down to the
consular service is superfluous and practically cashiered.
You tell me that the man is our natural enemy and that it
will soon be proved he is so and must remain so; I could
dispute this, or say with equal justice: " Austria, England, are our enemies, and that they are so has long ago been
proved,—naturally in the case of Austria, unnaturally in

that of England." But I will let that rest as it is, and, assuming that your contention were correct, I cannot even then regard it as politic, while peace still exists, to betray our apprehensions to others and to France herself; but I consider it expedient, until the breach foreseen by you really occurs, to go on allowing people to believe that we are not necessarily doomed to a war sooner or later with France, that it is at least nothing inseparable from the position of Prussia, and that the tension with regard to France is not an organic defect, an innate weakness of our nature, upon which every one else can speculate with safety. As soon as we are thought to be on cool terms with France my Federal colleague here will cool towards me. . . .

' v. B.'

Gerlach replied as follows:

' Berlin : May 6, 1857.

' Your letter of the 2nd gave me in one way much pleasure, since I gather from it that you heartily desire to remain or to become of one mind with me—a matter about which most people care but little; while, on the other hand, it called upon me to reply and to justify myself.

' To begin with, I flatter myself that at the very bottom I am still at one with you. Were that not the case, I would not undertake a thorough refutation, since it could after all lead to nothing. If you feel a need to remain in agreement with me on a matter of principle, it is incumbent upon us to seek out this principle first of all, and not to content ourselves with nègations, such as " ignoring facts" and the " exclusion of France from the political combinations." Just as little could we hope to find the common principle in " Prussian patriotism," in " hurtful-

181

ness or utility to Prussia," in the "exclusive service of the
King and of the country," for these are things which are
matters of course, and in regard to which you must be prepared for the answer that I believe I find these things better and in greater number in my policy than in yours or
any other. But for that very reason it is of the greatest
importance to me to seek out the principle, since, without
having found it, I regard all political combinations as
faulty, unsafe, and highly dangerous, having convinced myself of this during the last ten years, and that too by
results.

' Now I must make a rather wide digression, reaching
too as far as Charles the Great—that is, more than a thousand years back. At that time the principle of European
politics was the spread of the Christian Church. Charles
the Great devoted himself to this in his wars with the Sar-
acens, the Saxons, the Avars and others, and his policy was
really not unpractical. His successors fought among them·
selves, devoid of all principle, and again it was the great
princes of the middle ages who remained true to the old
idea. The foundations of the Prussian power were laid by
the struggles of the Brandenburg margraves and of the
Teutonic Order with those races who were unwilling to
submit to the Emperor, the Vicar of the Church, and this
lasted until the lapse of the Church into territorialism led
to the decline of the Empire and the split in the Church.
Since then there has no longer been one universal principle in Christendom. Of the original principle there
remained only resistance to the dangerous power of
the Turks, and Austria as well as Russia at a later period
were really not unpractical when they fought the Turks in
accordance with this principle. The wars against the

Turks founded the power of those Empires, and, had people been loyal to that principle, the destruction of the
Turkish Empire, Europe or Christendom would, humanly
speaking, have been in a better position with regard to the
East than at present, when we are threatened on that side
with the greatest dangers. Prior to the French Revolution, that abrupt and very practical revolt from the Church
of Christ, the foremost place in politics was held by a policy of "interests," of so-called patriotism, and whither this
led we have seen. Anything more wretched than Prussia's
policy from 1778 until the French Revolution there never
was; I may mention the subsidies paid by Frederick II to
Russia, which were equivalent to a tribute, and the hatred
against England. In Holland the old consideration for
Frederick II still held sway in 1787; the Convention of
Reichenbach had however already taken place—a disgrace
due to a deviation from the principle. The wars of the
Great Elector were in the Protestant interest, and those of
Frederick William III against France were in reality wars
against the Revolution. The three Silesian wars from
1740 to 1763 also had essentially a Protestant character,
even though territorial interests and the balance of power
played a part in them all.

' The principle that was instilled into European politics
by the Revolution, which made the tour of Europe, is that
which in my opinion still prevails to-day. It was, in truth,
not unpractical to remain faithful to this conception.
England, that remained faithful to the struggle against
the Revolution until 1815, and did not allow herself to be
misled by the old Bonaparte, rose to the highest power;
Austria, after many unfortunate wars, came out of the
arena fairly well; Prussia suffered heavily by the conse-

quences of the peace of Basle and only rehabilitated herself
by the events of 1813 to 1815; Spain suffered still more
and went to ruin; while, according to your own view, the
German middle states, the creatures, alas, of the Vienna
congress, the fruit of irresolution and jealousy, the protected products of the Revolution and of the Bonapartism
that followed upon it, are the *materia peccans* in Germany.
If, in accordance with principle, Belgium had been restored
to Austria, and the Franconian principalities to Prussia at
Vienna, Germany would be in a different position than it
now is, especially if those abortions, Bavaria, Wurtemberg,
Darmstadt, had been brought back to their natural size at
the same time; but in those days the idea of rounding off,
and other such purely mechanical interests, were preferred
to principle.

‘ You will, however, no doubt have been already bored
by my lengthy digression, and I will therefore turn to the
most recent period. Do you consider it a happy state of
things that now, when Prussia and Austria stand opposed
as foes, Bonaparte should rule as far as Dessau and nothing
should be done in Germany without asking his leave? Can
an alliance with France replace for us the condition of
things that existed from 1815 to 1848, when no foreign
Power interfered in German affairs? That Austria and
the German middle states will do nothing for us, of that I
am as convinced as you are. But, in addition to that,
I believe that France, which means Bonaparte, will also
do nothing for us. I approve as little as you of being
unfriendly and discourteous towards him, and to exclude
France from the political combinations is madness. It
does not, however, follow from this that we should forget
Bonaparte's origin, invite him to Berlin, and so confuse

every one's notions at home and abroad. In the Neuchâtel matter he behaved well in so far that he prevented war, and openly said that he would do no more. Whether that affair would, however, not have turned out better if we had not allowed ourselves to be swayed by a policy of sentiment, but had brought the matter to the European Powers that signed the London protocol without first taking shelter under Bonaparte's wing, is still very open to question, and after all that was what Austria really desired. No harm need have come to the prisoners, on whose behalf interest might have been made.

'Then you complain about our policy of isolation. The same complaint was made by Usedom, the freemason, when he wished to drive us into the treaty of December 2, and Manteuffel, now Usedom's sworn enemy, was very much impressed by the idea; you, however, thank God, at that time were not. Austria took part in that treaty of December, and what good has it done her? She is casting about in all directions for alliances. She entered into a quasi-alliance immediately after the peace of Paris, and now she is said to have concluded a secret one with England. I see no gain in this, but only difficulties. The last-named alliance can only be of avail in the event of that between France and England being dissolved, and Palmerston will not allow himself to be kept back from coquetting with Sardinia and Italy even as long as that.

'My political principle is, and remains, the struggle against the Revolution. You will not convince Napoleon that he is not on the side of the Revolution. He has no desire either to be anywhere else, for his position there gives him his decided advantages. There is thus no question either of sympathy or of antipathy here. This position of Bonaparte's is a "fact" which you cannot "ignore." From this, however, it by no means follows that we cannot show him courtesy and indulgence, recognition and consideration, but only that we cannot ally ourselves with him for definite objects. But if a principle like that of opposition to the Revolution is correct—and I believe that you also recognise it to be such—then we must also constantly stick to it in practice in order that, when the time comes for carrying it out—and that time must come, if the principle be correct—those who have to recognise it, as Austria and England too will perhaps soon have to do, may know what they have to expect from us. You say yourself that people cannot rely upon us, and yet one cannot fail to recognise that he only is to be relied on who acts according to definite principles and not according to shifting notions of interests, and so forth. England, and in her way Austria too, were from 1793 to 1813 perfectly trustworthy and therefore always found allies in spite of all the defeats which the French inflicted upon them.

' With regard now to our German policy I believe that it is still our vocation to show the small states the superiority of Prussia, and not to treat everything as all right, for instance in the affairs of the Zollverein and on many other occasions down to the hunting invitations and the princes who enter into our service, and so forth. Here— that is, in Germany—is also the place where, as it seems to me, we have to oppose Austria; at the same time we should carefully avoid exposing ourselves in any way to that country. This would be my answer to your letter.

'If I am, however, to speak further concerning our policy

outside Germany, I cannot regard it as striking or even as disquieting that we stand alone at a time when all relations are turned topsy-turvy, when England and France are for the present still so closely allied that France has not the courage to think of safeguards against the Swiss Radicals because England might take it amiss, though meanwhile she frightens that same England with her preparations for a landing, and takes decisive steps towards a Russian alliance; when Austria is in league with England, with the latter nevertheless continually stirring up Italy, &c. Whither, then, are we, in your opinion, to turn? Shall it be to an alliance with France and Russia against Austria and England such as Plonplon, who is at present here, is said to have suggested? From such an alliance, however, there would immediately result a preponderating influence of France in Italy, the total revolutionizing of that country, and likewise a preponderating influence of Bonaparte in Germany. Some share in this influence would be allowed us in the subordinate spheres, but neither a great nor a lasting one. We have indeed once already seen Germany under Russo-French influences from 1801 to 1803, when the bishoprics were secularised and distributed in accordance with rescripts from Paris and St. Petersburg. Prussia, which was then on a friendly footing with the two states and on unfriendly terms with Austria and England, also came in for a share at the distribution, but only for a small one, and her influence was less than ever.

'L. v. G.'

Without going fully into his letter, I wrote to the general on May 11 as follows:

BISMARCK

'. . . News from Berlin apprises me that they regard me at Court as a Bonapartist. In this they do me wrong. In the year '50 I was charged by our opponents with treasonable inclinations towards Austria, and we were called the Viennese in Berlin; it was subsequently discovered that we smelt of Russia leather, and they dubbed us " Cossacks of the Spree." To the question whether I was Russian or Occidental, I at that time always replied that I was a Prussian and that my ideal for one employed on foreign politics was freedom from prejudice, the habit of deciding independently of any feelings of antipathy to or preference for foreign states and their rulers. So far as concerns foreign countries I have, throughout my life, had a sympathy for England only and her inhabitants, and I am, in certain hours, not yet free from it; but the people there will not let us love them, and as soon as it were proved to me that it was in the interests of a sound and well-thought-out Prussian policy I would, with the same satisfaction, see our troops fire on French, Russians, English, or Austrians. In time of peace I consider it wanton self-debilitation to attract or encourage ill-temper, unless some practical political aim be connected therewith, and to sacrifice the liberty of one's future decisions and connections to vague and unrequited sympathies—concessions such as Austria now expects us to make with regard to Rastatt—purely out of good nature and love of approbation. If we cannot at once expect any equivalent for any politeness of that kind, then we ought also to withhold our concession; the opportunity to give it value as an article of exchange may perhaps present itself at a later time. The advantage accruing to the *Bund* can of course not be the exclusive clue of Prussian policy, for the greatest advantage of all to the *Bund* would undoubtedly be if we and all German governments submitted to Austria in military and political affairs and commercially in the Zollverein; under one leader the *Bund* would be capable of very different feats in peace and war, and become really stable when a *casus belli* arose. . . .'[1]

Gerlach replied to me under date of May 21 as follows:

'When I received your letter of the 11th inst., of course I thought it was an answer to my attempted refutation of your ample communication of the 2nd. I therefore felt very anxious, since it is painful to me to differ in opinion from you, and I hoped for an understanding. Your answer, however, to the charge of Bonapartism brought against you proves to me that we are still far apart. . . . That you are no Bonapartist I am as certain as that most statesmen, not only among us, but abroad, e.g. Palmerston, Bach, Buol and others are so in reality; I also know *a priori* that you will have seen many specimens of this kind in Frankfort and in Germany—I had almost said in the Confederation of the Rhine. The manner in which you regarded the Opposition in the last Diet would alone free you from the reproach of Bonapartism. But that is just the reason why the view which you take of our foreign policy is inexplicable to me.

'I too am of opinion that we ought not to be distrustful, stand-offish and cross-grained towards Bonaparte; we should behave in the best possible way towards him, only not invite him here, as you desire, since by doing so we should compromise ourselves somewhat, puzzle good inten-

[1] *Bismarck's Letters to L. v. Gerlach*, p. 324.

tions where they still exist, arouse suspicion, and lose our honour. For that reason I approve much that is in your memorandum;[1] the historical introduction, pages 1—5, is highly instructive, and most of the rest is very applicable; but you will excuse me for saying that the head and tail, the principle and aim of politics, are here wanting.

' 1. Can you deny that Napoleon III ("l'élu de sept millions") is like Napoleon I subjected to the consequences of his position—an absolutism based on the sovereignty of the people—and that he feels this as much as the old one did? . . .

' 2. A triple alliance of France, Russia, and Prussia, into which Prussia only enters with—" Let me be, I beg you, Sirs, in your league a humble third"—and remains the weakest, standing distrustfully on the defensive against Austria and England, directly brings about the triumph of " French interests," that is, the mastery in Italy in the first place, and then in Germany; from 1801 to 1804 Russia and France divided Germany and allotted a small portion to Prussia.

' 3. In what does the policy recommended by you differ from that of Haugwitz during the period of 1794 to 1805? At that time too there was talk only of a "defensive system." Thugut, Cobenzl, and Lehrbach were not a whit better than Buol and Bach; acts of perfidy on the part of Austria were also not wanting; Russia was even more untrustworthy than now; but England, it is true, more reliable. The King was also at heart opposed to that policy. . .

'In my difference with you the thought often occurs to me that I have become antiquated in my views and that,

---

[1] To Manteuffel, of May 18. See *Preussen im Bundestage*, iv. 262.

although I cannot consider my own policy wrong, it may perhaps be necessary to try a new, which must in the first place be gone through and mastered. In 1792 Massenbach was for the French alliance and wrote a treatise upon it in the middle of the war; from 1794 Haugwitz advocated the defensive system or neutrality, and so on. Revolutionary absolutism is by its nature given to conquest, since it can only maintain itself at home when a system similar to itself exists all around. Palmerston was obliged to support the demonstration against the Belgian press, and so forth. Against Swiss radicalism, although it is admittedly very inconvenient for Bonaparte, Napoleon III has been very weak. One parallel more. In 1812 Gneisenau, Scharnhorst, and a few others were opposed to the French alliance, which, as you know, was persevered with and made a reality by a contingent. The result spoke for those who had wanted the alliance. Yet I would very gladly have stood by Gneisenau and Scharnhorst. In 1813 Knesebeck was for the armistice and Gneisenau against it; as a 22-year-old officer I was at that time decidedly opposed to it, and in spite of the result I would venture to prove that I was right. "Victrix causa diis placuit victa Catoni" has indeed some significance. . .

'It will not be difficult for you to carry out the policy of the "defensive system" in the alliance with France and Russia—formerly that was called a policy of neutrality, and England would not tolerate any such in the Eastern question; the Manteuffels and many others as well are on your side (his Majesty not in his heart, it is true, but yet passively), and all of them too, so long as Bonapartism holds out. How many things, however, can happen in the meantime! I should, however, have been greatly pleased if you could have grasped the helm without the slightest aid from that force.

'The old Bonaparte reigned fifteen years, Louis Philippe eighteen; do you think that the present creature will last longer?

'L. v. G.'[1]

I replied in the following letter:

'Frankfort: May 30, 1857.

'In replying to your two last letters I labour under a sense of the imperfection of human expression, especially in writing; every attempt to make ourselves clear engenders fresh misunderstandings; it is not given us to commit to paper or to put into words our whole selves, and we cannot make others receive from the fragments which we bring forth precisely the same sensations as they gave ourselves. This arises partly from the inferiority of speech compared with thought, partly because the external facts to which we refer seldom present themselves to two persons in the same light, as soon as the one ceases to accept the view of the other on trust as though it were his own. This feeling came to the aid of the delays occasioned by business matters, visits, fine weather, indolence, children's ailments, and my own illness, and discouraged me from answering your criticism with further arguments, each of which will have its own weak points and imperfections. In pronouncing judgment upon them, please take into consideration that I am a convalescent, and that I have drunk my first Marienbad water to-day, and if my views diverge from yours you must seek the reason in the foliage and not in the root, for I claim that at bottom my convictions are in unison with yours. The principle of the battle

[1] Cf. *Bismarck-Jahrbuch*, ii. 242.

against the Revolution I acknowledge to be mine also, but I do not consider it right to set up Louis Napoleon as the sole or even only as the κατ᾽ ἐξοχήν representative of the Revolution, nor do I believe it possible to carry out principle in politics as something whose remotest consequences break through every other consideration and which forms to a certain extent the only trump suit in the game, the lowest card of which still beats the highest of every other suit.

' How many entities are there left in the political world to-day that have not their roots in revolutionary soil? Take Spain, Portugal, Brazil, all the American Republics, Belgium, Holland, Switzerland, Greece, Sweden, and England, the latter with her foot even to-day consciously planted on the glorious revolution of 1688; even for that territory which the German princes of to-day have won partly from Emperor and Empire, partly from their peers the barons, and partly from the estates of their own country, no perfectly legitimate title of possession can be shown, and in our own political life we cannot avoid the use of revolutionary supports. Many of the conditions referred to have become naturalized by antiquity and we have accustomed ourselves to them; it is with them as with all the marvels which surround us for twenty-four hours each day, and therefore cease to appear marvellous to us and deter no one from confining the idea of a " marvel " to phenomena which are by no means more wonderful than our own birth and the daily life of the individual.

' If, however, I acknowledge a principle to be supreme and universally pervading I can only do so in so far as it is verified under all circumstances and at all times, and the axiom " quod ab initio vitiosum, lapsu temporis convalescere nequit " is still correct in the view of the doctrinaires. But even at a time when the revolutionary phenomena of the past had not yet reached such a degree of antiquity that we could say of them like the witch in Faust of her hell-broth,

> Here is a flask,
> I taste myself, now and again—
> You'll not find any smell remain,

people were not always so chaste as to abstain from amorous contact; Cromwell was addressed as " brother " by very anti-revolutionary potentates, and his friendship was sought when it appeared to be of use; very honourable princes were in alliance with the States-General before they were recognised by Spain. In the eyes of our ancestors William of Orange and his successors in England passed current even while the Stuarts were still pretending, and we forgave the United States of America their revolutionary origin by signing the treaty of the Hague in 1785. The present King of Portugal has visited us in Berlin and we would have married into the House of Bernadotte had not hindrances accidentally intervened. When and by what tokens have all these powers ceased to be revolutionary? It appears that their illegitimate birth is pardoned them as soon as we have no apprehension of danger from them, and that no further exception is taken to them, even on principle, though they continue to acknowledge impenitently —nay, even boastingly—their illegitimate origin.

' I do not see how, before the French Revolution, a statesman, even were he the most Christian and conscientious, could have conceived the idea of subordinating his entire political aims, his conduct both in foreign and home politics, to the principle of fighting against the Revolution, and of testing the relations of his country to others solely by that touchstone; yet the principles of the American and English Revolutions were, independently of the measure of bloodshed and the religious disturbances that shaped themselves differently according to the national character, pretty much the same as those which in France caused an interruption in the continuity of the law.   I cannot suppose that before 1789 there were not some politicians quite as Christian and conservative, quite as able to recognise evil as we are, and that the truth of a principle to be laid down by us as the basis of all politics could have escaped them.   Nor do I find that we apply the principle with the same rigour to all revolutionary phenomena after 1789 as we do to France.   The analogous condition of justice in Austria, the prosperity of the Revolution in Portugal, Spain, Belgium, and in the now thoroughly revolutionary kingdom of Denmark, the open acknowledgment and propagation of the fundamental ideas of the Revolution on the part of the English government and the practical demonstration moreover of the same in the Neuchâtel question —all this does not deter us from judging the relations of our King with the rulers of those countries more kindly than those he maintains with Napoleon III.   What then is there peculiar to the latter and to the *French* Revolution generally?   The unprincely origin of the Bonapartes has a great deal to do with it, but the same conditions are found in Sweden without the same consequences.   Is the "peculiarity" an attribute of the Bonaparte family?   It did not call the Revolution into existence, nor would the Revolution be set aside or even rendered innocuous if that family were extirpated.   The Revolution is much older than the Bonapartes, and much broader in its foundations

than France. If one wants to attribute to it a terrestrial
origin, such origin must not be sought in France but rather
in England, if not still earlier in Germany or in Rome,
according as a preference may be shown for laying the
responsibility upon the outgrowths of the Reformation or
upon those of the Roman Church and the introduction of
Roman law into the Germanic world.

' The first Napoleon commenced by successfully utilising the Revolution in France for his ambition, and subsequently made attempts to conquer it unsuccessfully and
by wrong means; he would right gladly have cut it out
of his past, after he had plucked its fruits and put them
in his pocket. He, at least, did not further it in the
same degree as the three Lewises before him—by the
introduction of absolutism under Lewis XIV, by the in-
dignities of the Regency and of Lewis XV, and by
the weakness of Lewis XVI, who on September 14,
1791, proclaimed the Revolution at an end upon his
acceptance of the Constitution. The House of Bour-
bon has done more for the Revolution than all the
Bonapartes, even without crediting it with Philippe
Egalité. Bonapartism is not the father of the Revolution; it is, like every form of absolutism, only a fertile
field for its seed. In saying this I have not the slightest desire to place it beyond the domain of revolutionary phenomena, but only to bring it into view rid of the
accessories which are not necessarily proper to its essence. Among these I also count unjust wars and conquests. These are no peculiar attribute of the Bonaparte
family or of the system of government named after it.
Legitimate heirs to ancient thrones are capable of the
same. Lewis XIV carried on in Germany, so far as he

could, in no less heathen a fashion than Napoleon, and if the latter, with his disposition and inclinations, had been born a son of Lewis XVI he would presumably also have made our lives pretty sour for us.

'The impulse to conquest is no less an attribute of England, North America, Russia, and other countries than of Napoleonic France, and as soon as power and opportunity are at hand moderation and love of justice have a hard task in keeping even the most legitimate monarchy within bounds. The impulse in question does not seem to dominate Napoleon III as an instinct; he is no captain, and in a war on a great scale, with big results or risks, the eyes of the French army, the prop of his sovereignty, could scarcely fail to turn to a fortunate general rather than to the Emperor. He will therefore only seek war when he believes himself compelled to it by dangers at home. A compulsion of this kind would, however, exist from the outset for the legitimate King of France if he now came to the throne.

'Neither the remembrance of his uncle's passion for conquest nor the fact of the unrighteous origin of his power justifies me therefore in regarding the present Emperor of the French as the sole representative of the Revolution and as an object to be singled out in the fight against the latter. The second blemish he shares with many existing potentates, and with regard to the first he has not so far laid himself more open to suspicion than others. You, my respected friend, reproach him with being unable to maintain his power unless the condition of the surrounding countries resemble that of his own; if I acknowledged this to be correct, it would suffice to upset my view. But Bonapartism is distinguished from the Republic by the fact that it has no necessity to propagate its principles of government by the employment of violence. Even the first Napoleon did not attempt to obtrude his form of government upon those countries that were not directly or indirectly subjected to France; people vied in imitating it of their own free will. To threaten foreign states by the aid of the Revolution has now been for some years past the stock in trade of England, and if Louis Napoleon had been of the same mind as Palmerston, we should have witnessed an outbreak in Naples several years ago.

'By aiding the spread of revolutionary institutions among his neighbours the French Emperor would be creating dangers for himself; he will rather, in the interests of the maintenance of his rule and dynasty and with his conviction of the faultiness of present French institutions, seek to gain for himself firmer foundations than those of the Revolution. Whether he can, I admit, is another question, but he is by no means blind to the shortcomings and dangers of the Bonapartist system of government, for he himself dilates upon them and deplores them. The present form of government in France is not something arbitrary, something that Louis Napoleon might introduce or alter; it was a *datum* for him, and is probably the only method according to which it will be possible to govern France for a long time to come; the basis for anything else is either from the outset lacking to the national character or it has been crushed and become lost, and if Henry V came to the throne now he too would be unable to rule otherwise, if at all. Louis Napoleon did not call the revolutionary conditions of the country into existence, nor did he gain his sovereignty by opposition to a lawfully constituted authority; he fished it up as unclaimed property out of the whirlpool of anarchy. If he now desired to abdicate he would bring Europe into perplexities and he would be pretty unanimously begged to remain; even if he gave up the power to the Duke of Bordeaux the latter would no more be able to hold it than he was capable of acquiring it. When Louis Napoleon calls himself the "élu de sept millions" he alludes to a fact which he cannot disown; he cannot give himself any other origin than he has; but it cannot be said of him that now he is in possession of the power he continues practically to do homage to the principle of the people's sovereignty and to receive the law from the will of the masses—a system which is daily becoming more and more prevalent in England.

' It is in human nature that the oppression and shameful treatment of our country by the first Napoleon should have left behind an unextinguishable impression in all who went through it, and that in their eyes the evil principle which we combat in the form of the Revolution is alone identified with the person and the family of the man who is called " l'heureux soldat héritier de la révolution;" it appears to me, however, that you lay too much on the present Napoleon when you personify in him and in him alone the Revolution we have to fight against, and for that reason pronounce him a proscript with whom it is dishonourable to have intercourse. Every mark of the Revolution that he carries about him you also find in other places, though you do not direct your hatred thither with the same doctrinaire severity. The Bonapartist rule in home affairs with its crude centralisation, its extermination of all that is independent, its disregard of liberty and justice, its official lies, its corruption in the state and on the Stock Exchange, and its accommodating writers free from all

conviction, flourishes in that Austria which you regard
with such undeserved predilection just as much as in
France; on the Danube, however, it is consciously called
into existence out of free plenitude of power, while Louis
Napoleon found it waiting for him in France and, though
distasteful to himself, not easily to be altered.

' The specific quality which induces us to distinguish
the French Revolution in particular as *the* Revolution I
find not in the Bonaparte family but in the narrow limits
of time and space into which the events were compressed
and in the greatness and power of the country upon the
soil of which they took place. For that reason they are
more dangerous, but I do not on that account consider it
more wicked to stand in relation with Bonaparte than with
other bodies engendered by the Revolution or with governments which voluntarily identify themselves with it, like
Austria, and are active in the propagation of revolutionary
principles, like England.   In all this I have no desire to
make an apology for persons and conditions in France; I
have no predilection for the former and regard the latter
as a misfortune for that country; I only desire to explain
how I arrive at the conclusion that it is neither sinful nor
dishonourable to enter into closer connexion, should the
course of politics render it necessary, with the sovereign
of an important country who has been acknowledged by us.
That this connexion is in itself desirable I do not say, but
only that all other chances are worse, and that we must,
in order to improve them, go through with the reality or
the appearance of closer relations with France.   Only by
this means can we bring Austria so far on the road to reason and renunciation of its extravagant Schwarzenberg
ambition as to seek an understanding with us instead of

trying to circumvent us, and only by this means can we stop the further development of direct relations between the German middle states and France.   England too will begin to recognise how important an alliance with Prussia is when she begins to fear that she may lose it in favour of France.   Therefore, even if I took up your standpoint of inclination towards Austria and England, we should have to begin with France in order to bring them to a recognition of it.

'In your communication you anticipate, my respected friend, that we shall play a small part in a Prusso-Franco-Russian alliance.   I have, however, never put forward such an alliance as something to be striven for by us, but as a fact which will sooner or later spring from the present *décousu* without our being able to hinder it, which we must therefore take into account and about the effects of which we must be clear.   I added that we might perhaps prevent such an alliance or at least modify its results, and in any case avoid entering into it as a "third" by replying to the advances made by France for our friendship.   We shall appear relatively weak in every alliance with other Great Powers until we are stronger than we now are.   Austria and England, if we are leagued with them, will also not make their superiority felt exactly in our interest—that we experienced to our detriment at the Vienna congress. Austria grudges us any consideration in Germany, England any chances of maritime development in commerce or fleet, and she is envious of our industry.

'You draw a parallel between me and Haugwitz and the "defensive policy" of his time.   The conditions, however, were different in those days.   France was already in possession of the most menacing predominance, a notoriously dangerous conqueror being at its head, and England on the other hand might safely be reckoned on. I have the courage *not* to blame the peace of Basle; it was as impossible to make a lasting alliance with the Austria of that day and its Thugut, Lehrbach, and Cobenzl as it is now, and I cannot make the peace of Basle responsible for the fact that we came off badly in 1815; the reason was that we could not maintain our ground against the opposed interests of England and Austria because our physical weakness compared to the other Great Powers inspired no fear. The states of the Rhine Confederation had their Basle quite differently to us, and yet they came off exceedingly well at Vienna. It was, however, egregious stupidity on our part, in 1805, not to seize the opportunity to aid in breaking up the predominance of France; we ought to have made war upon Napoleon swiftly, vigorously, and to the last breath. To sit still was even more foolish than to take sides for France herself; but after we had let that opportunity go by, we ought to have kept the peace in 1806 *à tout prix* and waited for a better one.

'I am not at all in favour of a "defensive policy"—I only say that without any aggressive aims or obligations we can still respond to the advances of France, that such a line of conduct has the advantage of keeping every door open, every turning clear for us until the situation becomes firmer and more distinct, and that I regard the course I recommend not as a conspiracy against others but only as a precaution for our own defence.

'You say, "France will not do more for us than Austria and the middle states;" my belief is that no one does anything for us, unless he can at the same time serve his own interests. The direction, however, in which Austria and the middle states at present pursue their interests is quite incompatible with the tasks which are vital questions for Prussia, and a common policy is quite impossible until Austria adopts a discreeter system towards us, of which there is so far little prospect. You agree with me that we must show the small states the superiority of Prussia, but what means have we for doing so inside the Act of Confederation? Little can be done when we have but one voice among seventeen and Austria against us.

'A visit from Louis Napoleon would, for the reasons given by me elsewhere, render our voice more effective than it now is. They will become considerate and even affectionate to us in precise proportion to their fear of us; confidence in us they will never have. Every glance at the map robs them of that; they know that their interests and particular desires stand in the way of the general direction of Prussian policy, and that therein lies a danger against which only the disinterestedness of our most gracious master offers any security for the future. The visit of the Frenchman to us would not occasion any further distrust; such a feeling already exists wholly and completely against Prussia, and the sentiments of the King which might weaken it earn him no gratitude, but are only utilised and turned to the best account. Whatever confidence there may be will, in case of need, not bring a single man into the field for us; fear, if we but knew how to inspire it, would place the whole *Bund* at our disposal. That fear would be inspired by ostensible tokens of our good relations with France. If nothing of the kind happens, it might be difficult to carry on for long with that country those benevolent relations you too regard as desirable. For France is courting us, feeling the necessity of

having us as a set-off, and hoping for some understanding;
a refusal on our part to accept its advances would call forth
a coolness perceptible even in other courts, because the
"parvenu" would feel touched thereby on his most sensitive spot.

'Lay some other policy before me and I will discuss
it with you honestly and without prejudice, but we cannot exist in the centre of Europe in a state of passivity,
devoid of any plan and glad only to be left alone; such a
course might be as dangerous to us to-day as it was in
1805, and we shall have to serve as the anvil if we do
nothing to become the hammer. I cannot allow you the
consolation of "victa causa Catoni placuit" if therewith
you incur the danger of drawing our common Fatherland
into a "victa causa. . . ."

'If my ideas find no favour in your sight, do not, I
beg, condemn me altogether, but remember that for years
we not only trod the same soil in hard times but also
reared the same plants upon it, and that I am a man who
will listen to argument and put away error if conviction is
brought home to me. . . .

'v. B.'

Gerlach replied:

'Sans-Souci: June 5, 1857.

'. . . In the first place I want to acknowledge willingly the practical side of your view. Nesselrode, like
yourself, was quite right in saying here that so long as
Buol ruled (you correctly bracket Bach with him) it would
not be possible to get on with Austria. Austria, he
added, had hounded Europe against them (the Russians)
merely by assurances of friendship, had torn a portion of

Bessarabia from them, and was still causing them much heartburning. She behaves in a similar fashion towards us, and during the Eastern war her conduct was abominably perfidious. When, therefore, you say that we cannot go with Austria, that is relatively true, and it would be difficult for us to disagree about it *in casu concreto.* Do not, however, forget that sin always begets sin, and that in this respect Austria can confront us with a pretty long list, e.g. the objection we raised to her marching into the Lake Province * of Baden in 1849, which practically brought about the loss of Neuchâtel, for the Prince of Prussia might at that time have mastered it; then the Radowitz policy; then the arrogant treatment of the " Interim," in regard to which even Schwarzenberg was well disposed; and finally a host of less important details—all repetitions of the policy of 1793 to 1805. The notion, however, that our unfriendly relations towards Austria can only be relative becomes practical as often as an occasion arises, for one reason as checking us in taking revenge, which can only lead to misfortune, and for another as keeping up the desire for reconciliation and advances, and hence avoiding whatever makes such advances impossible. Both are wanting in our case, and why? Because our statesmen "donnent dans le Bonapartisme."

‘ In judging of these things, however, the old have an advantage over the young. The old actors on the stage are in this case the King and my humble self, the young ones Fra Diavolo [Manteuffel] and so on, for F. D. was in the Confederation of the Rhine from 1806 to 1814 and

---

* [That is the southern part, bordering on the Lake of Constance. The occasion was the rising in Baden, after the fiasco of the German Parliament.]

you were not yet born. But we made a practical study of Bonapartism for ten years; it was well thrashed into us. Agreeing as we do radically, our whole divergence of opinion lies solely in the different views we take of the essence of this phenomenon. You say that Lewis XIV was also a conqueror, that the Austrian "Viribus unitis" is also revolutionary, that the Bourbons are more responsible for the Revolution than the Bonapartes, and so on. You declare "quod ab initio vitiosum, lapsu temporis convalescere nequit" to be a phrase correct only from a doctrinaire point of view—I do not think it is even that, for from every injustice justice can grow and does grow in course of time; from the monarchy introduced into Israel in opposition to the will of God sprang the Saviour; the rights of the first-born, so generally acknowledged, were disregarded in the case of Reuben, Absalom, and others; Solomon, begotten of the adulteress Bathsheba, became the blessed of the Lord, and so on and so on—but you totally misunderstand the essence of Bonapartism if you throw it into the same pot with those cases. The Bonapartes, Napoleon I as well as Napoleon III, have not only an unlawful revolutionary origin, like William III, King Oscar, and others—they are themselves the Revolution incarnate. Both of them, No. 1 and No. 3, recognised and felt that to be an evil, but neither was able to shake himself free of it. Read a now forgotten book, *Relation et Correspondances de Nap. Bonaparte avec Jean Fiévée;* you will there find some profound glimpses of the old Napoleon into the nature of states, and the present Bonaparte impresses me in the same way with similar ideas, as, for example, the establishment of titles of nobility, the restoration of primogeniture, recognition of the danger

206

of centralisation, fight against stock-jobbing swindles, desire to re-establish the old provinces, and so on. This, however, does not alter the essence of his sovereignty any more than the essence of the House of Habsburg-Lothringen is altered by the liberal and even revolutionary Emperor Joseph II, or by Francis Joseph with his most noble Schwarzenberg and his barricade hero, Bach. " Naturam expellas furca," she comes back all the same. So no Bonaparte can disown the sovereignty of the people, nor does he do so. Napoleon I, as is proved by the book referred to above, gave up his efforts to get away from his revolutionary origin, as, for instance, when he had the Duc d'Enghien shot. Napoleon III will also do so, and has already done so, for instance in the Neuchâtel negotiations, when the best, and under other circumstances welcome, opportunity was afforded him of reforming Switzerland. He was, however, afraid of Lord Palmerston and the English press—a fact which Walewski honestly admitted; Russia was afraid of him and Austria both of him and of England, and thus that shameful compromise came to pass. How remarkable! We have eyes and see not, have ears and hear not. The Neuchâtel negotiations are immediately followed by the Belgian business, by the triumph of the Liberals over the Clericals, by the victorious alliance of the parliamentary minority and the street riots over the parliamentary majority. Here there can be no intervention on the part of the legitimate Powers; that would certainly not be tolerated by Bonaparte, though there will be an intervention, if it be not once more appeased, on the part of Bonapartism, hardly, however, in favour of the Clericals or of the Constitution, but in favour of the sovereign people.

207

BISMARCK

' Bonapartism is not absolutism, not even Cæsarism; the former may found itself a *jus divinum*, as in Russia and in the East, and therefore does not affect those who do not recognise this *jus divinum*, for whom, in fact, it does not exist, unless it occurs to this or that autocrat to regard himself, like Attila, Mohammed, or Timur, as a scourge of God; this, however, is an exception. Cæsarism is the arrogation of an *imperium* in a lawful republic and is justified by urgent necessity; to a Bonaparte, however, whether he like it or no, the Revolution—that is, the sovereignty of the people—represents an internal, and in any conflict or exigency also an external, legal title. For this reason your comparison of Bonaparte with the Bourbons and with absolutist Austria comforts me as little as does Napoleon III's individuality, which in many respects also impresses me. If he himself make no conquests, then must his successor do so, although the Prince Imperial has not much more chance of succeeding to the throne than many others, and certainly less than Henry V. In this sense Napoleon III is as much our natural enemy as Napoleon I was, and I only desire you to keep that fact in view; not, however, that we ought to sulk with him, tease him, vex him, and repel his advances, but we owe it to our honour and to justice to take up an attitude of reserve with regard to him. He must learn that we are not compassing his fall, that we are not hostile to him, that we have honest intentions towards him, but that, at the same time, we regard his origin as dangerous (which, mind you, he does himself), and that if he attempt to turn it to account we shall oppose him. He and the rest of Europe too have to give us credit for this without it being necessary for us to say so, otherwise he will put a halter upon us and drag us whithersoever he wishes. This is the very essence of a good policy, that without entering upon any conflict we inspire those with confidence with whom we are really at one. To bring this about, however, it is necessary to speak openly to people and not like F. D. exasperate them by silence and trickery. Prussia stands charged with the sin of having been the first of the three Powers of the holy alliance to recognise Louis Philippe, and of having moved the others to do the same. Louis Philippe would perhaps still be on the throne if we had been more honest towards him, if we had shown him our teeth more frequently, and thereby compelled him to think of his usurpation.

' The isolated position of Prussia has been spoken of; but how can we seek firm alliances, "si," as the Emperor Francis said in the Hungarian Diet, "totus mundus stulti. zat?" England's policy from 1800 to 1813 was directed towards keeping Bonaparte busy on the Continent in order to prevent him from landing in England, which he seriously wanted to do in 1805. Now Napoleon is arming in all his harbours in order to be able to effect a landing at some time or other, and Palmerston with his levity making enemies of all the Continental Powers. Austria is with reason afraid for her Italian possessions and is making enemies of Prussia and Russia, the only Powers that do not grudge them to her; she is making advances to France, which has cast longing eyes upon Italy since the fourteenth century; she is driving Sardinia to extremes—Sardinia, which has the custody of the gates and entrances of Italy; she casts sheep's eyes at Palmerston, who is busily engaged in stirring up and supporting rebellion in that country. Russia is beginning to liberalise at home and pays court to France. With whom are we to ally ourselves? Is there anything to be done except to wait?

' In Germany the Prussian influence is so slight because the King can never make up his mind to show the princes his displeasure. If they behave in ever such a worthless fashion they are still welcomed at hunting-parties and at Sans-Souci. In 1806 Prussia entered into war with France under very unfavourable auspices, and yet Saxony, the Electorate of Hesse, Brunswick, and Weimar followed her, while Austria had been without any adherents since 1805. . . .

'L. v. G.'

I had no reasons for continuing by a reply this correspondence, aimless in itself.

CHAPTER IX

TRAVELS—THE REGENCY

In the following year, 1856, the King began to approach me again, and Manteuffel (perhaps others too) feared that I might gain influence at his and their expense. Under these circumstances Manteuffel proposed to me that I should take over the Ministry of Finance whilst he would retain the Presidency and the Foreign department, making an exchange with me later on, so that he would preside in the council as Minister of Finance and I become Foreign Minister. He spoke as though the proposal came from himself, and although it seemed to me strange, I did not absolutely decline it, but only reminded him that when I was appointed envoy to the Federal Diet, the jest of the witty Dean of Westminster [*sic*] concerning Lord John Russell had been applied to me: ' The fellow would undertake to command a frigate or to operate for the stone.' If I became Minister of Finance some such verdict might be passed on me with greater validity, although I should in any case be able, as Finance Minister, to emulate Bodelschwingh's activity in signing his name. Everything depended upon how long the ' Interimisticum ' would last. In reality the proposal had emanated from the King; and when he asked Manteuffel what he had been able to effect, the latter replied, ' He absolutely laughed at me.'

Although I was repeatedly not offered, but verbally commanded by the King to take over Manteuffel's portfolio, in such words as ' Even if you grovel before me, it avails you nought, you have got to be minister,' I still could not rid myself of the impression that these demonstrations originated from the necessity of bringing Manteuffel to submission, to ' obedience.' Even if the King had been in earnest I should still have felt that any position I might hold as minister would not have been long acceptable to him.[1]

In March 1857 the conferences for the settlement of the dispute that had arisen between Prussia and Switzerland had been opened in Paris. The Emperor, ever well informed concerning events in Court and government circles of Berlin, evidently knew that the King was on a more confidential footing with me than with other delegates, and had repeatedly regarded me as a candidate for the ministry. After having in the negotiations with Switzerland observed to all appearance a benevolent attitude towards Prussia, especially as compared with that of Austria, he seemed to expect that in return for this he might rely on some complaisance on the part of Prussia in other matters, and explained to me that it was unjust to accuse him of having designs upon the Rhine frontier. The German left bank of the Rhine, with about three million inhabitants, would be an untenable frontier for France in the face of Europe; the nature of things would then drive France on to acquire, or at least to bring to a state of safe dependency, Luxemburg, Belgium, and Holland. The undertaking with regard to the Rhine frontier would therefore bring France, sooner or later, an increase of ten or eleven million active well-to-do inhabitants. Such a reinforcement of the French power would be re-

[1] See above, p. 152.

garded by Europe as intolerable—' devrait engendrer la coalition ; ' it would be more difficult to retain than to acquire
—' Un dépôt que l'Europe coalisée un jour viendrait re-
prendre.' Such a pretension, recalling Napoleon I, would
be too high for the present circumstances ; it would be said,
the hand of France is against every man, and consequently
every man's hand would be against France. Perhaps, in
certain circumstances, to soothe national pride he will
desire ' une petite rectification des frontières,' but he will
be able to live without it. If he should again need a
war, he would prefer to seek it in the direction of Italy.
Yet on the one hand that country had always had a great
affinity with France; on the other, the latter was rich
enough in land power, and in victories by land. The
French would find a much more piquant satisfaction in
an extension of their power on the sea. He did not exactly contemplate making the Mediterranean a French
lake, ' mais à peu près.' Frenchmen are no born sailors,
but good land soldiers, and for this very reason victories
at sea are much more flattering to them. This was the
only motive which could have induced them to help in
the destruction of the Russian fleet in the Black Sea, for
Russia, if once in possession of such an excellent material as the Greek sailors, would become too formidable
as a rival in the Mediterranean. I was under the impression that the Emperor was not quite straightforward on
this point, but rather that he was vexed at the destruction
of the Russian fleet, and that he was, moreover, endeav-
ouring to justify to himself the result of the war into
which, with his operation, England was driven like a rud-
derless ship, according to the expression of her Foreign
Minister—'we are drifting into war.'

As the result of a war in the near future, he contemplated for Italy a condition of intimacy and dependence towards France, and for himself perhaps the acquisition of a few points on the coast. It formed part of this programme that Prussia should not be opposed to him. France and Prussia supplement one another; he considered it a mistake that Prussia in 1806 did not side with Napoleon like other German powers. It was desirable to consolidate our territory by the acquisition of Hanover and the Elbe duchies, and thus lay the foundation for a stronger Prussian navy. There was a lack of maritime powers of the second rank, who, by the union of their active forces with those of the French, might put an end to the present oppressive preponderance of England. There could be no danger therein, either to them or to the rest of Europe, because they would by no means be taking part in one-sided selfish undertakings of the French, but only in freeing the seas from the prepotency of England. His first wish was to secure the neutrality of Prussia in the event of his incurring a war with Austria on account of Italy. I might sound the King about all this.

I answered, I was doubly delighted that the Emperor had given me these intimations, firstly because I was bound to see in them a proof of his confidence, and secondly because I was perhaps the only Prussian diplomatist who would engage to hold his tongue,[1] both at home and towards his sovereign, respecting the whole of this com-

---

[1] As a matter of fact there are no communications respecting this interview in the reports to Manteuffel of April 11 and 24, or May 1, 1857 (*Preussen im Bundestage,* iv. 257 &c., iii. 91 &c., 94 &c.); nor are there any in the letter to Gerlach of April 11, 1857 (*Briefe Bismarck's,* &c. p. 311 &c.). That Bismarck had told the latter about it is evident from Gerlach's *Denkwürdigkeiten,* ii. 521.

munication. I urgently besought him to put aside this idea; it was utterly impossible for King Frederick William IV to accede to such a thing; a negative answer was certain if the overture were made to him; while there remained in the latter case the great danger of an indiscretion in the verbal intercourse of princes, of some indication as to the temptations which the King had withstood. If one of the other German governments were put in a position to report such indiscretions to Paris, the good relations with France, which are so valuable to Prussia, would be disturbed. 'But that would be something more than an indiscretion, it would be treachery,' he broke in somewhat disturbed. 'You would get stuck in the mud!' I continued.

The Emperor thought this expression striking and shrewd, and repeated it. The interview concluded with his thanks to me for this frankness and my assurance of silence respecting his revelation.

In the same year I took advantage of the recess of the Federal Diet to make a hunting excursion into Denmark and Sweden.[1] At Copenhagen on August 6 I had an audience of King Frederick VII. He received me in uniform with his helmet on, and entertained me with exaggerated sketches of his experiences in various battles and sieges at which he had never been present. To my question whether he thought that the constitution (namely, the second joint one of October 2, 1855) would be maintained, he answered that he had sworn to his father upon his deathbed to maintain it, forgetting that at the time of his father's death (1848) this constitution

[1] Cf. the letters of August 6, 9, 16–19 in the *Bismarckbriefe*, 6th edit., p. 150 &c.

was not in existence. During the conversation I saw a
woman's shadow on the wall of an adjoining sunny gal-
lery; the King had not spoken for my benefit but for that
of Countess Dauner, respecting whose relations with his
Majesty I heard singular tales. I likewise had opportunities of conversing with notable Schleswig-Holsteiners.
They would not hear of a little German state; 'for the
morsel of European status at Copenhagen was still dearer
to them.'

While hunting in Sweden on August 17 I fell over
a corner of rock and severely injured my shin, and unfortunately I neglected it in order to go elk hunting
in Courland. On the way back from Copenhagen I arrived at Berlin on August 26, took part in a great review on September 3, at which I wore for the first time
the new white uniform of the 'heavy cavalry' regiment
of the period, and then pursued my journey to Courland.[1]

From Marienbad the King had paid a visit to the Emperor of Austria at Schönbrunn on July 8. On the way
back he went, on July 13, to visit the King of Saxony at
Pillnitz, where on the same day he was seized by an 'in-
disposition,' which the physicians in ordinary attributed
in their bulletins to his journey during very hot weather,
and his departure was postponed for several days. After
the King had returned to Sans-Souci on the 17th symptoms
of mental exhaustion were noticed by the persons about
him, and especially by Edwin Manteuffel, who anxiously
endeavoured to hinder or interrupt all conversation between the King and other persons. The political impressions which the King received among his relations at

[1] Cf. letter from Königsberg of September 12, 1857. *Bismarckbriefe*,
p. 154.

Schönbrunn and Pillnitz had acted upon his disposition and rendered discussions odious to him. While riding beside him at parade on July 27 I felt, in the course of conversation, impressed by his diminished flow of thought, and had occasion to interfere in his management of his horse while at a walk.

His condition was rendered worse by the fact that on October 6 the King had accompanied the Emperor of Russia, a hard smoker, to the Lower Silesia and Brandenburg railway station, in the imperial closed saloon carriage, in a reek of tobacco, which was just as intolerable to him as the smell of sealing-wax.*

As is well known an apoplectic fit ensued. In high military circles the statement was current that he had had a similar attack once before during the night of March 18-19, 1848. The physicians consulted whether they should open a vein or not, as they dreaded in the first case disturbance in the brain, in the second death; and it was only after several days that they decided upon bleeding, which restored the King to consciousness. During these days, and therefore with the possibility of an immediate entrance upon the government before his eyes—on October 19—the Prince of Prussia took a long walk with me through the new pleasure grounds, and discussed with me whether, if he undertook the government, he should accept the constitution unaltered, or first of all demand its revision. I said a refusal of the constitution could be justified if the feudal law were applicable by which an heir, while bound by his father's enactments, was not bound by those of his brother. But for reasons of state my advice

* [That even letters in his own hand were not sealed in his presence, had a very serious side to it.]

was, not to meddle with the matter, and not to introduce
into our political condition the insecurity attached to even
a conditional refusal. The fear of the possibility of a
change of system at every change of sovereign should not
be aroused. The authority of Prussia in Germany and
her capacity for action in Europe would be diminished
by a struggle between the Crown and the Diet; sides
would be taken throughout Liberal Germany against the
contemplated step. In my sketch of the consequences to
be apprehended, I started from the same idea which I had
to explain to him in 1866, when it was a question of the
Indemnity Bill : namely, that questions of constitution were
subordinate to the necessities of the country and its political position in Germany, and that there was no urgent
necessity to touch ours at present; and that for the time
being the question of forces and internal self-reliance
was the chief thing.

When I returned to Sans-Souci I found Edwin Manteuffel agitated with apprehension about my long conversation with the Prince and the possibility of further interference on my part. He asked me why I did not go to
my post, where I should be very much wanted in the
present state of affairs. I replied : I am much more necessary here!

By royal decree of October 23 the Prince of Prussia
was charged to act for the King for the next three months,
and this was renewed three times for three months, but not
being again extended it lapsed in October 1858. In the
summer of 1858 a strong effort was being made to induce
the Queen to obtain the King's signature to a letter to
his brother, saying that he felt himself sufficiently recovered to undertake the government, and that he thanked

the Prince for having represented him. The appointment had been introduced by a letter from the King, and could therefore, it was argued, be terminated in the same way. The government would then, under control of the royal signature, be carried on through her Majesty the Queen by those gentlemen of the Court who might be called upon or might offer to undertake it. My participation in this plan was also requested verbally, but I absolutely refused; it would be a government by harem. I was summoned from Frankfort to Baden-Baden, and there I informed [1] the Prince of the plan, without naming its originators. 'Then I take my departure,' exclaimed the Prince. I represented to him that separation from his military employments was of no avail, but would make matters worse. The plan could only be carried out if the ministry of state quietly submitted to it. My advice, therefore, was to send a telegram to summon the minister Manteuffel, who was at his own estate awaiting the result of the plan, with which he was acquainted. The threads of the intrigue might then be cut by suitable instructions. The Prince agreed to do so. On my return to Frankfort [2] I received the following letter from Manteuffel:

'Berlin: July 20, 1858.

'Sir,—I beg to inform you that it is my intention to go from here to Frankfort next Thursday, the 22nd inst., at 7 A.M., and to proceed as early as possible on the following morning to Baden-Baden. I should be pleased if it should suit your convenience to accompany me. My wife and son, who, at the present moment, are still in the

---

[1] Cf. Bismarck's letter to Gerlach, December 19, 1857. H. Kohl's edit., p. 337 &c.
[2] On July 15, 1858.

country, but arrive here to-morrow, will probably be with me. I do not want my journey to be talked about in Frankfort beforehand, but venture to give you a little intimation by these lines.'

The further course of the question about a deputy for the Sovereign is shown in the following letter from Manteuffel :

'Berlin : October 12, 1858.

' Our great historical drama has meanwhile been played out at least in the first act. The affair has caused me much anxiety, unpleasantness, and undeserved vexation. Only yesterday I received a very touchy letter from Gerlach upon the subject. He thinks that the sovereignty has been half thrown out of window through it. This, with the best will in the world, I cannot admit; my idea of the business is the following : We have a king capable of disposing but incapable of governing; he says to himself, and must say to himself, that he has been unable to govern for more than a year, that the physicians and he himself have to recognise that the date when he will again be able to govern in person cannot be even remotely specified; that an unnatural extension of the allotment of plenary power made up to the present time is not convenient, and that a head responsible to himself alone is needed by the state. From all these considerations, the King gives orders to the next heir to the throne to do what is laid down in the constitution of the country to meet such a case. The directions of the constitution which, precisely on this point, have been drawn up in the interests of the monarchy, will then be brought into operation, and the vote of the Diet which, though superfluous after the King's declaration, is nevertheless on good ground prescribed in the constitution, will be obtained. But it will be strictly limited to an answer to the question : Is the establishment of a regency necessary ? in other words : Is the King removed from the management of affairs upon satisfactory grounds ? How this question can be answered in the negative is more than I can see; in any case there will still be many difficulties to overcome, especially in matters of form. For instance, a form of procedure is wanting for the joint sitting provided in the constitution. This will have to be improvised; nevertheless, I hope that it will be possible to arrive at a resolution in about five days, so that the Prince can then take the oath and close the Assembly. Other measures, especially such as relate to votes of money, naturally do not, in any way, concern this sitting. If your engagements permit, I shall be glad if you will be present at the Diet, and if possible, be on the spot before its opening. I hear of extraordinary proposals on the Extreme Right; which, in the interest of the public, as well as in that of those gentlemen themselves, it might perhaps be possible to obstruct.

' Westphalen's dismissal just at the present moment has been very contrary to my wishes. I had already prevented it once when he himself asked for it. Now the Prince, by an entirely unbiassed decision, and without his application, desired to send it to him, and sent me a private letter to Westphalen upon the subject, with orders to proceed to carry it out at once. This, however, I did not do, nor did I forward the autograph letter, but made remonstrances to the Prince as to the suitability of the moment, remonstrances which, after no slight trouble, were effectual. I was empowered at ail events to suspend the measure and retain the letter in my possession. Then

Westphalen wrote on the 8th inst. to the Prince as well as to myself a most extraordinary letter, in which, while withdrawing former declarations, he made his counter-signature to the order, which was about to be issued, and was already settled, conditional upon the special orders that might be issued by the Prince being first of all submitted to the King for approval. This was a demand which, in view of the recent deterioration in the King's mental condition, really bordered on the preposterous. Then the Prince lost patience, and reproached me for not having forwarded his letter at once, and the matter could no longer be delayed. The choice of Flottwell has proceeded from the Prince alone, entirely without my assistance; it has much against it and also much in its favour.'

I went to the Diet, and took part in the meeting of a group opposed to the members from whom the attempt proceeded to resist the constitutional vote for the Regency, being confident in the acceptance of the Regency which then took place.

After the Prince of Prussia had undertaken the Regency on October 26, Manteuffel asked me what he should do in order to avoid an involuntary dismissal, and, at my request, gave me his last correspondence with the Regent to read. My answer, that it was quite clear that the Prince would dismiss him, he regarded as not straightforward and, perhaps, as covetous. He was dismissed on November 6. Prince von Hohenzollern succeeded him with the ministry of the ' New Era.'

In January 1859, at a ball at Moustier's or Karolyi's, Count Stillfried made jocular allusions to me from which I concluded that my removal from Frankfort to St. Petersburg, which had already often been projected, was to be carried out, and he added the friendly remark : ' Per aspera ad astra.' The information of the Count was doubtless derived from his intimate relations with all the Catholics in the Princess's household, from the first chamberlain down to the lackey. My relations with the Jesuits were as yet undisturbed, and I still possessed Stillfried's good-will. I understood the transparent allusion, betook myself on the following day (January 26) to the Regent, said openly that I heard that I was to be transferred to St. Petersburg, and begged permission to express my regret, in the hope that it could still be reversed. The first counter-question was : ' Who told you that ? ' I replied that it would be indiscreet on my part to mention the person, but I had heard it from the Jesuit camp, with which I had long-standing associations, and I regretted it because I thought that in Frankfort, the Federal Diet's own ' earth,' with the exits and entrances of which I had be-come acquainted down to the very soil-pipes, I could render more useful service than any possible successor, who would first have to learn the very complicated position due to relations with numerous Courts and ministers. I could not bequeath my eight years' experience in this sphere, which I had acquired in stirring times. I was personally acquainted with every German prince and every German minister, and with the Courts of the capitals of the princes of the Confederation, and I enjoyed, as far as it was at-tainable for Prussia, an influence in the Assembly of the Confederation and at the separate Courts. This fund of Prussian diplomacy, after its acquisition and conquest, would be ruined to no purpose by my recall from Frank-fort. The appointment of Usedom would weaken the confidence of the German courts, because he was a doubt-

ful Liberal, and more of a gossiping courtier than a statesman, while Frau von Usedom, through her eccentricity,
would embarrass us and create undesirable impressions in
Frankfort.

To this the Regent answered: ' That is as much as to
say that the high qualification of Usedom can be utilised
nowhere else because his wife would cause difficulties in
every Court.' This, however, happened not only in Courts,
but even in much-enduring Frankfort, and the unpleasantness which she caused to private persons by overrat-
ing her ambassadorial privilege even degenerated into
public scandals. But Frau von Usedom was an English-
woman by birth, and therefore, owing to the inferiority
of German self-esteem, experienced at Court a forbear-
ance which no German lady would have been able to
enjoy.

My reply to the Regent was pretty much as follows:
' Then in that case it is a defect that I too have not married a tactless lady, for otherwise I should have the same
claim to the post where I feel myself at home as Count
Usedom has.'

To which the Regent answered: ' I do not understand
how you can take the matter up so bitterly; St. Petersburg has surely always ranked as the highest post of Prussian diplomacy, and you should accept it as a proof of high
confidence that I am sending you there.'

To which I replied: ' Directly your Royal Highness
gives me this testimony I must naturally say no more;
nevertheless with the freedom of speech which your Royal
Highness has always allowed me I cannot help expressing
my anxiety respecting the situation at home and its influence on the German question. Usedom is a *brouillon* and

no man of business. He will receive his instructions from Berlin; if Count Schlieffen remains as Minister for German Affairs the instructions will be good; I do not believe in their conscientious execution by Usedom.'

Nevertheless, he was appointed to Frankfort. His subsequent conduct in Turin and Florence showed that I had done him no injustice in my judgment. He delighted to pose as a strategist, also as a ' devil of a fellow,' and a deeply initiated conspirator; he had dealings with Garibaldi and Mazzini, and prided himself somewhat upon them. From his inclination for underground connexions he engaged at Turin as private secretary a pretended Mazzinist, but really an Austrian spy, gave him the official documents to read, and put the cipher into his hands. He was absent from his post for weeks and months, and left signed blanks, upon which the secretaries of the Legation wrote reports; and thus reports with his signature reached the Foreign Office respecting conversations which he was supposed to have had with the Italian ministers, whereas he had not seen those gentlemen at the time in question. But he was a high Freemason. In February 1869, when I demanded the recall of such a useless and irresolute employé, the King, who fulfilled his duties towards the brethren with an almost religious fidelity, offered a resistance which was not to be overcome even by my protracted withdrawal from official activity, and which reduced me to the intention of soliciting my discharge.[1]

Now, after more than twenty years, when I again read the papers upon the matter, I am struck with regret that, being then placed between my conviction of the interest of the state and my personal affection for the

[1] Cf. *Bismarck-Jahrbuch*, i. 76 &c.

King, I followed, and was compelled to follow, the former. To-day I feel myself shamed by the amiability with which the King bore my official pedantry.   I ought to have sacrificed the service in Florence to him and his masonic faith.   On February 22 his Majesty wrote to me: ' The bearer of these lines [Privy Councillor Wehrmann] has informed me of the commission which you have given him on your own account.   How can you even think that I could yield to your views!   My greatest happiness is to live and be always on the best understanding with you.   How can you let yourself be so upset, that my only instance of disagreement leads you to the most extreme step!   Even from Varzin, during our difference, you wrote to me respecting the reimbursement of the deficit, that you are indeed of a different opinion from mine, but that upon accepting your post, you laid it down as an obligation, after dutifully expressing your views, to submit to my decisions.   What then has now so entirely altered the intention you so nobly expressed three months ago? There is but one single difference, I repeat it, namely, that at Frankfort[1] I settled the Usedomiana yesterday in writing and quite in accordance with your desire; the domestic matter will right itself; we were agreed as to the appointments, but the individuals are not willing.   Where then is your ground for the extreme?   Your name shows brighter in the history of Prussia than that of any Prus-

[1] On February 1, 1869, the government had brought forward in the Diet a bill respecting the separation of the state and city of Frankfort, which was based on an opinion of the Crown syndics, was advised by the ministry, and approved by the King.   The magistrates of Frankfort, while the discussions upon the bill were still going on, obtained the King's promise that 2,000,000 gulden from the state exchequer should be assigned to the city of Frankfort, as balancing settlement of the claims she had raised. The bill had to be altered accordingly.

sian statesman. Is that the one I am to let go? Never.
Rest and prayer will settle everything.

'Your most sincere Friend,

'W.'

The following letter from Roon is of the next day's
date:

'Berlin : February 23, 1869.

'Since I left you yesterday evening, my honoured
friend, I have been continually occupied about you and
your resolution. It leaves me no rest; I must once more
appeal to you to word your letter in such a manner that
a reconciliation may be possible. Perhaps you have not
yet sent it and can still alter it. Just reflect that the
almost tender note received yesterday lays claim to veracity,
even if not fully justified. It is so written and claims
not to be regarded as false coin, but as genuine and of full
value; and do you remember that the alloy mixed with it
is nothing more than the copper of false shame, which will
not, and, in view of the rank of the writer, perhaps even
cannot confess: "I, I have done very wrong and will
amend." It is quite unallowable for you to burn your
ships, you ought not to do it. You would thereby ruin
yourself before the country and Europe would laugh.
The motives which guide you would not be appreciated;
it would be said: he despaired of finishing his work; that
is why he retired. I must not further repeat myself save
at most in the expression of my unchangeable and sincere
attachment.   Yours

'VON ROON.'

After I had withdrawn my request to retire, I received the following letter:

227

BISMARCK

'Berlin : February 26, 1869.

' When, in my consternation at Wehrmann's communication, I wrote you on the 22nd a very hasty but all the more urgent letter in order to deter you from your intention which threatened ruin, I ventured to assume that your answer, in its final form, would be influenced by my remonstrances—and I have not been mistaken. Thanks, heartiest thanks, for not disappointing my expectation!

'And now as regards the chief reasons which led you momentarily to think of retiring; I fully acknowledge their weight, and you will recollect how urgently I called upon you in December last, when you again took up affairs, to provide every possible alleviation for yourself, so that you might not sink afresh under the weight and mass of work which was to be anticipated. Unfortunately, it appears that you have not found such an alleviation feasible (not even the getting rid of Lauenburg), and that my fears in this instance have been verified to the utmost, to such a degree indeed, that you are said to have arrived at ideas and conclusions pregnant with mischief. If, according to your statement, still further difficulties have arisen in overcoming individual disturbances to the equilibrium of business, no one regrets it more than I do. One such is the position of Sulzer.[1] I offered, some time ago, to aid in removing him to a post elsewhere, so that it is not my fault if it has not been done, Eulenburg being also convinced of the same thing. If a similar increase of work was brought upon you by the Usedom affair, it, too, cannot be laid to my account, seeing that what he wrote in his defence—of which I certainly could not be the cause—demanded an examination

---

[1] Under-Secretary of State in the Ministry of the Interior.

on your side. If I did not at once set about the execution of the job you proposed, you must surely have been prepared for it from the surprise with which I received your communication when you indicated to me the step you had already taken against Usedom. It was the middle of January when you gave me this intimation, scarcely three months had elapsed since the La Marmora episode began to settle down, so that the opinion I had written to you in the summer respecting Usedom's continuance at Turin was still the same. The communications made to me under date of February 14 respecting the way Usedom did business, which more than ever called for his removal from office, even if he were to escape a criminal investigation, I left untouched for a few days, as in the meantime I had received information that Keudell, with your cognisance, had invited Usedom to make a counter-move. Yet even before an answer arrived from Turin, I asked you as early as February 21 how you thought of filling up this embassy, thus expressing my consent to the vacating of it. Yet as early as the 22nd of the same month you took the decisive step to Wehrmann for which the Usedom epic was to be the joint motive. You seek to find another motive in the circumstance that, after receiving the report of the minister of state on the affair of Frankfort-on-Main, before coming to a decision, I had not so much as asked you to state your views. But as your reasons and those of the ministers of state were so decidedly shown by the presentation of the bill and accompanying report, and as my signature was actually desired within an hour of its presentation, so that it might be carried at once to the Chambers, I did not think a further statement of views necessary for

strengthening my own view and intention. If a report
had been made* to me before a decision as to the course
to be taken in the Frankfort question—which was entirely different from my earlier declaration—had been
adopted in the ministry, then, by interchange of ideas,
a way out of the various views would have been aimed at,
and the divergence and lack of joint action, the remodel-
ling, &c. which you justly regret so much could have been
avoided. To all that you say on this occasion respecting
the difficulty of keeping the constitutional machine of
state in working order **etc.,** I entirely subscribe; only I
cannot accept as valid the view that I am wanting in that
confidence towards you and the other advisers of the
Crown which is so absolutely necessary. You yourself
say that this is the first occasion since 1862 that a difference has arisen between us, and is that to be a sufficient
proof that I no longer felt confidence in my Executive?
No one appreciates more highly than I do the good fortune that, in a period of six such troubled years, disagree-
ments of this kind have not arisen; but we are spoilt by
it—and so the present impulse causes a greater shake
than is justified. Is it possible for a monarch to show
greater confidence in his premier than I do, by sending you at such various times, and finally in this present
instance, private letters which treat of floating questions
of the moment so that you may be satisfied that I do nothing of the kind behind your back? If I sent you General
von Manteuffel's letter on the Memel affair,† because it
seemed to me to contain a new point, and I therefore

* [Some free time would have been required for that purpose.]
† [About the Memel-Tilsit railway. A letter from General von Manteuffel had disposed the King to recede from a decision that had been
arrived at upon a report from the departmental minister.]

wished to hear your opinion; if I communicated to you General von Boyen's letter, and likewise some newspaper cuttings, with the remark that these pieces accurately reproduced what I had expressed without variation generally and officially for a long time past—I might be justified in thinking that I could hardly increase my confidence. But that I should, in general, shut my ear to the voices which in certain important moments address themselves to me in full confidence, even you yourself will not demand.

If I bring forward some of the points which your letter adduces as causes which have brought about your present frame of mind, while leaving others untouched, then I come back to your own expression when you call your present state of mind morbid; you feel tired and exhausted, and the longing for rest creeps over you. All this I perfectly understand, for I feel it like you; but can and ought I on that account to think of laying down my office? Just as little ought you to do so. You do not belong to yourself alone; your existence is bound up too closely with the history of Prussia, of Germany, and of Europe, to allow of your withdrawal from a scene which you have helped to create. But in order that you may be able to dedicate yourself entirely to this creation, you must manage to have less work, and I most urgently beg you to submit proposals to me to this effect. You should disengage yourself from the cabinet councils when ordinary matters are being discussed. Delbrück stands so faithfully at your side that he might relieve you of much. Reduce your reports to me to the most vital points, and so on. But, above all, never doubt my unchanged confidence and my indelible gratitude! Yours

'WILLIAM.'

Usedom was put on the Reserve list. His Majesty, in this instance, so far overrode the tradition of the administration of the royal personal estate, that he caused the financial difference between the official income and the pension to be paid regularly out of the privy purse.

I now return to the conversation with the Regent. After I had expressed myself concerning the post at the Federal Diet, I passed on to the general situation and said: ' Your Royal Highness has not a single statesman-like intellect in the whole ministry, nothing but mediocrities and limited brains.'

The Regent.—' Do you consider Bonin's a limited brain ? '

I.—'By no means; but he cannot keep a drawer in order, much less a ministry. And Schleinitz is a courtier, but no statesman.'

The Regent (irritably).—' Do you perchance take me for a sluggard? I will be my own Foreign Minister and Minister of War; that I comprehend.'

I apologised, and said: 'At the present day the most capable provincial president cannot administer his district without an intelligent district secretary, and will always rely upon such an one; the Prussian monarchy requires the analogue in a much higher degree. Without intelligent ministers your Royal Highness will find no satisfaction in the result. I feel less anxiety about the Home Office; but when I think of Schwerin I do feel uneasy. He is honourable and brave, and if he were a soldier, would fall like his ancestor at Prague; but he lacks prudence. Look, your Royal Highness, at his profile: immediately above his eyebrows springs forth swiftness of conception, the quality which the French call *primesautier;* but the forehead over it, in which phrenologists look for prudence, fails. Schwerin is a statesman without discernment, and has more capacity for pulling down than for building up.

The Prince acknowledged the limitations of the rest. On the whole he stuck to his endeavour to make me regard my mission to St. Petersburg in the light of a distinction, and gave me the impression of feeling relieved that by my initiative the question of my displacement, by no means cheering to him either, had been kept out of the conversation. The audience terminated in gracious form on the Regent's part, and on my side with the feeling of undisturbed attachment to the master and heightened contempt for the wirepullers to whose influence, supported by the Princess, he was then subject.

In the new era that illustrious lady had from the first a ministry in her eye, of which she might regard herself as founder and patroness. Even in this cabinet, however, her influence did not remain permanently governmental, but soon took the form of favouritism towards those ministers who were distasteful to the supreme head of the state. Most of all might this be said of Count Schwerin, who was under the influence of Winter, the then chief Burgomaster of Dantzig, and other Liberal officials. He pushed ministerial independence towards the Regent so far that he answered written orders in writing, discharging them by saying that they were not countersigned. On one occasion when the ministry had forced the Regent to sign a document that was repugnant to him, he did so in an illegible form and smashed the pen on it.

BISMARCK

Count Schwerin caused a second fair copy to be made, and insisted on a legible signature. The Regent now signed as usual, but crumpled up the paper and threw it into the corner, from which it was rescued, and, after being smoothed, was then added to the records. In the case of my resignation of 1877, it was again evident that the Emperor had reduced it to a ball before he answered it.

I was appointed ambassador at St. Petersburg on January 29, 1859, but did not leave Frankfort until March 6, and stayed in Berlin until the 23rd of the same month. During this time I had an opportunity of obtaining a practical impression of the application of the Austrian secret service money, which, up to that time, I had only encountered in the press. Levinstein, a banker who for decades had had dealings with my superiors, and, in their confidential commissions in Vienna and Paris, with the leaders of foreign policy, and with the Emperor Napoleon in person, addressed the following letter to me on the morning of the day for which my departure was fixed:

' Your Excellency,—I take the liberty most humbly herewith to wish good luck to your journey and mission, hoping that we shall soon greet you here again, since you can do more valuable work in the fatherland than abroad. Our time needs men and needs energy, which will perhaps be perceived here too late. But events in our day move rapidly, and I fear that peace will hardly be obtainable permanently, however it may be cemented for a few months.

' I have to-day carried out a little operation, which I trust will bear good fruit. I shall have the honour of informing you about it later on.

' There is great uneasiness felt in Vienna respecting
234

your St. Petersburg mission, because you are regarded as an antagonist on principle. It would be a very good thing to be on good terms there, because sooner or later those Powers will come to a good understanding with us.

'If your Excellency would only write me a few lines, in any form you please, saying that you are not *personally* prejudiced against Austria, it would be of incalculable service. Herr von Manteuffel always says that I am tenacious in carrying out an idea, and do not rest until I reach the goal. But he added that I am neither ambitious nor avaricious. Up to the present, thank God, it is my boast that no one has suffered any kind of detriment from connexions with me.

'For such time as you are absent I have the pleasure to offer you my services in looking after your affairs, whether here or elsewhere. You would certainly not be served more honourably and disinterestedly by any one else.

'With sincere esteem, I am
'Your Excellency's
'Most obedient
'LEVINSTEIN.'

B. 23. 3. 59.

I left the letter unanswered, and in the course of the day, before starting for the railway station, I received Herr Levinstein's visit at the Hôtel Royal, where I was staying. After he had justified his visit by showing an autograph letter of introduction from Count Buol, he proposed that I should take part in a financial transaction which would bring me '20,000 thalers a year with certainty.' To my reply that I had no capital to invest came

235

the answer that payments on account were not necessary in the transaction, but that what I put into the concern would consist in becoming the advocate of Austrian together with Prussian policy at the Court of Russia, because the transactions in question could only succeed provided the relations between Russia and Austria were favourable. It was of importance to me to get into my hands some kind of evidence in writing respecting this offer, in order to prove to the Regent how well grounded was my distrust of Count Buol's policy. I therefore represented to Mr. Levinstein that in such a risky transaction I must have a stronger security than his verbal statement, on the strength of the few lines from Count Buol's hand which he had retained. He would not consent to get me a written promise, but raised his offer to 30,000 thalers a year. When I had made sure that I should not obtain any evidence in writing, I entreated Levinstein to leave me and prepared to go out. He followed me to the staircase with varying phrases on the theme: ' Be careful; it is not pleasant to have the " Imperial Government" for an enemy.' It was not until I called his attention to the steepness of the staircase, and to my physical superiority, that he bolted down the stairs and left me.

This intermediary had become personally known to me through the confidential position he had occupied for years past with the Foreign Office, and the commissions he had received from it for me in Manteuffel's time. He cultivated his relations among the lower grades by lavish gratuities.

When I had become minister and had broken off the connexion between the Foreign Office and Levinstein,

repeated attempts were made to set it going again, especially by Consul Bamberg at Paris, who came to me several times and reproached me for being able to treat so
harshly 'such a distinguished man' as Levinstein, who
held such a position in the European Courts.

  —   I also found further occasion to abolish customs which
had prevailed in the Foreign Office. The porter of the
office, an old drunkard who had been there for many
years, could not, as an employé, be dismissed without
further cause. I forced him to resign by the threat that
I would have him brought up on the charge of showing
me for money, since he admitted any one for a tip. I
silenced his protest with the remark: ' Did you not, when
I was ambassador, take me into Herr von Manteuffel on
every occasion for a thaler, and when it was especially
strictly forbidden, for two thalers?' I heard on that occasion from my own domestics what excessive gratuities
Levinstein lavished upon them. Active agents and re-
cipients of money in this direction were some of the chancery servants taken over by Manteuffel and Schleinitz, and
among them one prominent as a mason, considering his
subordinate official position. Count Bernstorff could not
put a stop to the corruption in the Foreign Office during
his short period there, and was, besides, far too much
occupied with his business and with his rank to deal with
these things minutely. I subsequently told the Regent,
in full detail, about my meeting with Levinstein, my
opinion of him and his relations with the Foreign Office,
as soon as I found it possible to do so verbally, which was
not until some months later. I could anticipate no result
from a report in writing, as the protection of Levinstein
by Herr von Schleinitz did not simply extend to the

Regent, but likewise to those about the Princess,* who in her representations of the case felt no need to investigate the objective reality on which it rested, but was inclined to hold a brief for my opponents.

* Cf. what was talked about in the action against Hofrath Manché, October 1891.

CHAPTER X

IT has assuredly hardly happened twice in the history of the European states that a sovereign of a Great Power has done such service to a neighbour as the Emperor Nicholas did to the Austrian monarchy. In the perilous position in which the latter found itself in 1849 he came to its assistance with 150,000 men, subdued Hungary, re-established the King's authority there, and withdrew his troops without asking for any advantage or indemnity, and without mentioning the Eastern and Polish questions at issue between the two states. This act of disinterested friendship in the region of the domestic politics of Austria-Hungary was continued in undiminished measure by the Emperor Nicholas, to Prussia's cost, in her foreign politics during the days of Olmütz. Even if he was not influenced by friendship but by considerations of imperial Russian policy, it was in any case more than one sovereign usually does for another, and is only intelligible in such an absolute and excessively chivalrous autocrat. Nicholas at that time regarded the Emperor Francis Joseph as his successor and heir in the leadership of the Conservative triad. He considered the latter as solid against revolution, and with regard to the continuation of the hegemony, had more confidence in Francis Joseph than in his own successor. Still lower was his opinion of the fitness of our King, Frederick William, for the part of leader in the region of practical politics; he considered him to be as little suited to guide the monarchical triad as his own son and successor. He acted in Hungary and at Olmütz under the conviction that he was called by divine will to be the leader of the monarchical resistance against the revolution advancing from the West. He was naturally an idealist, but hardened in the isolation of the Russian autocracy, and it is wonderful enough that he retained throughout this idealistic impetus, among all his experiences, from the Dekabrists onward, and through all succeeding experiences.

How he felt as regards his position towards his subjects is shown by a circumstance which Frederick William IV himself related to me. The Emperor Nicholas asked him to send two corporals of the Prussian guard for the purpose of performing a certain massage treatment prescribed by the doctors, which was to be carried out on the back of the patient while he lay on his stomach. He added: 'I can always manage my Russians when I can look them in the face, but on my back and without eyes, I should not like them to come near me.' The corporals were sent confidentially, and were employed and handsomely paid. This shows how, in spite of the religious devotion of the Russian people to their Czar, the Emperor Nicholas did not absolutely trust his personal safety in a *tête-à-tête* even to the ordinary man among his subjects; and it is a sign of great strength of character that up to the very end of his life he did not allow himself to be depressed by these feelings. If we had then had on the throne a personality with whom he could have felt the same sympathy as with the young Emperor Francis Joseph, he would perhaps in the struggle for hegemony in

Germany at that time have taken the side of Prussia, just as he took that of Austria. It would have been a preliminary condition to this that Frederick William IV should have maintained and utilised the victory of his troops in March 1848; which was quite possible, without further repressions such as Austria was compelled to effect in Prague and Vienna by Windischgrätz and in Hungary by Russian assistance.

In St. Petersburg society during my time three generations could be distinguished. The one of highest quality, that of the European and classically cultured *grands seigneurs* from the reign of Alexander I, was dying out. It could still count Mentchikoff, Woronzoff, Bludoff, Nesselrode, and, as regards intellect and culture, Gortchakoff, whose standing, owing to his overweening vanity, was somewhat lowered in comparison with those named above—men who were classically educated, who spoke well and fluently not only French, but German also, and belonged to the cream of European civilisation.

The second generation which was contemporary with the Emperor Nicholas, or at all events bore his stamp, usually limited themselves in conversation to affairs of the court, theatres, promotions, and military events. Among them are to be mentioned as exceptions standing intellectually nearer to the older category, old Prince Orloff, whom we found remarkable in character, courtesy, and trustworthiness; Count Adlerberg the elder, and his son, the future governor, who, with Peter Shuvaloff, was the keenest intellect with whom I had relations there, and who only lacked industry to play a leading part; Prince Suworoff, the best disposed towards us Germans, in whom the Russian general of the Nicholas tradition was strongly, but not disagreeably, tempered by student reminiscences of German universities; Chevkin, the railway ' general,' always quarrelling with Suworoff, and yet his firm friend, a man of a keenness and delicacy of intelligence such as are not infrequently found in deformed persons, with that clever shape of head that is peculiar to them. Lastly, Baron Peter von Meyendorff, to me the most sympathetic figure among the older politicians, formerly ambassador at Berlin. By his culture and the elegance of his manners, he belonged rather to the Alexandrine period. In those days he had by intelligence and bravery worked himself up from the position of a young officer in a line regiment, in which he served in the French war, to that of a statesman whose word was of notable weight with the Emperor Nicholas. The charm of his hospitable house in Berlin, and in St. Petersburg, was materially heightened by his wife, a woman of masculine shrewdness, distinguished, honourable, and amiable, who in a still higher degree than her sister, Frau von Brints, of Frankfort, gave proof that in the family of Buol the hereditary intelligence was a fief passing on the distaff side. Her brother, the Austrian minister Count Buol, had not inherited the portion of it which is indispensable for guiding the policy of a great monarchy. The two, brother and sister, stood personally no nearer to one another than the Russian and the Austrian policies. When I was accredited to Vienna in 1852, on a special mission, the relationship between them was still of such kind that Frau von Meyendorff was inclined to facilitate the success of my friendly mission to Austria; in which sense the instructions of her husband were doubtless couched. The

Emperor Nicholas at that time desired our good understanding with Austria. A year or two later, when, at the time of the Crimean war, there was a question of my appointment to Vienna, the relations between her and her brother found expression in the words: she hoped I was coming to Vienna ' and would irritate Charles into a bilious fever.' Frau von Meyendorff was, as her husband's wife, a patriotic Russian; and even without this, simply from her personal feeling, she would not have approved of the hostile and ungrateful policy to which Count Buol· had committed Austria.

The third generation, that of the young men, showed for the most part in its social demeanour less courtesy, occasionally bad manners and as a rule stronger antipathy towards German and especially Prussian elements, than the two elder generations. If any one ignorant of Russian addressed them in German, they were inclined to disclaim a knowledge of the language and to answer uncivilly, or not at all; and as regards civilians, to fall below the measure of courtesy which they observed in uniform- or order-wearing circles. It was a judicious regulation of the police that the servants of the representatives of foreign governments should be distinguished by lace, and the dress of the *chasseur* in livery reserved for the diplomatic service. Those who belonged to the diplomatic body would otherwise, not being accustomed to wear uniforms or orders in the street, have been exposed, both from the police and from members of the higher society, to the same unpleasantness and the resulting altercations which a civilian without an order, and who was not known as an eminent man, might easily experience in the traffic of the streets and on the steamboats.

In Napoleonic Paris I observed the same thing.[1] If I had lived there longer I should have had to become used, according to the French custom, to not going on foot in the streets without some indication of a decoration. I have seen on the boulevards, during a festival, some hundreds of people unable to move either backwards or forwards, because, owing to defective arrangements, they had come between two detachments of troops marching in opposite directions; while the police, who had not perceived the obstruction, charged violently upon the crowd, striking out with their fists and with the *coups de pied* so usual in Paris, until they came upon a *monsieur décoré*. The red ribbon induced them at least to listen to the protestations of the wearer, and to allow themselves at length to be convinced that the apparently refractory mob was wedged between two bodies of troops, and consequently could not budge. The leader of the excited police got out of the difficulty by a joke, for catching sight of the Chasseurs de Vincennes going by at the double, he pointed to them and said: 'Eh bien, il faut enfoncer ça!' The public, including those who had been maltreated, laughed, and those who had escaped violence moved away with a feeling of gratitude towards the *décoré*, whose presence had saved them.

In St. Petersburg, too, I should have considered it expedient to wear the indication of a high Russian order in the street, if the great distances had not caused one to appear more frequently in a carriage, with lace liveries, than on foot. Even on horseback, if in civil dress and without a groom, one ran a risk of being roughly treated, both in word and deed, by the coachmen of the higher

[1] See above, p. 89.

dignitaries, recognisable by their livery, if one came un-
avoidably into collision with them; and any one sufficiently
master of his horse, and having a riding-whip in his hand,
did well in such encounters to establish the equality of
his rights with those of the people in the carriages. The
few riders in the environs of St. Petersburg, one could
perceive, were for the most part German and English
merchants, who, from their position, avoided as much as
possible all contact likely to cause quarrels, and preferred
to suffer rather than complain to the authorities. Only a
very small number of officers made use of the good bridle-
paths on the islands and further outside the city, and those
who did so were in general of German extraction. Efforts
in high quarters to bring about an increased taste for riding among the officers had no lasting result, and the only
effect was, that, after every attempt of the kind, the imperial equipages met more riders than usual for a day or
two. It was a remarkable thing that the best riders among
the officers were admittedly the two admirals, the Grand
Duke Constantine and Prince Mentchikoff.

But, even apart from carriages and horses, one could
not help perceiving that in good manners and the tone of
good society the younger contemporary generation was
behind as compared with the preceding one of the Emperor Nicholas, and these again were, both in European
culture and thorough breeding, behind the old school of
the time of Alexander I. Nevertheless within the circle
of the court and of 'society' perfect high tone still prevailed, and also in the homes of the aristocracy, especially
as far as the ladies held the sway. But politeness of
manners decreased considerably when one met younger
men in places uncontrolled by the influence of the Court

or of distinguished ladies. I will not decide how far what I observed is to be explained by a social reaction of the younger stratum of society against the German influences which had previously prevailed, or by a lowered standard of breeding in the younger Russian society since the period of the Emperor Alexander I, or perhaps by the contagion which social developments in Parisian circles usually exercise on the members of the upper society of Russia. Good manners and perfect courtesy are not so general now in the dominant circles of France, outside the Faubourg Saint-Germain, as was formerly the case, and as I have learnt to appreciate them by contact with older Frenchmen and French ladies, and still more charmingly among Russian ladies of every age—as, moreover, my position in St. Petersburg did not oblige me to close intercourse with the youngest adult generation, I have only retained from my sojourn there the pleasing recollection which I owe to the amiability of the Court, to the men of the old school, and to the ladies of society.

The anti-German tone of the younger generation made itself perceptible in a higher degree to myself and others, and even in the domain of political relations, very soon after my Russian colleague Prince Gortchakoff turned his predominant vanity also upon me. So long as he had the feeling of looking upon me as a younger friend, in whose political training he claimed a share, his benevolence towards me was unlimited; and the ways in which he showed me confidence overstepped the boundaries allowed among diplomatists. This was possibly from calculation, or perhaps from ostentation towards a colleague, of whose admiring intelligence I had succeeded in persuading him. These relations became untenable directly

I could, as a Prussian minister, no longer leave him the illusion of his personal and political superiority. *Hinc iræ.* Immediately I began to step forward independently as German, or Prussian, or as rival in the sight of Europe and in the records of political history, his benevolence turned to disfavour.

Whether this change first commenced after 1870, or whether it had escaped my attention before that year, I must leave uncertain. If the former was the case, I can adduce as an honourable, and to a Russian chancellor a justifiable motive, his error of calculation that the estrangement between us and Austria would exist permanently even after 1866. We readily supported the policy of Russia in 1870 in order to release her from the limitations which the treaty of Paris had imposed upon her in the Black Sea. These were unnatural, and the prohibition of free movement on her own coast could not be long endured by a Power like Russia, because it was a humiliation. Besides which it was not, and is not, to our interest to stand in the way of Russia turning her surplus forces towards the East. In our position and with our historical development in Europe, we ought to rejoice whenever we find Powers in whom we encounter no sort of competition of political interests, as is the case, so far, with us and Russia. With France we shall never have peace; with Russia never the necessity for war, unless Liberal stupidities or dynastic blunders falsify the situation.

At St. Petersburg, whenever I happened to be at one of the imperial palaces of Sarskoe or Peterhof, if only to confer with Prince Gortchakoff, who had his summer quarters there, I used to find a lunch of several courses with three or four kinds of excellent wine prepared for myself and a companion in the apartments assigned to my use in the palace. Nothing except the best wine ever came my way in the imperial commissariat. No doubt a good deal of stealing went on in the household, but it was not the Emperor's guests who suffered from it; on the contrary, their entertainment was calculated with a liberal allowance of perquisites for the ' service.' Kitchen and cellar were absolutely above reproach, even in contingencies where no control was exercised over them. Perhaps the employés, who had the right to drink the wine that was left, had by long experience developed too exquisite a taste to put up with any irregularities which might injure the quality of the supplies. Certainly, from the information I received, the prices of the articles must have been enormously high. I gained some conception of the hospitality of the household when my patroness, the Empress Dowager Charlotte, our King's sister, sent me an invitation. On those occasions two dinners were supplied from the imperial kitchen for the gentlemen of the embassy, who were invited with me, and three for myself. In my own quarters luncheons and dinners were served and charged for, and probably also eaten and drunk, as though I and my companions had received no invitation from the Empress. One cover was laid for me in my own quarters, with all the usual accessories. Another was served for me at the table of the Empress, as well as for my suite, and even there I was not brought into contact with it, since I had to dine beside the bed of the invalid Empress *en petit comité*, without my suite. On these occasions Princess Leuchtenberg, afterwards wife of Prince William of Baden, at that time in the first bloom of youthful beauty, used to do the honours in her grandmother's place with the grace and liveliness which were peculiar to her. I also remember that on another occasion a little grand-duchess, four years of age, was moving about a table at which four persons were seated and refused to show a great general the same civility which she bestowed on me. I felt greatly flattered when this grand-ducal child, in answer to her grandmother's admonition, said, referring to me, *on milü* (he is nice), but was naïve enough to say of the general, *on wonajet* (he stinks), which resulted in the removal of the grand-ducal *enfant terrible.*

It happened once that some Prussian officers, who had lived for a long while in one of the imperial palaces, were asked in confidence by some of their Russian friends whether they had really consumed as much wine, &c., as was requisitioned for their use; in that case they could only envy their powers of consumption and take care that the supplies continued in future. This confidential inquiry was addressed to gentlemen of very temperate habits, and, with their consent, the apartments in which they were living were examined. It turned out that cupboards in the wall, of which they were not even aware, were filled with stores of valuable wines and other articles of consumption.

There is a well-known story how the Emperor once remarked upon the extraordinary quantity of tallow that always appeared in the bills whenever the Prince of Prussia came on a visit; at last it turned out that on the occasion of his first visit he had ridden himself sore, and in the evening had asked for a little tallow. The ounce of this stuff which was then required was transformed, on the occasions of future visits, into a pood. The illustrious personages had an oral explanation about the matter, resulting in considerable amusement, of which the offenders reaped the benefit.

At the time of my first stay at St. Petersburg, in 1859, I had an example of another Russian peculiarity. During the first spring days it was then the custom for every one connected with the court to promenade in the Summer Garden between Paul's Palace and the Neva. There the Emperor had noticed a sentry standing in the middle of a grass plot; in reply to the question why he was standing there, the soldier could only answer, ' Those are my orders.' The Emperor therefore sent one of his adjutants to the guard-room to make inquiries; but no explanation was forthcoming except that a sentry had to stand there winter and summer. The source of the original order could no longer be discovered. The matter was talked of at court, and reached the ears of the servants. One of these, an old pensioner, came forward and stated that his father had once said to him as they passed the sentry in the Summer Garden : ' There he is, still standing to guard the flower; on that spot the Empress Catherine once noticed a snowdrop in bloom unusually early, and gave orders that it was not to be plucked.' This command had been carried out by placing a sentry on the spot, and ever since then one had stood there all the year round. Stories of this sort excite our amusement and criticism, but they are an expression of the elementary force and persistence on which the strength of the Russian nature depends in its attitude towards the rest of Europe. It reminds us of the sentinels in the flood at St. Petersburg in 1825, and in the Shipka Pass in 1877; not being relieved, the former were drowned, the latter frozen to death at their posts.

ST. PETERSBURG

At the time of the Italian war I still believed in the possibility of influencing the discussions at Berlin, while in the position of an ambassador at St. Petersburg, as I had tried with varying results to do when I was at Frankfort. I had not realised that the extraordinary exertions which I had imposed upon myself in my dispatches with this end in view must be absolutely fruitless, because my direct reports and my communications made in autograph letters reached the Regent either not at all or else accompanied by comments which prevented them from making any impression. The only result of my labours, besides a complication of the disease which medical poisoning had induced in me, was that suspicion was cast on the accuracy of my reports as to the inclinations of the Emperor, in consequence of which Count Münster, formerly Military Plenipotentiary at St. Petersburg, was sent there to keep control over me. I was in a position to prove to this supervisor, who was a friend of mine, that my communications were based upon a view of the autograph remarks made by the Emperor on the margin of the reports of Russian diplomatists which Gortchakoff had shown me, and also on verbal communications made by personal friends in the cabinet and at court. The Emperor's autograph marginal notes had perhaps been communicated to me by a calculated indiscretion in order that their contents should reach Berlin in this less vexatious manner.

These and other modes by which I was made acquainted with specially important communications are characteristic of the political game of chess as it was played in those days. A gentleman, who on one of these occasions made a confidential communication to me, turned round as

he reached the door and said : 'My first indiscretion neces-
sitates a second. You will of course communicate this
matter to Berlin. In doing so, do not make use of your
cypher, number so-and-so; we have been in possession of
that for years, and as matters stand our people would at
once conclude that I was the source of information. You
must further oblige me by not suddenly giving up the compromised cypher, but using it a few months longer for unimportant telegrams.' At the time I thought, in the tran-
quillity resulting from this communication, that I might
infer the probability of only one of our cyphers being in
Russian hands. It was specially difficult to keep a cypher
secure at St. Petersburg, because all the embassies were of
necessity obliged to employ Russian servants and subordinates in their households, and it was easy for the Russian police to procure agents among these.

At the time of the war between Austria and France,
the Emperor Alexander, in the course of a confidential
chat, complained to me of the violent and offensive tone in
which Russian politics were criticised in the correspondence between German princes and members of the imperial
family. He ended his complaint of his relations by the
indignant words : ' What is specially offensive to me in
the matter is that my German cousins send their rude
remarks through the post in order that they may be sure of
coming to my personal knowledge.' There was no malice
in the Emperor's admission; he was simply under the impression that it was his right as a monarch to make himself acquainted, even by such means as these, with the correspondence which passed through the Russian post office.

In Vienna, too, similar arrangements used to subsist.
Before the construction of railways there were times when

an Austrian official would enter the carriage of the Prussian courier as soon as the frontier had been passed, and with his assistance open the dispatches with professional skill, make extracts, and close them again before ever they reached the embassy at Vienna. Even after the cessation of this practice it was considered a prudent mode of making official communications to the cabinet of Vienna or St. Petersburg to send letters through the ordinary post to the Prussian ambassador in the place. The contents were then regarded by both sides as imparted, and this mode of imparting was occasionally employed when the effect of a disagreeable communication had to be weakened in the interests of the courtesy required by formal intercourse. How epistolary secrecy fared in the Thurn and Taxis post office may be seen from a letter I wrote on January 11, 1858, to the minister Manteuffel: ' I have already expressed by telegraph my urgent request that you will not send my confidential report on Lord Bloomfield's complaint in the Bentinck case by post to Count Flemming at Carlsruhe, since in this way it would be brought to the knowledge of Austria. If my request arrives too late I shall be brought in various directions into unpleasant perplexities, the only way out of which seems to be a personal conflict between Count Rechberg and myself. As far as my knowledge of him goes, and in view of the Austrian view as to the secrecy of letters in general, he will not be prevented from producing this proof by the fact that they have been taken from an opened letter. I rather expect he will expressly appeal to the fact that the dispatch could only have been passed through the post with a view of bringing it to the knowledge of the imperial government.'

253

BISMARCK

In 1852, when I had the direction of the embassy at Vienna, I found it was the practice, whenever the ambassador had a communication to make, to hand over to the Austrian Minister for Foreign Affairs the original of the instructions he had received from Berlin. This custom, which was unquestionably disadvantageous for the service, since it made the intermediary functions of the ambassador appear superfluous, had become so deeply rooted that the chancery officials of the embassy, who for decades had been natives of Vienna, hearing that I had forbidden the practice, called upon me, and represented that the mistrust of the imperial chancery would be great indeed were we suddenly to make a change in a practice of many years' standing; in my case specially it would be a matter of doubt whether the effect produced by me on Count Buol really corresponded to the text of my instructions and thus to the intentions of Berlin policy.

In order to protect themselves against treachery on the part of officials of the Foreign Office, very drastic remedies have sometimes been used in Vienna. I once had in my hands a secret Austrian official document, and this sentence has remained in my memory:

'Kaunitz, not being able to find out which of his four clerks had betrayed him, had them all four drowned in the Danube by means of a boat with a valve.'

There was a question of drowning too in a jocular conversation which I had with the Russian ambassador at Berlin, Baron von Budberg, in 1853 or 1854. I mentioned that I suspected one official of representing the interests of another state in the business with which he was entrusted. Budberg said: 'If the man is in your way send him as far as the Ægean Sea; we have means there of helping him to disappear;' and upon my saying somewhat anxiously, ' You don't mean to drown him, do you?' he continued, laughing, ' He would disappear somewhere mysteriously in the interior of Russia, and as he appears to be a useful person, he would reappear again as a contented Russian official.'

In the beginning of June 1859 I went on a short excursion to Moscow. During this visit to the ancient capital, which happened to fall at the time of the Italian war, I witnessed a remarkable instance of the hatred which at that time prevailed in Russia against Austria. As the governor, Prince Dolgorouki, was showing me round a library I noticed that a subaltern officer among several military decorations wore the Iron Cross upon his breast. To my inquiry how he came by it, he named the battle of Kulm, after which Frederick William III had distributed to Russian soldiers iron crosses, differing slightly from the ordinary shape and known as Kulm crosses. I congratulated the old soldier on being so hearty after forty-six years, and his reply was that, did the Emperor but permit it, he would be glad enough to take part in the present war. I asked him which side he would take, that of Italy or Austria, whereupon he drew himself up and declared with enthusiasm, 'Always against Austria.' I pointed out to him that at Kulm Austria had been on our side and Russia's, while Italy was our enemy. Whereupon he continued in his stiff military attitude, and with the loud and penetrating voice with which the Russian soldier always addresses his officer, he

replied: 'An honest enemy is better than a false friend.'
This straightforward answer delighted Prince Dolgorouki
so much that in a moment the general and subordinate officer
were in each other's arms and exchanging cordial kisses
on both cheeks. Such at that time was the Russian feeling
towards Austria among generals and subordinate officers.

The following correspondence * with Prince Obolenski
is a souvenir of my journey to Moscow:

' Moscow: June 2, 1859.

' When visiting recently the antiquities of Moscow,
your Excellency paid great attention to the monuments
of our ancient life as bearing on politics and character.
The old buildings of the Kremlin, the objects connected
with the home life of the Czars, the precious Greek manuscripts in the library of the patriarchs of Russia—everything aroused your intelligent curiosity. Your scientific
remarks on the subject of these monuments proved that,
apart from your knowledge of diplomatic affairs, you had
an equally profound knowledge of archæology. Such attention to our antiquities on the part of a stranger is doubly
delightful to me, as a Russian and as a man who dedicates
his leisure to archæological research. Permit me to offer
your Excellency, as a souvenir of your short stay at Moscow and of the pleasant acquaintance which I had the
honour to make with you, a copy of the book containing
the description of the " Election and Accession of the
Czar Michael Feodorowitch." You will see in the cuts,
inartistic but curious for their antiquity, the same buildings and objects which interested you in the Kremlin.

' Believe me, &c.,

' P. M. OBOLENSKI.'

*[French in the original.]

'St. Petersburg : July 1859.

'I should be indeed ungrateful if, after all your kindness at Moscow, I had let four weeks pass, save for urgent reasons, before replying to the letter with which your Excellency has honoured me.   After my return I was attacked by serious illness, a form of gout, which has kept me crippled and in great pain for nearly a month with insignificant intervals, and those absorbed by arrears of current work.   Even to-day I am not equal to walking, but otherwise I am so much better that I shall try to obey an order of my government calling me to Berlin.   Pardon these details, Prince; they are necessary to explain my silence.

'I had hoped that by this delay in my answer I should have been enabled to enclose the reply which I expect from Berlin to the message which you kindly entrusted to me for the King.   I have not yet got it, but I cannot go away, Prince, without telling you how much I am touched by the manner, at once dignified and kind, in which you do the honours of the department which you direct and of the capital in which you dwell, showing a noble model of national hospitality to foreigners.   The magnificent work which you have so kindly given me will always remain a valued ornament of my library and an object recalling a Russian nobleman who is so well able to reconcile the enlightenment of the *savant* with the qualities that distinguish the man of high birth.

'Believe me, &c.

'VON BISMARCK.'

One day, when I was fresh to the climate of St. Petersburg, in June 1859, after riding for some time in an overheated riding-school, I returned home without a fur and stopped a little on the way to watch some recruits at drill. Next day I had rheumatism in all my limbs, which gave me trouble for a long while. When the time came for setting out to fetch my wife to St. Petersburg I had quite recovered, except for a slight pain still noticeable in my left leg, which I had injured in 1857 by a fall over a rock during a hunting expedition in Sweden,[1] and which, in consequence of careless treatment, had become *locus minoris resistentiæ*. Dr. Walz, who had been recommended to me when I set out, by the former Grand Duchess of Baden, offered to prescribe a remedy for me, and when I said that I thought it unnecessary since the pain was but slight, he assured me that the matter might become worse on the journey, and it was advisable to take precautions. The remedy was a simple one; he would put a plaster in the knee-hollow, which would cause me no annoyance, and after a few days would fall off of its own accord and only leave a slight redness behind. Being unacquainted with the previous history of this doctor, who came from Heidelberg, I unfortunately yielded to his persuasion. Four hours after I had put on the plaster I woke up from a sound sleep in violent pain and tore off the plaster, but without being able to remove it entirely from the knee-hollow, into which it had already burnt a wound. Walz came a few hours afterwards and assured me that he could scrape away the black plaster mass from the wound, which was as big as a hand, with some sort of metallic blade. The pain was unbearable and the result unsatisfactory, since the corrosive action of the poison continued. I realised the ignorance and unconscientiousness of my physi-

[1] See p. 214.

cian, in spite of the recommendation from high quarters which had determined me in choosing him. He himself assured me, with an apologetic smile, that the ointment had been peppered rather too strongly; it was a mistake of the chemist's. I sent to the latter for the prescription, and he sent the answer that Walz had taken it back again, but, according to his own statement, the doctor no longer possessed it. I was therefore unable to discover who was the poisoner, and could only learn from the chemist that the chief ingredient of the ointment was the stuff which was used in making cantharides ointment, and as far as he could remember there was an unusually strong dose of it set down in the prescription. I have been asked since whether this poisoning might have been done on purpose; for my part, I merely ascribe it to the ignorance and audacity of this medical swindler.

Upon the recommendation of the Dowager Grand Duchess Sophie of Baden, he had been made director of all the children's hospitals in St. Petersburg; further inquiries on my part resulted in the discovery that he was the son of the university confectioner at Heidelburg, had been an idle student, and failed in his examination. His ointment had destroyed a vein and it caused me many years' suffering.

With a view to seeking help from German doctors, I set out in July for Berlin, travelling by sea to Stettin. Violent pain induced me to consult the celebrated surgeon Pirogow, who was one of the passengers. He wanted to amputate the leg, and on my asking where he would take it off, above or below the knee, he pointed to a place a long way above it. I declined, and after trying various kinds of treatment at Berlin in vain, I was so far restored

by the baths of Nauheim under the treatment of Professor
Benecke of Marburg, that I was able to walk and ride, and
in October to accompany the Prince Regent to Warsaw to
a meeting with the Czar.   On my way back to St. Petersburg in November, when I was on a visit to Herr von
Below at Hohendorf, the clot which had formed and settled
in the injured vein, becoming detached, according to the
medical view, entered the circulation and brought about
inflammation of the lungs.   The doctors expected it to
be fatal, but it was cured after a month of grievous sickness.   The impressions which a dying Prussian had at
that time on the subject of trusteeship seem very strange
to me now.   My first desire, after my condemnation by
the doctors, was to write down a last direction which
should exclude all interference by the courts with the
trustees appointed by me.   Satisfied on this point I anticipated my end with that calmness which is induced by
unendurable pain.   At the beginning of March 1860 I was
well enough to be able to travel to Berlin, where I awaited
the completion of my cure, taking part in the sittings of
the Upper House.   Here I stayed until the beginning
of May.

CHAPTER XI

THE INTERMEDIATE YEARS

DURING this period Prince Hohenzollern and Rudolf von Auerswald suggested to the Regent that I should be appointed Minister of Foreign Affairs. The result of that proposal was a sort of conference at the palace attended by the Prince, Auerswald, Schleinitz, and myself. The Regent introduced the discussion by calling upon me to sketch out the programme which I should approve. I expounded it plainly on the lines which I afterwards followed as minister, pointing out that the weakest side of our policy was the feeble attitude towards Austria which had prevailed since Olmütz, and especially of late years during the Italian crisis. If we could accomplish our German task in agreement with Austria, so much the better. But this would not be possible until the conviction had gained ground in Vienna that in the opposite case we should shrink from neither rupture nor war. The *rapprochement* with Russia, which was so desirable for the accomplishment of our policy, could be more easily preserved by acting against Austria than with her. But even in the latter case it did not seem to be impossible, in the light of the experience I had gained at St. Petersburg of the Russian court and the influences prevailing there. The Crimean war and the Polish complications left us with a balance in hand which, if skilfully used, would enable us to come to an understanding with Austria without break-

ing with Russia. I was only afraid that the understanding with Austria might come to grief on account of the
exaggerated idea prevalent there of the greatness of their
own power and the smallness of the Prussian; until, at any
rate, Austria was thoroughly convinced that we were seriously prepared, if necessary, even for rupture and war.
Our policy at Vienna during the last ten years had removed all belief in any such possibility; they had grown
to regard the basis of Olmütz as permanent, and they
either failed to notice or had forgotten that the convention
of Olmütz had its chief justification in the temporary disadvantage of our position caused by the dispersal of our
cadres, and by the fact that at the time of that convention
the whole weight of Russian power had fallen into the
scale of Austria, which since the Crimean war was no
longer the case. But Austria was just as exacting in her
policy towards us in 1856 as at the time when the Emperor
Nicholas helped her against us. I maintained that our
submission to the Austrian illusion recalled the experiment of fixing a hen to the spot by drawing a chalk line
in front of it. Austrian confidence, a skilful use of the
press, and a plentiful supply of secret service money enabled Count Buol to keep up the Austrian phantasmagoria
and to ignore the strong position in which Prussia would
be placed as soon as she was ready to break through the
witchcraft of the chalk line. The Regent knew perfectly
well what I meant by the reference to Austrian secret
funds.[1]

After I had developed my views, Schleinitz was called
upon to bring his forward. He did this by a reference
to the will of Frederick William III, thus skilfully touch-

[1] See pages 233-5.

ing a chord which never failed to find a response in the mind of the Regent. He described the anxieties and dangers which threatened us from the West, from Paris, and at home, if our relations with Austria, in spite of all justifiable grounds for sensitiveness, failed to be maintained. The dangers of a combination between Russia and France, which even at that time was openly discussed, were set forth, and the possibility of an alliance between Prussia and Russia was said to be condemned by public opinion. It was characteristic of the Regent that, as soon as Schleinitz had spoken the last word of a fluent and evidently carefully-prepared speech, he at once declared in a lucid statement that in accordance with the traditions of his ancestors he decided in favour of the minister von Schleinitz. This brought the discussion to a speedy conclusion.

The rapidity with which he had made his decision as soon as the minister had uttered his last word led me to suppose that the whole *mise en scène* had been arranged beforehand, and had been carried out according to the wish of the Princess, so as to preserve some appearance of regard to the opinions of Prince Hohenzollern and Auerswald, although even at that time she was not in agreement with them or with their inclination to strengthen the cabinet by adding me to it.

The policy of the Princess, which had considerable weight with her husband and the minister, was determined, as it seemed to me, rather by special dislikes than by any positive aims. Her objects of dislike were Russia, Louis Napoleon, with whom I was suspected of keeping up relations, and myself, on account of my inclination to an independent opinion and my refusal to present the illustrious lady's opinions to her husband as my own.

263

Her likes were of a similar character. Herr von Schleinitz was politically her creature, a courtier who depended on her without any political opinion of his own.

The Prince of Hohenzollern, who was convinced that the Princess and Schleinitz were stronger than he, soon withdrew from all active participation in affairs, although he bore the name of Minister-President until 1862. The nominal leadership then also passed to Auerswald, and during the rest of my stay in Berlin I was on a very pleasant footing with him. He had a special charm of manner besides unusual political gifts, and two years afterwards, when I became Minister-President, he lent me his kindly assistance, especially in combating the Crown Prince's anxieties and scruples as to the future of our country, which were instilled into him from England in opposition to me as a friend of Russia, and which afterwards led to the *pronunciamiento* of Dantzic. On his deathbed[1] he begged the Crown Prince to come to him, warned him earnestly against the dangers which his opposition might cause the monarchy, and besought the Prince to cling to me.[2]

In the summer of 1861 a quarrel had arisen within the ministry which is described in the following letter of June 27, from von Roon, the Minister of War:[3]

'Berlin: June 27, 1861.

'I suppose that you are acquainted with the general features of the Homage question, which has become so critical.* It is almost ripe for an explosion. The King

[1] R. v. Auerswald died January 15, 1866.

[2] Cf. *Aus dem Leben Theodor von Bernhardis*, vi. 227, 228, 234.

[3] *Bismarck-Jahrbuch*, vi. 194 &c.

* [The King of Prussia had usually indicated his accession by receiving formal homage. William I ultimately decided on coronation, but put on the crown with his own hands.]

cannot give way without ruining himself and the crown for ever. Nor can the majority of the ministers yield; if they did they would slit open their own immoral bellies and commit political suicide. They are forced to be, and to remain, disobedient. Hitherto I, who have taken up an entirely opposite position on this burning question, and (Edwin) Manteuffel have had the greatest difficulty in preventing the King from giving way. He would do it if I advised it, but I pray that God will take away the use of my tongue before it gives assent. But I stand alone—quite alone, for to-day Edwin Manteuffel is put under arrest.[1] It was not until yesterday that the King permitted me to look out for other ministers. He holds the gloomy view that, except Stahl and Co., he will find no one who judges the homage with the oath of allegiance to be admissible.

' Now I ask you, do you regard the ancient traditional hereditary homage as an attack on the constitution? If you answer my question with Yes, I shall have made a mistake in assuming you were of my opinion; but if you agree with me and think this view is mere doctrinaire humbug, resulting from political engagements and political party-grouping when our dear comrades think that they are not in position, you will have no objection to entering the King's council and solving the homage question in correct fashion. Then you will also find means of setting out without delay on your proposed holiday and sending me word by telegraph immediately. The words " Yes, I am coming," are sufficient; better still if you can add the date of your arrival. Schleinitz goes under any circum-

[1] On account of a duel with Twesten as author of the pamphlet *Was uns noch retten kann.*

stances, quite independently of the homage question; that much is certain. But the question is whether you will have to take over his portfolio or Schwerin's. His Majesty seems more inclined to the latter than the former. But that is *cura posterior.* Our business is to convince the King that even without advertising a change of system he can find such a ministry as he requires. I have also addressed similar questions to President von Möller and to von Selchow, but am still without an answer. It is a hopeless state of things! The King suffers terribly. His nearest relations are against him, and counsel a rotten peace. God grant that he may not give way! If he did we should be steering under full sail into the morass of parliamentary government.

'I dread all business excitement, for the accumulated burdens together with this political worry are almost crushing me; still, a good horse may break down but does not give in. Therefore, let my business troubles excuse the shortness of these lines. Only one word more: I have broken down the bridge behind me and must there-fore go, if the King gives way; but this is really a matter of course.

'This letter is to reach you by the English courier: so Schlieffen promises. Send me an immediate answer by telegraph.'

I answered on July 2:

'Your letter sent by the English courier arrived here yesterday in storm and rain, and disturbed me in my pleasant anticipation of the quiet time I intended to spend in Reinfeld with Kissinger, and afterwards in Stolp-münde. Torn by affectionate feelings for young caper-cailzie on the one hand and the return to wife and children on the other, your order " to horse " struck me as a discordant note. I have become indolent, weary, and dispirited since I lost my foundation of good health. But to business! As to the homage quarrel, I scarcely understand how it can have become so important for both sides. There is not the least doubt in my own mind that the King does nothing repugnant to the constitution in accepting the homage in the traditional manner. He has the right to receive homage from each individual among his subjects, and from every corporation in the land, whenever and wherever he pleases, and if any one denies my sovereign a right which he is willing and able to exercise, I feel myself bound to assert it, even though I am not convinced of the practical importance of its exercise. In accordance with this view I telegraphed to Schlieffen that I consider the " title of possession," on the basis of which a new ministry is to be established, as lawful, and regard the refusal of the other party and the importance it attaches to preventing the act of homage as mere doctrinaire ill-temper. When I added that I "am not acquainted with the lie of the rest of the property " I did not mean by that the persons and capacities with whom we should have to do business, but rather the programme on the basis of which we should have to work. Therein, in my opinion, lies the difficulty. My impression is that the chief fault of our policy hitherto has been this : it has been liberal in Prussia and conservative in foreign parts ; we have esteemed the rights of our King too cheaply and those of foreign princes too highly. This is a natural result of the dualism between the constitutional tendencies of the ministers and the legitimist direction which the personal will of his Majesty gave our foreign policy. I should not easily make up

my mind to inherit from Schwerin, if only because I
do not consider my present capital of health sufficient.
But even were I to do so, I should still feel in internal
affairs the need for a different colouring of our foreign
policy. My belief is that nothing but a change in our
"foreign" attitude can liberate the position of the Crown
in domestic matters from the pressure which it will otherwise be actually impossible to resist; though I have
no doubt as to the sufficiency of the means for the
purpose. The domestic steam must be at extremely
high pressure, else it is impossible to understand how
our public life could have been so disturbed by such
trumpery stuff as Stieber, Schwark, Macdonald, Patzke,
Twesten, and the like; and in other countries no one
will understand how the homage question could have
blown up the cabinet. It will surely be thought that
grievous misrule had so embittered the people against
the authorities, that the flame was ready to burst forth
at the first breath. Political unripeness has a good
deal to do with this stumbling over mere threads; but
during the last fourteen years we have been teaching the
nation a taste for politics without satisfying its appetite,
and it has to seek its nourishment in the sewers. We
are almost as vain as the French; if we can talk ourselves into the belief that we are respected outside our
country we are ready to put up with a good deal at home;
but if we have the feeling that every little Würzburger
despises and jeers at us, and that we must put up with
it from fear, in the hope that the army of the *Reich* will
protect us against France, then we find at home something wrong in every corner, and every booby of the press
who opens his mouth against the government is in the

right.* Not one of the royal houses from Naples to Hanover will thank us for our affection, and in their case we love
our enemies in truly gospel fashion at the cost of the security of our own throne. I am faithful to my Prince to the
very marrow, but as far as all the others are concerned I do
not feel in a single drop of blood the least trace of obligation to raise a finger for them. I fear that this attitude of
mine is so far removed from that of our most gracious
master that he will scarcely consider me a suitable adviser
for the crown. Therefore, if he employs me at all, he
will prefer to use me in internal affairs. But according to
my view that makes no difference, for I do not believe that
the collective government will produce any satisfactory results unless our attitude in foreign affairs becomes stronger
and less dependent on dynastic sympathies. Our want of
self-confidence causes us to seek in them a support which
they cannot give us, and which we do not require. It is
a pity on account of the elections that the split has taken
just this form; the loyal and monarchical mass of electors
will not understand a quarrel about homage, and the democracy will distort it. It would have been better to hold
out firmly against Kühne in the military question, to break
with the chamber, dissolve it, and thus show the nation
what is the King's position towards the people. Will the
King be willing to adopt this measure in the winter when
it would be suitable? I do not believe in good elections
this time, although the homage ceremonies should give
the King many opportunities of influencing them. But
a timely dissolution after palpable excesses on the part
of the majority is a very wholesome remedy, perhaps

* ['Ed un Marcel diventa
Ogni villan che parteggiando viene.']
269

the best that can be obtained for restoring a healthy circulation.

' I cannot express myself fully in writing about a situation with which I am but insufficiently acquainted, nor
do I like setting down on paper everything which I might
wish to say. As I have received my leave of absence to-
day, I shall set out on Saturday by water and hope to be
at Lübeck Tuesday morning, and at Berlin in the evening. I cannot come earlier because the Emperor still
wishes to see me. The English courier will take these
lines back. Further details by word of mouth. Pray
give my kindest regards to your wife.

' In true friendship, yours,

' v. BISMARCK.' [1]

I had not seen any newspapers for five days when I
reached Lübeck at five o'clock in the morning on July 9,
and I learnt from the Swedish ' Ystädter' journal, which
alone was procurable at the station, that the King and
ministers had left Berlin, and the crisis was therefore apparently averted. On July 3 the King had issued the
manifesto saying that he adhered to the original form of
hereditary homage, but in view of the changes which had
been made in the constitution of the monarchy under his
brother's rule, he had determined, instead of holding the
ceremony of homage, to revive the solemn coronation on
which the hereditary dignity of the sovereign was based.
In a letter dated July 24, from Brunnen (Canton Schwyz),
Roon decribed to me the course of the crisis.[2]

' I made a vow to answer your letter on the first rainy

[1] Given in full in the Bismarck letters (6th ed.), p. 213 sqq. Now
also in Roon's *Denkwürdigkeiten*, ii.[4]
[2] *Bismarck-Jahrbuch*, vi. 196 sqq.

day, and unfortunately I am obliged to do so as early as to-day, with the help of a half-dry inkpot which, if I cannot fill it in any other way, will have to be held outside the window for a few minutes in order to help its deficiencies. Our constantly missing one another seems to be anything but providential, rather let us say most disastrous. The dispatch from Frankfort, owing to the stupidity of the officials, did not reach me until the 17th after eight o'clock in the morning, and a few hours afterwards my reply, which had been sent immediately, was returned with the comment that it could not be delivered. That made me all the more anxious about my departure. But I could not put it off. Schleinitz, in the service of Queen Augusta, has done us a good deal of immediate harm. The swelling had come to a head. Schleinitz himself, convinced that the present system is untenable, has given in his resignation principally on that account, just as rats forsake a rotten ship. But both he and von der Heydt agreed in thinking that dead and used-up persons ought not to be resuscitated by the galvanic shock of a supposed martyrdom, and therefore they voted against me. Schleinitz, supported by the Queen and the Grand Duchess Helene, has conquered by the help of the revived coronation idea, for which the mantles had been ordered as early as February. The ill-disguised retreat was now begun, and the all but completed list of ministers placed *ad acta.* I am also much inclined to believe that Schleinitz, like the Queen, and even Prince Hohenzollern, believes in the speedy destruction of the present system of lies, and is inclined to further it. Schleinitz's resignation is in every respect an advance, although he does not take up the same doctrinaire position as Patow, Auerswald, and Schwerin.

BISMARCK

Apart from his impotence in action, his presence gave the ministry support from above. Their pet could not be allowed to fall; well, he has got to port. If Count Bernstorff is but half the man that many people maintain, this second wedge will be more efficacious than the first, else he will not remain in office four months. You will doubtless have heard from Manteuffel or Alversleben that I have split with my comrades permanently on the homage question. If I still remain in this company, it is because the King insists upon it, and I, being exempt from all scruple under the present circumstances, can now go on fighting with my vizor up. It suits my nature better that these gentlemen shall *know* I am opposed to their prescriptions than that they should, as hitherto, only *believe* it. May God help us in future! I can do little more than remain an honest man; work in my own department, and do what is sensible. The greatest misfortune, however, in all this worry is the weariness and languor of our King. He is more than ever under the orders of the Queen and her accomplices. If he does not recover his physical vigour everything will be lost, and we shall totter on into the yoke of parliamentarism, the Republic, and the Presidency of Patow. I can see no means of safety whatever, unless the Lord our God help us. In the process of universal dissolution I can recognise only one organism with any power of resistance, and that is the army. To maintain this untainted is the problem which I regard as still soluble, but certainly only for a short time. It too will become plague-stricken if it does not get to action, unless healthy air is breathed into it from above, and that too becomes more difficult every day. If I am right in this, and I think I am, I cannot be blamed for continu-

272

ing to serve in this company. I do not mean to say that another man could not fill my office with equal or superior insight and energy, but even the most capable person will require a year to find his way about, and—"dead men ride fast." There is no need for me to assure any one who knows me well how glad I should be to resign. There is much more inclination to ease in my nature than I can justify before Heaven; and the considerable pension which I have earned would help me to this, since I am neither luxurious nor ambitious. How much I am inclined to idleness I feel now that, like a discharged cart-horse, free from harness and bridle, I am turned out on the common. If nothing particular happens I shall not return to my collar till the middle of September; then I hope we shall not miss each other again. I shall certainly have to go off again to the Rhine for the manœuvres on September 9, but only for ten or eleven days. Whether the King will go as he intends for a few days to Berlin at the beginning of September seems an open question. It appears to me indispensable if there is to be any further idea of government by a King in Prussia.

‘ Your letter leads me to hope that you will not return to St. Petersburg before the coronation. I consider that the "Kreuzzeitung" made a great political blunder in its unsparing criticism of the coronation manifesto.* It would be just as great a blunder if the supporters of the paper were not to be represented at the ceremony. You may tell Moritz so. We have lost a good deal of ground by that unfortunate article, and we shall have to win it back.

‘ Let me conclude with my best wishes for your vari-

* [After the appearance of the article the King never again read the *Kreuzzeitung.*]

ous cures. I hope you will return from them with renewed health. The time is approaching when all your
powers will be needed for the well-being of your country.
Give my (our) most respectful salutations to your wife.

‘I am sending this letter by way of Zimmerhausen,
registered; it *must* not fall into wrong hands!’

At Schleinitz's telegraphic request I went on July 10
to Baden-Baden, to report myself to the King. He seemed
unpleasantly surprised to see me, supposing I had come on
account of the ministerial crisis. I said I had heard that
it had been averted, and stated I had only come in order
to request his personal consent to an extension of my
leave until after the coronation, which was to take place
in the autumn, accordingly beyond the three months already accorded me. The King granted this in the kindest manner, and himself invited me to dinner.

After spending August and September in Reinfeld
and Stolpünde I reached Königsberg on October 13, for
the coronation which was to take place on the 18th.

During the festivities I noticed that a change had
taken place in the disposition of the Queen, perhaps connected with the withdrawal of Schleinitz which had occurred in the meantime. She took the initiative in dis-
cussing national German politics with me. There, for
the first time, I met Count Bernstorff as minister. He
did not seem yet to have come to any definite conclusion
about his policy, and in conversation he gave me the impression of a man struggling after an opinion. The Queen
was more friendly to me than she had been for many
years; she showed me marked attentions, which apparently
went beyond the line traced at that time by the King. At
a moment whose ceremonial character scarcely gave any

opportunity for conversation, she remained standing in front of me, while I was in the crowd, and began a conversation about German politics, which the King, who was with her, tried for some time in vain to bring to an end. The conduct of both royal personages on this and other occasions proved that at that time there was a difference of opinion between them as to the treatment of the German question; I conjecture that Count Bernstorff was not congenial to her Majesty. The King avoided talking politics with me, probably because he feared that relations with me would cause him to be regarded in a reactionary light. This anxiety prevailed with him as late as May 1862, and even September of that year. He thought me more fanatical than I was. Probably his remembrance of my criticism of the capacity of the new cabinet, before my departure for St. Petersburg, had some influence with him.[1]

The summons to Prince Adolf of Hohenlohe-Ingelfingen, in March 1862, to take the post of President of the Ministry as substitute for Prince Hohenzollern already suggested a sort of ministerial bill-jobbing calculated on an early date of maturing. The Prince was clever, amiable, entirely devoted to the King, and had taken part in our home politics, in a somewhat dilettante fashion, it is true, but still more ardently than most of his compeers of the old imperial nobility. Physically, however, and perhaps also intellectually, he was not equal to the post of Minister-President, and when I saw him in May 1862 he tried purposely to strengthen this impression of mine by conjur-

[1] See page 230.

ing me to deliver him from his martyrdom by immediately
taking over the post, which was breaking him down.

At that time I was not yet in a position to fulfil his
wishes, nor had I any inclination to do so. Even at the time
of my summons from St. Petersburg to Berlin I was able to
assume, from the tortuous windings of our parliamentary
policy, that I should have to face this question.   I cannot
say that I found this prospect attractive, nor that it stimu-
lated me to action; I had no belief in the permanence of any
firm resistance on his Majesty's part to domestic influences.
I remember that at Eydtkuhnen I did not pass the toll-gate
of my native frontier with the same sensation of pleasure
that I had always felt hitherto.   I was oppressed by the
anxiety of going to meet difficult and responsible business,
and of having to renounce the pleasant and not necessarily responsible position of an influential ambassador.
Nor could I calculate with any security on the weight and
tendency of the assistance which I should receive from the
King and his consort, from my colleagues and the country
in general, in my combat with the rising tide of parliamentary government.   My pride was offended by a position
which obliged me to lie at anchor in a Berlin hotel, like one
of the intriguing ambassadors of the Manteuffel *régime*, in
the light of a suitor for office.   I begged Count Bernstorff
to procure me either an office or my dismissal.   He had
not yet abandoned the hope of being able to remain; he
asked and obtained in a few hours my appointment to Paris.

I was appointed on May 22, 1862, and on June 1 I
handed in my letters of credence at the Tuileries.   The
following letter to Roon[1] was written on the next day:—

[1] *Bismarck Letters* (6th ed.), pp. 242, 243. Now also published in
Roon's *Denkwürdigkeiten*, ii.[4] 91, 92.

' I have arrived safely, and am living here like a rat in an empty barn, confined by the cold, rainy weather. Yesterday I had a formal audience, drove up in imperial carriages, ceremony, procession of dignitaries. Otherwise it was short and satisfactory, no politics, as they were postponed for *un de ces jours*, and a private audience. The Empress looks very well, as she always does. Yesterday evening the King's messenger arrived; he brought me nothing from Berlin except some " leathery stuff "—dispatches about Denmark. I had been looking forward to a letter from you. From a communication which Bernstorff has made to Reuss, I learnt that the writer counts with certainty upon my continued stay here and his at Berlin, and that the King is mistaken if he assumes that Bernstorff is anxious to return to London as soon as possible. I cannot understand why he does not say quite openly, " I should like to stay," or " I should like to go," for neither is a disgrace. To keep both posts at the same time exposes him to far more reproach. As soon as I have anything to report, i.e. have had a private audience with the Emperor, I shall write with my own hand to the King. I still flatter myself with the hope that I shall seem less indispensable to his Majesty when I have been out of his sight for a while, and that some hitherto unrecognised statesman will be found to supplant me, so that I may ripen a little more here. I am waiting quietly to see whether any arrangements will be made about me, and of what kind. If nothing is done in a few weeks, I shall ask for leave of absence to fetch my wife, but must in that case have some security as to the length of my stay here. I cannot settle down here on the terms of a week's notice.

' The proposal to give me a post in the ministry without a portfolio will not, I hope, find favour in the highest quarters; it was not mentioned in my last audience. The post is unpractical; to say nothing, and to put up with everything; to meddle uninvited in everything and be cut short by everybody where one really wants to get in a word. I value a portfolio above the Presidency, for the latter after all is only a reserve post; nor should I care to have a colleague who spent half his time in London. If he does not want to live there altogether, I am heartily willing that he should stay where he is, and should regard it as unfriendly to urge him away.

' My kindest regards to your family. Your faithful friend and willing but not daring comrade in war, if war it must be; but rather in winter than in hot weather!'

Roon wrote to me from Berlin under date June 4:[1]

'. . . On Sunday Schleinitz spoke to me about a successor for Hohenlohe, and thought your time had not yet come. When I asked him who, in his opinion, ought to act as head of the ministry, he shrugged his shoulders; and when I added that then there would be nothing for it but for him to take pity on the post himself, he evaded my remark, neither refusing nor agreeing. You will not be surprised that this makes me feel anxious. I therefore found an opportunity yesterday of raising the question of the Presidency in the proper quarter, and found the old inclination towards you along with the old indecision. Who can help us there? and how is this to end? . . . . No party fit to govern! The democrats are excluded as a matter of course, but the great majority consists of democrats and those who intend to become such,

---

[1] The letter has been published in full in the *Bismarck-Jahrbuch*, iii. 233, 234. Now also in Roon's *Denkwürdigkeiten*, ii.[4] 93 &c.

even though the rough drafts of their addresses are saturated with assurances of loyalty. Next to them come the constitutionalists, i.e. the real ones, a little troop of not much more than twenty persons with Vincke at their head; about fifteen Conservatives; thirty Catholics; some twenty Poles. Where then can any possible government find the necessary support? Which party can govern with this grouping, except the democrats? and these cannot and must not. Under these circumstances, according to my logic, the present government must stay in office, however difficult it may be. And just for that reason it must absolutely be reinforced, and the sooner the better. . . . It certainly does not appear to me to be for the interest of Prussia that Count Bernstorff should still hold two important posts. I shall therefore be very glad if you are soon appointed President of the Ministry, although I am quite convinced Bernstorff will quickly abandon his dual position and no longer play the part of Colossus with one foot in London and one in Berlin. I appeal to your conscience not to make any counter-move, since it might and would result in driving the government into the open arms of the democrats. . . . Hohenlohe's leave of absence is up on the 11th inst. He will not return, but only send his resignation. And then, yes, then I hope the telegraph will summon you hither. This is what all patriots long for. How could you then hesitate and manœuvre?'

My answer was as follows:

'Paris: Whitsuntide 1862.[1]

'Dear Roon,—I received your letter duly through

[1] June 8 or 9. *Bismarck Letters* (6th ed.), pp. 243, 244. Now also in Roon's *Denkwürdigkeiten*, ii.[4] 95 &c.

Stein (at that time Military Plenipotentiary) obviously unopened, for I could not open it without partially destroying it. You may rest assured that I shall not make any counter-moves and manœuvres; if I could not see from all the indications that Bernstorff has no thought of resignation I should expect with certainty to leave Paris in a few days, in order to go *via* London to Berlin, and I should not stir a finger to prevent it. As it is I am stirring none, but I cannot after all advise the King to give me Bernstorff's place, and if I were to enter without a portfolio, we should have, including Schleinitz, three Ministers for Foreign Affairs, two of whom, in face of any responsibility, might withdraw at an hour's notice, one into the Household Ministry, the other to London. With you I believe I am in accord; with Jagow I believe I can become so. The Departmental Ministers would not cause me any difficulty; but I have tolerably distinct opinions about foreign affairs, so probably has Bernstorff, but I am not acquainted with them, and I am not able to accommodate myself to his methods and his forms. Nor have I any confidence in his just estimate of political affairs, and presumably he has none in mine. However, the uncertainty cannot go on much longer; I shall wait until the 11th, to see whether the King will abide by his views of the 26th ult.,[1] or supply himself elsewhere. If nothing is done by then I shall write to his Majesty on the assumption that my position here is permanent and that I can make my domestic arrangements with a view to staying here till the winter at any rate, or longer. My luggage and carriages are still at St. Petersburg; I must find

[1] The date of the special audience at the Castle of Babelsberg before his departure for Paris.

a place for them somewhere. Besides, mine are the habits of a respectable *paterfamilias*, including the need for a settled habitation, and I have really had none since July of last year when Schleinitz first told me that I was to be moved. You do me wrong if you think I am unwilling. On the contrary I have lively attacks of the adventurous spirit of that animal which goes and dances on the ice when it is feeling too happy.

' I have followed the debates on the Address to some extent, and am under the impression that the government surrendered more than was desirable in committee, perhaps also in the whole House. After all, what does a bad Address matter? The people fancy that by the adoption of another they have won a victory. In an Address a chamber does its manœuvring with dummy enemies and blank cartridges. If people mistake the sham fight for a serious victory, and scatter themselves to plunder and maraud on royal territory, the time will doubtless come when the dummy enemy will unmask his batteries and begin serious fighting. I notice a lack of geniality about our point of view; your letter breathes forth honest martial anger sharpened by the dust and heat of the battle. Without flattery, you gave an admirable answer, but really it is wasted, these people do not understand German. I have found our friendly neighbour calm and accommodating, very well disposed towards us, very much inclined to discuss the difficulties of the " German question." He can refuse his sympathies to none of the existing dynasties, but he hopes that Prussia will solve successfully the great problem set her, namely, the German one; then the government would also win confidence at home. Nothing but fine words. I tell people who ask why I have not settled down here comfortably, that I am thinking of taking a few months' leave before long, and then returning here with my wife.

'*June* 10.—His Majesty's answer to the address makes a very dignified impression in its reserve and moderation; it is calm without any irritation. Several papers contain allusions to Schleinitz's entrance in place of Hohenlohe. I do not grudge it him, and he will still remain treasurer of the household.

' I shall send this letter to-morrow by the King's messenger, he will then wait at Aachen until he has something more to bring from Berlin. Remember me very kindly to the ladies of your family. Mine are all well.

' In old friendship, your

' v. B.'

On June 26, the Emperor had invited me to Fontainebleau, and took a long walk with me. In the course of conversation about the political questions of the day and the last few years, he asked me suddenly whether I thought the King would be inclined to enter into an alliance with him. I answered that the King had the most friendly feelings towards him, and that the prejudices which formerly prevailed in the public mind against France had almost disappeared; but alliances were the result of circumstances, which determined their need or their utility. An alliance assumed a motive—a definite object. The Emperor disputed the necessity of any such assumption; there were, he said, Powers that stood in friendly relations to one another, and others with whom this was less the case. In view of the uncertain future confidence must be directed towards some one side. He did not

speak of an alliance with a view to any adventurous project, but he thought that between Prussia and France there
was a conformity of interests in which lay an element of
an *entente intime et durable.* It would be a great mistake
to try to create events; it would be impossible to calculate their tendency and strength in advance; but it was
possible to make arrangements to meet them—to be fore-
armed while considering means to confront them and
profit by them. This idea of a ' diplomatic alliance,' in
which the custom of mutual confidence was assumed and
the two parties learnt to count on one another in difficult
situations, was further developed by the Emperor. Then
suddenly he stood still and said, ' You cannot imagine
what singular overtures Austria made to me a few days
ago. It appears that the coincidence of your appointment with the arrival of Herr von Budberg has caused a
regular panic in Vienna. Prince Metternich told me he
had received instructions which went so far that he himself was alarmed by them; he had authorisation as unlimited as a sovereign had ever entrusted to his representative
in respect to all and every question which I might raise,
so that he might come to an agreement with me at any
cost.' This revelation placed me in some perplexity, for
apart from the incompatibility of the interests of the two
states, I have an almost superstitious dislike to being entangled with the fortunes of Austria.[1]

These deliverances of the Emperor's could not have
been entirely without foundation, even though he might
expect that I should not take advantage of my social

[1] Compare this with report of June 20, 1862, to Bernstorff, which
agrees with the above almost word for word, although Prince Bismarck
cannot have had it at hand when his reminiscences were being taken down.
I have published it in the *Bismarck-Jahrbuch*, iv. 152 &c.

relations with Metternich to the extent of breaking the
confidence reposed in me.   In any case this revelation to
the Prussian ambassador was imprudent, whether it was
true or exaggerated.   Even at Frankfort I had become
convinced that Viennese policy under certain circumstances would shrink from no combination; and would
sacrifice Venetia or the left bank of the Rhine, if by these
means they could purchase a confederacy on the right
bank securing the preponderance of Austria over Prussia.
I knew that German phrases would pass current at the
Hofburg so long as they could serve as a leash for us or
the Würzburgers.   If a Franco-Austrian coalition was not
already in existence against us we owed this not to Austria but to France, yet not to any special affection for us
on Napoleon's part, but to his doubts whether Austria
would be in a position to sail with the nationality breeze
then blowing strong.   In the report which I made to the
King, my deduction from all this was not that we ought
to enter into an agreement with France, but that we could
not count upon Austria's loyalty to the Confederation as
against France, nor could we hope to win Austria's free
consent to the improvement of our position in Germany.

In the lack of any kind of political task or business I
went for a short time to England, and on July 25 started
for a longish tour in the south of France.   To this period
belongs the following correspondence :

'Paris : July 15, 1862.[1]

' Dear Roon,—I have been wondering a good deal
lately why you inquired by telegraph whether I had got

[1] *Bismarck Letters* (6th edit.), p. 250 &c.; Roon, *Denkwürdigkeiten*,
ii.[4] 102 &c.

your letter of the 26th (ult.). I did not answer it because I could give no news about the subject of chief importance, but could only receive it. Since then a courier has reached me who was announced to me by telegraph a fortnight ago, and in expectation of whom I returned a week too soon from England. He brought me a letter from Bernstorff in answer to my request for leave. I am quite superfluous here now, because there is neither Emperor, minister, nor ambassador here. I am not in very good health, and this provisional existence, with the suspense of "whether and how" without any regular business, is not calming to the nerves. I thought that I was coming here for ten days or a fortnight, and now I have been here seven weeks without ever knowing whether I shall have to stay another twenty-four hours. I do not want to force myself on the King by lying at anchor in Berlin, and I will not go home because I am afraid of being stuck fast for an unlimited time in the hotel, on my way through Berlin. From Bernstorff's letter[1] I learn that it is not at present the King's pleasure to make over foreign affairs to me, and that his Majesty has not yet decided whether I am to take Hohenlohe's place; but does not want to prejudice this question negatively by giving me six weeks' leave. The King is doubtful, according to Bernstorff, whether I can be of any use in the present session, and whether my appointment, if it takes place at all, ought not to be postponed till the winter. Under these circumstances, I am repeating my request for six weeks' leave,[2] which I put on the following grounds. In the first place, I really need to recruit my health in moun-

---

[1] Of July 12. *Bismarck-Jahrbuch*, vi. 155, 156.
[2] Letter to Bernstorff of July 15. *Bismarck-Jahrbuch*, vi. 156 &c.

tain and sea air; if I am to take an oar in the galley I must
collect some store of health, and Paris has hitherto suited
me badly, with this confounded lounging bachelor's life.
In the second place, the King must have time to come to
a quiet decision on his own initiative, else his Majesty
will make those persons who urged him on responsible for
the conclusions.   In the third place, Bernstorff does not
intend to go now: the King has repeatedly invited him
to stay, and declared that he never spoke to me at all
about the Foreign Office; but I do not consider the position of a minister without portfolio tenable.   In the fourth
place, my joining it would appear at the present time pur-
poseless and casual, but may be used later on as an im-
pressive manœuvre.

'I imagine that the ministry will quietly and distinctly oppose all attempts at retrenchment in the army budget,
but not let them lead to a crisis, rather permitting the
Chamber to discuss the whole budget in detail.   I suppose that will be finished by September.   Then the budget, which I assume will not be acceptable to the government, will be sent up to the Upper House, in case it is
quite certain that the mutilated budget draft will be rejected there.   Then, or at any rate before the discussion
in the Upper House, it might be returned to the Chamber
of Deputies, with a royal message explaining the reasons
why the Crown cannot give its assent to a budget bill of
this nature, and they might be called upon to discuss the
matter afresh.   Perhaps at this point, or earlier, it might
be well to adjourn the Diet for thirty days.   The longer
the matter is drawn out, the more the Chamber will lose
in public esteem, since it has made and will continue to
make the mistake of taking its stand on foolish trifles, and

has not a single orator who does not increase the boredom of the public. If they can be brought to take their stand on such rubbish as the continuity of the Upper House, and begin a conflict on this subject, delaying the business proper, it will be a great piece of good fortune. They will grow tired, hope that the government's wind will give out, while the district judges will be getting alarmed at the expense of finding substitutes. When they grow mellow, feel that they are boring the country, and are urgently hoping for concessions on the part of the government, to deliver them from their false position, then, in my opinion, comes the moment to prove to them by my nomination that we are very far from giving up the contest, but are rather returning to it with fresh forces. The appearance of a new battalion in the ministerial ranks would then make an impression which could not be obtained now. Especially if there was a good deal of clatter made before-hand with talk about granting charters, and *coups d'état*, my old reputation for light-hearted violence will come in useful, and they will think " Now for it ! " Then all the Centre and the " halfs " will be ready for negotiation.

'All this depends more on my instinctive feeling than on any proof that I could bring forward; and I should not go so far as on my own responsibility to say " No " to any order of the King's. But if I am asked for my opinion, I shall give it in favour of keeping in the background a few months longer.

' Perhaps all this is reckoning without my host; per-haps his Majesty will never make up his mind to appoint me, for I really do not see why he should do it at all, after not doing it during the last six weeks. But there is abso-lutely no reason why I should be either here, swallowing the hot dust of Paris, yawning in cafés or theatres, or camping at Berlin in the Hôtel Royal as a political dilettante. I could spend my time better at the baths.

' I am really amazed at the political incapacity of our Chambers, and yet we are a highly cultured country; doubtless too highly; other countries are certainly not wiser than the flower of our class-elected representatives, but they do not possess the childlike self-confidence with which our people will make a public exhibition of their impotency in complete nakedness as a standard of how to do it. How have we Germans come by our reputation for retiring modesty? There is not one of us who does not think that he knows better about everything, from managing a war to picking fleas from a dog, than all the learned specialists; while in other countries there are many people who admit that they know less about some things than other people, and are therefore ready to give in and keep silence.

' *The* 16th.—I must close quickly to-day, for my time is required for other business. With kindest regards for your family, I remain in old friendship,

' Your

' v. B. '

Roon answered me under date August 31, 1862:

'My dear Bismarck,—You will be pretty well able to imagine why I did not answer you before; I was always hoping and hoping for a decision, or else for a situation which would bring about an acute solution. Unfortunately my, or rather our, troubles still preserve their chronic character. Now a new complication has arisen—the acquittal of von der Heydt's slanderers—but this too will be dissipated in the sand of the Mark. I have withdrawn for a few days from the *misère générale*, taking flight to this place (Zimmerhausen) to shoot partridges, when the King set out for D[oberan]. Bernstorff, whom I found quite determined three or four weeks ago to give up his post, which is becoming much too difficult and troublesome for him, told me a week ago that after all he was not sure whether at the conclusion of the parliamentary session he should not yield to the King's wish (supposing it to be expressed) and remain, although his longing for deliverance was by no means extinguished. Translated into facts, this means that the session had been drawn out so long that its conclusion will probably coincide with the confinement of the Countess, and that therefore a removal involving a winter journey would be even more inconvenient than under other circumstances. He had told me even before this that his removal to London must take . place at the latest in September, if it was to be acceptable to him. This perhaps condemnable self-seeking on the one hand, and the indecision of the King on the other, combined with the declaration of von der Heydt that he could and would put up with a President, but not with one taken from among his younger colleagues, makes me return to my former assertion that you will have to enter the ministry as President, and for the present without a portfolio; this will come of its own accord later. I consider it quite unreasonable and impossible that we should enter upon the winter session in our former incomplete and unsatisfactory condition, and more than one person in the highest quarters agrees with this view. There must and will be fighting. Concessions and compromises are not to be thought of; least of all is the King disposed towards

them. We may therefore look with certainty for dangerous catastrophes quite independently of the complications
in our foreign policy, which already exhibits some very
interesting entanglements.

'I can imagine that you, my old friend, are greatly
disgusted; I can measure your vexation by my own.
But I still hope that you will not sulk on that account,
but rather remember the ancient knightly duty of hew-
ing out a way for the King, even when, as at present,
he has gone into danger wantonly. But you are only
a human being, and, what is more, a husband and a
father. You want besides all your work to have a home
and a family life. You have a right to it, *c'est convenu !*
You want therefore to know, and to know soon, where
your bed and writing-table are to be set up, whether
in Paris or Berlin. And the King's word that you are
not to establish yourself at Berlin has as yet, as far
as I know, not been recalled; but you must have certainty. I will do my part—and this not from selfishness
but from patriotic interest—to procure you this certainty
before long. I am therefore pretending, and shall continue to do so until you forbid it, that I have been privately
instructed by you to procure this certainty. After my
last conversations with the Most Serene about you, I was
in any case obliged to use my special personal interest on
your behalf. I can therefore speak also of your unendurable position, which is specially due to your being
distinctly prevented from establishing yourself in Paris.
Motives of this kind are comprehensible, and might therefore have the effect of political considerations. I am therefore pretending that I have your consent in advising your
appointment, *for the present*, to the presidency without a

portfolio, which I have hitherto avoided doing; it cannot be managed in any other way! If you absolutely decline this, then you can throw me over, or order me to keep silence. I shall speak to his Majesty on the 7th, at a very confidential audience which he has promised me on that day, when he passes through on his way to the christening at Carlsruhe (on September 9). So you will still have time for protesting.

'Of the general situation I do not mean to speak to-day. The internal catastrophe, in my opinion, will not take place now, but early in the spring, and then you must necessarily be present. It will be absolutely decisive for our future. . . .

'Your

'v. ROON.'[1]

I replied:

'Toulouse : September 12, 1862.

'I have been travelling hither and thither in the Pyrenees, and in consequence have only to-day received your letter of the 31st [August]. I had also hoped to find one from Bernstorff, who wrote to me four weeks ago that the question of the ministerial changes must certainly be decided in September. Your letter, unfortunately, leads me to suppose that the uncertainty will be just as great at Christmas as it is now. My belongings are still at St. Petersburg, and will be snowed up there. My carriages are at Stettin, my horses in the country near Berlin, my family in Pomerania, and I myself on the high-road. I am going back now to Paris, although I have less than ever to do there, but my leave is at an end. My plan is now to propose to Bernstorff that I shall go to Berlin to discuss

[1] *Bismarck-Jahrbuch*, iii. 237, 238. Now also Roon's *Denkwürdigkeiten*, ii.[4] 109 &c.

future arrangements verbally with him.' I feel the necessity of spending a few days at Reinfeld, for I have not
seen my family since May 8. On that occasion I must
get matters cleared up. I should like nothing better than
to remain in Paris, but I must know that the move and
settling in are not only for a few weeks or months; for
that my household is too large. I have never refused to
accept the presidency without a portfolio, as soon as the
King commands it. I only said that I considered the arrangement unsatisfactory. I am still prepared to enter
without a portfolio, but I cannot see any serious intention
of it. If his Majesty would say to me, November 1, or
January 1, or April 1—then I should know what I was
about, and I am not a man to make difficulties; I only ask
for a hundredth part of the consideration of which Bernstorff received such rich measure. This uncertainty takes
away all my pleasure in business, and I thank you from
my heart for every friendly service that you undertake in
order to put an end to it. If this does not soon succeed,
I must take matters as they stand, and say to myself: I
am the King's ambassador in Paris, and I will send for
chick and child to join me there on October 1. When
that is done his Majesty can dismiss me from my office,
but he can no longer compel me to move again immediately; I would rather go home to the country, for then I
should know where I am living. In my solitude I have,
with God's help, recovered my former health, and I am
better than I have been for the last ten years; but I have
not heard a single word about our political world. I
have learnt to-day, from one of my wife's letters, that the

' This was done in a letter sent from Montpellier on the same day.
Bismarck-Jahrbuch, vi. 162 &c.

King was at Doberan, else I should not have understood the D. in your letter. Nor yet had I heard that he was going to Carlsruhe on the 13th. I should no longer find his Majesty if I wanted to go there. I know, too, from experience, that apparitions of this sort are unwelcome; they lead his Majesty to assume ambitious and pushing intentions on my part, which, God knows, are very far from me. I am so well satisfied to be his Majesty's am- bassador in Paris that I would ask for nothing but the cer- tainty of remaining in this position till 1875. Procure me this or any other certainty, and I will paint angels' wings on your photograph! . . .

'What do you mean by "end of this session"? Can that be so definitely fixed beforehand? Will it not rather be merged in the winter session without any interval? And can the Chambers be closed without any conclusion about the budget? I do not want to answer with a dis- tinct negative, it depends upon the plan of campaign. I am just setting out for Montpellier, thence by way of Lyons to Paris. Please direct to me there, and give my kindest regards to your family.

' In faithful friendship,

' Your

' v. B.' [1]

In Paris I received the following telegram, the signa- ture of which had been agreed upon:

' Berlin : le 18 Septembre.

' Periculum in mora. Dépêchez-vous.

' L'oncle de Maurice,

' HENNING.'

[1] *Bismarck Letters* (6th edit.), pp. 263, 264. Also Roon's *Denkwürdig- keiten*, ii.[4] 117 &c.

Henning was the second name of Moritz Blanckenburg, Roon's nephew. Although the wording left it doubtful whether the invitation was given on Roon's own initiative, or was suggested by the King, I did not hesitate to set out.

I arrived at Berlin in the morning of September 20, and was summoned to the Crown Prince. To his question as to my view of the situation, I could only give a very cautious answer, because I had read no German papers during the last few weeks, and from a sort of *dépit* had neglected to inform myself about home affairs. The cause of my vexation was the King's having led me to believe that in six weeks at latest he would come to a decision about my future—i.e. whether I was to take up my residence in Berlin, Paris, or London—that a quarter of a year had already passed away, and that autumn was come before I knew where I was to spend the winter. I was not sufficiently acquainted with the particulars of the situation to be able to give the Crown Prince a detailed opinion; nor did I consider myself justified in expressing my views to him before I had done so to the King. The impression which the fact of my audience had made was at once discernible from Roon's statement that the King had said to him, referring to me: ' He is no good either; you see he has already been to see my son.' The bearing of this remark was not at once comprehensible to me, because I did not know that the King, having conceived the idea of abdication, assumed that I either knew or suspected it, and had therefore tried to place myself favourably with his successor.

As a matter of fact, however, the idea of the King's abdication was fresh to me when I was received at Babelsberg on September 22, and the situation only became clear to me when his Majesty defined it in some such words as these : ' I will not reign if I cannot do it in such a fashion as I can be answerable for to God, my conscience, and my subjects. But I cannot do that if I am to rule according to the will of the present majority in parliament, and I can no longer find any ministers prepared to conduct my government without subjecting themselves and me to the parliamentary majority. I have therefore resolved to lay down my crown, and have already sketched out the proclamation of my abdication, based on the motives to which I have referred.' The King showed me the document in his own handwriting lying on the table, whether already signed or not I do not know. His Majesty concluded by repeating that he could not govern without suitable ministers.

I replied that his Majesty had been acquainted ever since May with my readiness to enter the ministry; I was certain that Roon would remain with me on his side, and I did not doubt that we should succeed in completing the cabinet, supposing other members should feel themselves compelled to resign on account of my admission. After a good deal of consideration and discussion, the King asked me whether I was prepared as minister to advocate the reorganisation of the army, and when I assented he asked me further whether I would do so in opposition to the majority in parliament and its resolutions. When I asserted my willingness, he finally declared, ' Then it is my duty, with your help, to attempt to continue the battle, and I shall not abdicate.' I do not know whether he destroyed the document which was lying on the table, or whether he preserved it *in rei memoriam.*

BISMARCK

The King invited me to accompany him into the park. During the walk he gave me a programme to read, which filled eight pages of his close writing, embraced all eventualities of the politics of the time, and went into such details as the reform of the district sub-Diets. I cannot say whether this elaboration had already served as the basis of discussion with my predecessors, or whether it was to serve as a security against a policy of conservative thoroughness such as I was credited with. At the time when he was meditating my appointment, some fear of this nature had doubtless been aroused in him by his wife, of whose political understanding he had originally a very high opinion, dating from the time when his Majesty was only permitted a Crown Prince's privilege of criticising his brother; without the obligation to do better himself. In criticism the Princess was her husband's superior. The first doubts as to her intellectual superiority were wakened in him when he was compelled, instead of criticising, to act himself, and to bear the official responsibility for improvements. As soon as the tasks of the two royal persons became practical, the King's sound common sense had begun gradually to emancipate itself more and more from her ready feminine volubility.

I succeeded in convincing him that, so far as he was concerned, it was not a question of Liberal or Conservative of this or that shade, but rather of monarchical rule or parliamentary government, and that the latter must be avoided at all costs, if even by a period of dictatorship. I said: ' In this situation I shall, even if your Majesty command me to do things which I do not consider right, tell you my opinion quite openly; but if you finally persist in yours, I will rather perish with the King than forsake your Majesty in the contest with parliamentary government.' This view was at that time strong and absolute in me, because I regarded the negations and phrases of the Opposition of that day as politically disastrous in face of the national task of Prussia, and because I cherished such strong feelings of devotion and affection for William I, that the thought of perishing with him appeared to me, under the circumstances, a natural and congenial conclusion to my life.

The King tore the programme to pieces, and was about to throw them down from the bridge into the dry ditch in the park, when I reminded him that these papers in his well-known writing might fall into very wrong hands. He saw that I was right, put the pieces in his pocket to commit them to the flames, and on the same day ratified my appointment as minister and interim chairman of the ministry, which was made public on the 23rd. The King kept my nomination as President in reserve, until he had completed the correspondence on the subject with Prince von Hohenzollern, who still occupied this post constitutionally. [1]

[1] Cf. 'Kaiser Wilhelm I. und Fürst Bismarck,' in the *Münchener Allg. Zeitung*, October 7, 1890, M.A.

CHAPTER XII

RETROSPECT OF PRUSSIAN POLICY

THE royal authority with us had been weakened by a want of independence and energy in our foreign and still more in our domestic policy; and the same cause had fostered the unjust middle-class opinions about the army and its officers, and the aversion to military proposals and expenditure. In the parliamentary groups the ambition of the leaders, orators, and ministerial candidates found nourishment, and took shelter behind the national ill-temper. Since the death of Frederick the Great our policy had either lacked definite aims, or else chosen or pursued them unskilfully; the latter was the case from 1786 to 1806, when our policy began in confusion and ended in disaster. Before the definite outbreak of the French Revolution there is not a trace of a national German tendency to be found in it. The first indications of anything of the kind to be found in the confederation of princes, in the ideas of a Prussian empire, in the line of demarcation, in the acquisition of German territory, are the results, not of German, but of Prussian particularist efforts. In 1786 the chief interest was not as yet centred in national German territory but rather in the idea of territorial acquisition in Poland and before the war of 1792 the distrust between Prussia and Austria was fed less by the German than the Polish rivalry of the two Powers. In the disputes of the Thugut-Lehrbach period, the struggle for the

298

possession of Polish territory, Cracow in particular, played a more striking part than that for the hegemony of Germany, which was prominent in the second half of the present century.

At that time the question of nationality was kept more in the background; the Prussian state incorporated fresh Polish subjects quite as readily as German, if not more so, so long as they were subjects. Austria, too, had no hesitation in risking the results of the common war against France, as soon as she began to fear that the necessary forces for opposing Prussia in order to secure her own Polish interests would not be forthcoming, if they had to be employed on the frontiers of France. It is hard to say whether the situation at that time, judged by the opinions and capacities of the persons who directed it in Russia and Austria, offered any opportunity to Prussian policy to enter upon a path more profitable than that of a veto on the Oriental policy of its two Eastern neighbours, such as it exercised at the convention of Reichenbach, July 27, 1790. I cannot resist the impression that this veto was an act of unprofitable self-assertion, recalling the French *prestige*, which used up to no purpose all the authority inherited from Frederick the Great, without giving Prussia any advantage from this exhibition of power except the satisfaction of her vanity in asserting her position as a Great Power in face of the two imperial Powers' ' show of power.'

If Austria and Russia found occupation in the East, it would, I imagine, have been to the interest of their neighbour—whose power at that time was inferior to theirs—not to disturb them in it, but rather help and confirm them in their eastward aspirations, and thus weaken their pressure on our own borders. At that time Prussia, in consequence of her military arrangements, was more quickly ready to strike than her neighbours, and might, as on many subsequent occasions, have profited by this readiness, could she have refrained from premature partisanship, and, in accordance with her comparative weakness, placed herself *en vedette* instead of assuming the *prestige* of an arbiter between Austria, Russia, and the Porte.

The mistake in such situations has usually lain in the aimlessness and irresolution of the mode in which they were used and turned to advantage. The Great Elector and Frederick the Great had a clear conception of the mischief of half-measures in cases where there is a question of taking a side or threatening to do so. So long as Prussia had not attained the form of a state corresponding to some extent to German nationality; so long as—to use the expression which Prince Metternich employed to me—it was not one of the ' saturated' states, it was obliged to manage its policy *en vedette*, according to the saying of Frederick the Great quoted above. But a *vedette* has no right to exist without a fully equipped force behind it. Without this, and without the determination to make an active use of it, whether for or against one of the combatants, Prussian policy could derive no material advantage, either in Poland or Germany, from the interposition of its European influence on such occasions as that of Reichenbach; it could but awaken the annoyance and mistrust of both neighbours. To this day we can discern in the historical judgments of our chauvinistic countrymen the satisfaction with which the *rôle* of arbitrator as it might have been exercised from Berlin on the Eastern quarrel inspired Prussian self-satisfaction; in their eyes the convention of

Reichenbach is a point of maximum on the scale of ' Frederickian' policy, after which followed the descent and
downward course through the negotiations of Pillnitz, the
peace of Basle, down to Tilsit.

Had I been a minister of Frederick William II, my
advice would rather have been to support the ambition of
Austria and Russia in an eastward direction; but in return
to demand material concessions, if only in regard to the
Polish question, at that time popular, and rightly so, as
long as we did not possess Dantzic and Thorn, and the
German question had not yet been raised. At the head
of 100,000 or more capable soldiers, with the threat of
putting them into action if necessary, and leaving Austria to carry on the war against France alone, Prussian
policy in the situation then prevailing could still have
attained better results than the diplomatic triumph of
Reichenbach.

The history of the house of Austria from Charles V
onward is held to point to a whole series of neglected opportunities, for which in most cases the royal confessor for the
time being was made responsible; but the history of Prussia, even if we consider only the events of the last hundred
years, is no less rich in similar omissions. If the opportunity offered at the time of the Reichenbach convention,
rightly used, could bring about some advance, although
not a satisfactory one, in the career of Prussia, an evolution on a larger scale would have been possible as early as
1805, when Prussian policy could have been played against
France on behalf of Austria and Russia, in the military
field better than in diplomacy, but not gratis. The conditions on which the assistance was to be, or to have been,
afforded, could not be insisted on by a minister like

Haugwitz, but only by a general at the head of 150,000 men in Bohemia or Bavaria. What was *post festum* in 1806, would have had decisive results in 1805. As in Austria the confessors, so in Prussia the privy councillors and honest but *borné* adjutants-general were responsible for the neglected opportunities.

There was all the less need to give gratuitously the services which Prussian policy rendered to Russian at the peace of Adrianople in 1829 and at the suppression of the Polish rising in 1831, that the unfriendly intrigues which had occurred a little while before between the Emperor Nicholas and King Charles X were not unknown to the Berlin cabinet. The family relations between the princes were, as a rule, sufficiently genial among us to cover Russian sins, but there was a lack of reciprocity. In the year 1813 Russia had doubtless won a claim on Prussian gratitude. In February 1813, and down to the congress of Vienna, Alexander I had remained, on the whole, faithful to his promise to restore Prussia to the *status quo ante*, doubtless without neglecting Russian interests. Still it was natural that Frederick William III should entertain grateful remembrances of him. Such remembrance was still very lively among us during my childhood, until the death of Alexander in 1825. Russian Grand Dukes, generals, and detachments of soldiers, who appeared from time to time at Berlin, still enjoyed a legacy of the popularity with which the first Cossacks were welcomed among us in 1813.

Flagrant ingratitude, such as Prince Schwarzenberg proclaimed, is not only unlovely but unwise in politics as in private life. But we paid our debt, not only when the Russians were in difficulties at Adrianople in 1829, and by our attitude in Poland in 1831, but also during the whole reign of Nicholas I, who appealed less to German romanticism and good nature than Alexander I, though he was on friendly terms with his Prussian relations and with Prussian officers. During his reign we lived like Russian vassals, even in 1831, when Russia could scarcely have made way against the Poles without our help, but especially in all European combinations between 1831 and 1850, when we always accepted and honoured Russian cheques; until after 1848, when the young Austrian Emperor found more favour in the sight of the Russian than the King of Prussia, and the Russian arbitrator gave his decisions in cold and hard terms against Prussia and the German aspirations, taking full payment for the friendly services of 1831 by forcing on us the humiliation of Olmütz. Afterwards we became considerable creditors of Russia in the Crimean war and in the Polish insurrection of 1863, and though in that year we did not accept Alexander II's personal summons to war, and he showed his annoyance at this, and on the Danish question, this only proves how far Russian claims had advanced beyond equality and how they were beginning to demand actual subordination.

The deficit on our side was caused in the first place by a feeling of kinship and the habit of dependence, in which the lesser energy stood to the greater; secondly, by the mistaken supposition that Nicholas entertained the same feelings for us as Alexander I, and had the same claims on our gratitude as had originated at the time of the war of liberation. As a matter of fact, during the reign of the Emperor Nicholas, no cause rooted in the German nature presented itself to place our friendship with Russia on a footing of equality and enable us at any rate to get an advantage from it corresponding to that which Russia had derived from our assistance. A little more self-respect and confidence in our own power would have led to the recognition at St. Petersburg of our claims to reciprocity, the rather that in 1830, after the July revolution, Prussia, in spite of its cumbrous Landwehr system, was, in face of this astonishing event, for at least a year unquestionably the strongest military state in Europe, perhaps the only one that was ready to strike a blow. How greatly military preparations had been neglected during fifteen years of peace, not only in Austria but in Russia (with the sole exception perhaps of the Imperial Guard and the Grand Duke Constantine's Polish army), was proved by the weakness and dilatoriness of the preparations made by the mighty Russian Empire against the little kingdom of Warsaw.

Similar conditions prevailed at that time in the French, and still more in the Austrian army. After the July revolution Austria took more than a year to repair the damage done to the organisation of her army, sufficiently to enable her to protect her Italian interests. Austrian policy under Metternich was skilful enough to postpone any decision of the three great Eastern Powers until she herself should feel prepared to put in her word. It was only in Prussia that the military machine, cumbrous as it was, operated with precision; and had Prussian policy been able to form its own decisions, it would have had strength enough to prejudice according to its own discretion the situation of 1830 in Germany and the Netherlands. But an independent Prussian policy did not even exist in the period between 1806 and the 'forties; our policy was made alternately in Vienna and St. Petersburg.

As far as it went its independent way at Berlin between 1786 and 1806, and 1842 and 1862, criticism from the point of view of an energetic Prussian can scarcely approve it.

Before 1866 we could only claim the title of a Great Power *cum grano salis,* and after the Crimean war we considered it necessary to sue for an outward recognition of this position, by dancing attendance at the congress of Paris. We confessed that we required the testimony of other Powers in order to look upon ourselves as a Great Power. We did not feel up to the standard of Gortchakoff's speech about Italy, *une grande puissance ne se reconnaît pas, elle se révèle.* The *révélation* that Prussia was a Great Power had been previously recognised on occasion in Europe (compare Chapter v), but it was weakened by long years of cowardly policy which at last found expression in the pitiful part played by Manteuffel at Paris. Her belated admittance could not obscure the fact that a Great Power requires for its recognition, above all else, the conviction and the courage to be one. I regarded it as a deplorable lack of self-knowledge that, after all the slights that had been put upon us by Austria and all the Western Powers in general, we still felt the necessity of gaining admittance to the congress and adding our signatures to its conclusions. Our position at the Black Sea conference in London in 1870 would have proved the correctness of this view, had Prussia not pushed her way in an undignified fashion into the Paris congress. When Manteuffel returned from Paris and was my guest at Frankfort on April 20 and 21, I took the opportunity of expressing to him my regret that he had not taken *victa Catoni* for his motto, and so paved the way for our proper independent position in the eventuality of the Russo-French *rapprochement*, which the position of affairs rendered probable. There could be no doubt in the Berlin Foreign Office that the Emperor Napoleon even at that time had his eye on Russian friendship, and that authoritative circles in London regarded the conclusion of peace as premature.* How dignified and independent would have been our position if we had not forced our way in a humiliating fashion into the Paris congress, but had rather declined participation, when our invitation did not arrive at the proper time! Had we shown a suitable reserve we should have been courted when the new grouping took place; and even outwardly our position would have been more dignified, if we had not made our inclusion among the great European Powers dependent upon our diplomatic opponents, but had based it simply upon our own self-knowledge; refraining from any claim to participate in European negotiations, which were of no interest for Prussia, instead of seeking, on the analogy of the Reichenbach convention, after the vanity of *prestige*, and the discussion of things which did not concern us.

The neglected opportunities which belong to the two periods 1786 to 1806 and 1842 to 1862 were seldom understood by contemporaries, and still rarer was it for the responsibility for them to be rightly assigned. Fifty to a hundred years later the opening of archives and memoirs of those persons who had shared in the action or the knowledge, put public opinion in a position to recognise the πρῶτον ψεῦδος for the several blunders, the point of divergence into the wrong path. Frederick the Great

* ['We have been infernally humbugged,' Lord Clarendon is said to have remarked.]

left behind him a rich inheritance of authority and a belief in Prussian policy and power. His heirs, like the new
generation of to-day, were able to live for a couple of decades on the legacies of the old, without realising the
weakness and errors of their latter-day *régime*. Even
down to the battle of Jena they continued to overvalue their
own military and political ability. It was only the collapse of the following weeks that forced the court and the
people to realise the clumsiness and error which had prevailed in the management of the state. Whose clumsiness
and whose error? who was personally responsible for this
unexpected and tremendous collapse?—these are matters
which are undecided to this day.

Under an absolute monarchy—and at that time Prussia
was one—no one except the sovereign can be proved to
have any definite share of responsibility for its policy.
If the King comes to any unfortunate decisions, no one
can judge whether they are due to his own moral will, or
to the influence which the most various personalities of
male and female gender—aides-de-camp, courtiers and
political intriguers, flatterers, chatterboxes and tell-tales
—may have had upon the monarch. In the last resort
the royal signature covers everything; how it has been
obtained no one ever knows. From the monarchical point
of view, the most natural expedient is to place the responsibility for every event on the minister for the time
being. But even when the form of absolutism has made
way for the form of a constitution, the so-called ministerial responsibility in no way depends on the will of the
irresponsible monarch. True, a minister can resign if he
cannot obtain the royal signature where he considers it
necessary; but by his resignation he takes upon himself

the responsibility for its consequences, which may be much farther-reaching in other domains than in the one under dispute.

Moreover, the board character of the ministry, with its majority votes, daily compels him to compromise and surrender to his colleagues, in accordance with the Prussian ministerial constitution. A real responsibility in high politics can only be undertaken by one single directing minister, never by a numerous board with majority voting. The decision as to paths and bypaths often depends on slight but decisive changes, sometimes even on the tone and choice of expressions in an international document. Even the slightest departure from the right line often causes the distance from it to increase so rapidly that the abandoned clue cannot be recovered, and the return to the bifurcation, where it was left behind, becomes impossible. The customary official secrecy conceals for whole generations the circumstances under which the track was left; and the result of the uncertainty in which the operative connexion of things remains, produces in leading ministers, as was the case with many of my predecessors, an indifference to the material side of business, as soon as the formal side has been settled by a royal signature or by parliamentary votes. In the case of others, the conflict between their own feeling of honour, and the complications caused by the questions of jurisdiction, induces fatal nervous fevers, as in the case of Count Brandenburg, or symptoms of brain-disease, as in some of his predecessors.

It is hard to assign justly the responsibility for our policy during the reign of Frederick William IV. Humanly speaking, it must rest mainly on the King, for he never at any time had superior advisers who could direct him and his business. He retained in his own hands the power of selection among the advice, not only given by each individual minister, but also offered him with far greater frequency by more or less clever aides-de-camp, privy councillors, scholars, dishonest pushers, honest visionaries, and courtiers. And he was often a long time about selecting. It is frequently less disastrous to do the wrong thing than nothing at all. I never had the courage to profit by the opportunities which this very amiable gentleman several times gave me, occasionally in the most pressing manner, to become his minister in the years 1852 to 1856, or to further the realisation of his wishes. From the way in which he regarded me, I should have had no authority in his eyes, and his rich phantasy lacked wings as soon as it ventured on the domain of practical resolve; while I lacked the accommodating disposition which would enable me to take over and represent as a minister political tendencies in which I did not believe, or in the carrying out of which I thought the King deficient in resolution and consistency. He supported and furthered the elements of strife between his individual ministers; the friction between Manteuffel, Bodelschwingh, and Heydt, who carried on a sort of triangular duel, was agreeable to the King and served as a political aid in little private contests between royal and ministerial influence. It was with full knowledge that Manteuffel put up with the camarilla activity of Gerlach, Rauch, Niebuhr, Bunsen, Edwin Manteuffel. His policy was rather defensive than directed at any particular object; muddling along, as Count Taaffe would say, satisfied if he was protected by the royal signature. Still, pure absolutism with a par-

liament has this advantage, that it gives a feeling of responsibility for one's own actions. Far more dangerous
is the absolutism that is supported by accommodating
parliaments, and which needs no other justification than
a reference to the assent of the majority.

The next favourable situation after the Crimean war was
offered to our policy by the Italian war. Not that I believe that King William, even as Regent in 1859, would
have been disposed to cross by a sudden decision the gulf
which separated his policy at that period from that which
afterwards brought about the re-establishment of the German Empire. If the situation of that time is judged by
the standard which characterises the attitude of the Foreign Minister, von Schleinitz, in the ensuing conclusion
of the guarantee treaty of Teplitz with Austria, and its
refusal to recognise Italy, we may well doubt whether it
would have been possible at that time to urge the Regent
to a policy which would have made the employment of the
Prussian armaments dependent on concessions in the policy of the German Federation. The situation was not regarded from the point of view of a forward Prussian policy,
but rather in the light of the customary endeavours to
win the applause of the German Princes, the Austrian
Emperor, and the German press, and of the undignified
striving after an ideal prize of virtue for devotion to Germany. There was no clear conception of the nature of
the goal, the direction in which it was to be sought, or
the means of attaining it.

Under the influence of his wife and the party of the
' Wochenblatt,' the Regent was very near taking part in
the Italian war of 1859. Had he done so, the war would
have been transferred in its chief issues from an Austro-

French to a Prusso-French contest, on the Rhine. Russia, in her hatred to Austria, which at that time was still very lively, would at any rate have made a demonstration against us and Austria as soon as we had become entangled in war with France, and, from her position at the longer end of the political lever, would have calculated how far we might be permitted to be victorious. What Poland was at the time of Thugut, Germany was at this time, on the chess-board. My idea was that we ought at any rate to prepare for war, but at the same time send an ultimatum to Austria, either to accept our conditions in the German question or to look for our attack. But the fiction of a continuous and self-sacrificing devotion for ' Germany' in words only, never in deeds, the influence of the Princess and of her minister von Schleinitz, who was devoted to the Austrian interest, as well as the phrase-mongering of parliaments, associations, and the press, at that time customary, made it difficult for the Regent to test the situation by his own clear homely common sense; and there was no one in his political or personal surroundings who could explain to him how meaningless was all this phrase-making, and represent the cause of a healthy German interest. The Regent and his minister at that time believed in the truth of the saying: 'Il y a quelqu'un qui a plus d'esprit que Monsieur de Talleyrand, c'est tout le monde.' *Tout le monde*, however, in point of fact takes too long about finding out what is right, and as a rule the moment when the knowledge might be useful is already gone by before *tout le monde* gets at the back of what ought really to have been done.

It was only the internal struggles which he had to encounter as Regent and afterwards as King; only his con-

viction that his ministers of the new era were not yet in
a condition to render his subjects happy and contented, or
maintain them in obedience, and to win at the elections
and in parliament an expression of the contentment for
which he had striven and hoped; only the difficulties
which in 1862 had brought the King to resolve on abdication, that were able so far to influence his spirit and
sound judgment as to help his monarchical views of 1859
across the bridge of the Danish question, to the point of
view of 1866, i.e. from speaking to doing, from phrase to
action.

The direction of foreign policy in the very difficult
European situation was rendered even more laborious for
a minister who wished to pursue a calm and practical
policy without any dynastic sentimentality and courtier-
like Byzantinism, by powerful cross-currents. Of these
the strongest and most effectual were due to Queen Augusta and her minister Schleinitz, but there were also
other princely influences, as well as family correspondence, the insinuations of hostile elements at the court,
and no less of the Jesuit organs (Nesselrode, Stillfried,
&c.) of intriguers and capable rivals, such as Goltz and
Harry Arnim, or incapable ones, such as the former ministers and parliamentarians who wished to attain that dignity. It required all the King's honest and noble fidelity
for his first servant, to keep him from wavering in his
confidence towards me.

In the beginning of October I went as far as Jüterbogk to meet the King, who had been at Baden-Baden
for September 30, his wife's birthday, and waited for him
in the still unfinished railway station, filled with third-
class travellers and workmen, seated in the dark on an

overturned wheelbarrow. My object in taking this opportunity for an interview was to set his Majesty at rest
about a speech made by me in the Budget Commission on
September 30, which had aroused some excitement, and
which, though not taken down in shorthand, had still been
reproduced with tolerable accuracy in the newspapers.

For people who were less embittered and blinded by
ambition, I had indicated plainly enough the direction in
which I was going. Prussia—such was the point of my
speech—as a glance at the map will show, could no longer
wear unaided on its long narrow figure the panoply which
Germany required for its security; that must be equally
distributed over all German peoples. We should get no
nearer the goal by speeches, associations, decisions of
majorities; we should be unable to avoid a serious
contest, a contest which could only be settled by blood
and iron. In order to secure our success in this, the
deputies must place the greatest possible weight of blood
and iron in the hands of the King of Prussia, in order
that according to his judgment he might throw it into
one scale or the other. I had already given expression to the same idea in the House of Deputies in 1849,
in answer to Schramm on the occasion of an amnesty
debate. [1]

Roon, who was present, expressed his dissatisfaction
with my remarks on our way home, and said, among other
things, that he did not regard these ' witty digressions ' as
advantageous for our cause. For my part, I was torn between the desire of winning over members to an energetic
national policy, and the danger of inspiring the King,
whose own disposition was cautious, and shrank from

[1] Cf. the speech of March 22, 1849. *Politische Reden*, i. 76, 77.

violent measures, with mistrust in me and my intentions. My object in going to meet him at Jüterbogk was
to counteract betimes the probable effect of press criti-
cisms.

I had some difficulty in discovering from the curt
answers of the officials the carriage in the ordinary train,
in which the King was seated by himself in an ordinary
first-class carriage. The after-effect of his intercourse with
his wife was an obvious depression, and when I begged
for permission to narrate the events which had occurred
during his absence, he interrupted me with the words: ' I
can perfectly well see where all this will end. Over
there, in front of the Opera House, under my windows,
they will cut off your head, and mine a little while afterwards.'

I guessed, and it was afterwards confirmed by witnesses, that during his week's stay at Baden his mind
had been worked upon with variations on the theme of
Polignac, Strafford, and Lewis XVI. When he was silent, I answered with the short remark, '*Et après, Sire.*'
'*Après*, indeed; we shall be dead,' answered the King.
' Yes,' I continued, ' then we shall be dead; but we must
all die sooner or later, and can we perish more honourably? I, fighting for my King's cause, and your Majesty
sealing with your own blood your rights as King by the
grace of God; whether on the scaffold or the battlefield,
makes no difference to the glory of sacrificing life and
limb for the rights assigned to you by the grace of God.
Your Majesty must not think of Lewis XVI; he lived
and died in a condition of mental weakness, and does not
present a heroic figure in history. Charles I, on the
other hand, will always remain a noble historical charac-

314

ter, for after drawing his sword for his rights and losing
the battle, he did not hesitate to confirm his royal intent
with his blood. Your Majesty is bound to fight, you cannot capitulate; you must, even at the risk of bodily danger,
go forth to meet any attempt at coercion.'

As I continued to speak in this sense, the King grew
more and more animated, and began to assume the part
of an officer fighting for kingdom and fatherland. In presence of external and personal danger he possessed a rare
and absolutely natural fearlessness, whether on the field of
battle or in the face of attempts on his life; his attitude
in any external danger was elevating and inspiring. The
ideal type of the Prussian officer who goes to meet certain death in the service with the simple words, 'At your
orders,' but who, if he has to act on his own responsibility, dreads the criticism of his superior officer or of
the world more than death, even to the extent of allowing
his energy and correct judgment to be impaired by the fear
of blame and reproof—this type was developed in him to
the highest degree. Hitherto, on his journey, he had
only asked himself whether, under the superior criticism
of his wife and public opinion in Prussia, he would be able
to keep steadfast on the road on which he was entering with
me. The influence of our conversation in the dark railway compartment counteracted this sufficiently to make
him regard the part which the situation forced upon him
more from the standpoint of the officer. He felt as
though he had been touched in his military honour, and
was in the position of an officer who has orders to hold
a certain position to the death, no matter whether he
perishes in the task or not. This set him on a course
of thought which was quite familiar to him; and in a few

minutes he was restored to the confidence which he had
lost at Baden, and even recovered his cheerfulness. To
give up his life for King and Fatherland was the duty of
an officer; still more that of a King, as the first officer in
the land. As soon as he regarded his position from the
point of view of military honour, it had no more terror for
him than the command to defend what might prove a desperate position would have for any ordinary Prussian offi·
cer. This raised him above the anxiety about the criticism which public opinion, history, and his wife might
pass on his political tactics. He fully entered into the
part of the first officer in the Prussian monarchy, for whom
death in the service would be an honourable conclusion to
the task assigned him. The correctness of my judgment
was confirmed by the fact that the King, whom I had
found at Jüterbogk weary, depressed, and discouraged,
had, even before we arrived at Berlin, developed a cheer-
ful, I might almost say joyous and combative disposition,
which was plainly evident to the ministers and officials
who received him on his arrival.

Even if the alarming historical reminiscences which
had been presented to the King at Baden as proofs of
short-sighted blundering could only dishonestly or fan-
cifully be applied to our conditions, our situation was still
sufficiently serious. Some progressive journals hoped to
see me picking oakum for the benefit of the state; and
on February 17, 1863, the House of Deputies declared
by 274 to 45 that ministers were responsible with their
persons and fortunes for unconstitutional expenditure. It
was suggested to me, that for the sake of securing my
estate I should make it over to my brother. But the ces-
sion of my property to my brother in order to avoid its

confiscation, which on a change of sovereign might not have been impossible, would have given an impression of alarm and anxiety about money matters which were repugnant to me. Besides this, my seat in the Upper House was attached to Kniephof.

CHAPTER XIII

DYNASTIES AND STOCKS

NEVER, not even at Frankfort, did I doubt that the key to German politics was to be found in princes and dynasties, not in publicists, whether in parliament and the press, or on the barricades. The opinion of the cultivated public as uttered in parliament and the press might promote and sustain the determination of the dynasties, but perhaps provoked their resistance more frequently than it urged them forward in the direction of national unity. The weaker dynasties leant for shelter upon the national cause, rulers and houses that felt themselves more capable of resistance mistrusted the movement, because with the promotion of German unity there was a prospect of the diminution of their independence in favour of the central authority or the popular representative body. The Prussian dynasty might anticipate that the hegemony in the future German Empire would eventually fall to it, with an increase of consideration and power. It could foresee its own advantage, so far as it were not absorbed by a national parliament, in the lowering of status so much dreaded by the other dynasties. From the time that the idea of the dual entity, Austria-Prussia, under the influence of which I had come to the Frankfort Federal Diet, had given place to the sense of the necessity of defending our position against attacks and stratagems on the part of the president, when once I had received the impression that the mutual support of Austria and Prussia was a youthful dream, resulting from the after effects of the war of liberation and the notions of schools, and had convinced myself that the Austria with which I had until then reckoned did not exist for Prussia, I acquired the conviction that on the basis of the authority of the Federal Diet it would not be possible even to recover for Prussia that position which she had held in the *Bund* before the events of March, to say nothing of such a reform of the federal constitution as might have afforded the German people a prospect of the realisation of their pretension to a position recognised by international law as one of the great European nations.

I remember a crisis in my views which occurred in Frankfort when Prince Schwartzenberg's dispatch of December 7, 1850, till then unknown to me, first came under my eyes. In this he represents the results of Olmütz as if it had depended upon him to ' humiliate' Prussia or magnanimously to pardon her. The Mecklenburg envoy, Herr von Oertzen, my honourable Conservative confidant and colleague in dualist policy, with whom I discussed the dispatch, attempted to salve my wounded Prussian feelings. Notwithstanding the poor show, so humiliating to those feelings, which we had made at Olmütz and Dresden, I had come to Frankfort well disposed towards Austria. The insight into Schwartzenberg's policy of *avilir puis démolir*, which I there obtained by documentary evidence, dispelled my youthful illusions. The Gordian knot of German circumstance was not to be untied by the gentle methods of dual policy, could only be cut by the sword: it came to this, that the King of Prussia, conscious or unconscious, and with him the Prussian army, must be gained for the national cause, whether from the

'Borussian' point of view one regarded the hegemony of Prussia or from the national point of view the unification of Germany as the main object: both aims were co-extensive. So much was clear to me, and I hinted at it when in the budget committee (September 30, 1862) I made the much misrepresented deliverance concerning iron and blood (p. 313).

Prussia was nominally a Great Power, at any rate the fifth. The transcendent genius of Frederick the Great had given her this position, and it had been re-established by the mighty achievements of the people in 1813. But for the chivalrous attitude observed under the influence of Stein, or at any rate under German influence, by the Emperor Alexander I from 1812 to the Congress of Vienna, it would have remained a question whether the diplomatic methods of the Humboldts and Hardenbergs of that day, and the timidity of Frederick William III, would have sufficed to turn the national enthusiasm of four million Prussians—the population was no larger at the peace of Tilsit—and of perhaps an equal number of sympathisers in Old-Prussian or German lands, to such practical account as to effect even the re-modelling of the Prussian state as it took place in 1815. Prussia's material weight did not then correspond to her moral significance and her achievement in the war of liberation.

In order that German patriotism should be active and effective, it needs as a rule to hang on the peg of dependence upon a dynasty; independent of dynasty it rarely comes to the rising point, though in theory it daily does so, in parliament, in the press, in public meeting; in practice the German needs either attachment to a dynasty or the goad of anger, hurrying him into action: the latter phenomenon, however, by its own nature is not perma-

nent. It is as a Prussian, a Hanoverian, a Wurtem-
berger, a Bavarian or a Hessian, rather than as a German,
that he is disposed to give unequivocal proof of patriotism; and in the lower orders and the parliamentary groups
it will be long before it is otherwise. We cannot say
that the Hanoverian, Hessian, and other dynasties were
at any special pains to win the affections of their subjects; but nevertheless the German patriotism of their
subjects is essentially conditioned by their attachment to
the dynasty after which they call themselves. It is not
differences of stock, but dynastic relations upon which in
their origin the centrifugal elements repose. It is not
attachment to Swabian, Lower Saxon, Thuringian, or other
particular stock that counts for most, but the dynastic
incorporation with the people of some severed portion of a
ruling princely family, as in the instances of Brunswick,
Brabant, and Wittelsbach dynasties. The cohesion of the
kingdom of Bavaria does not rest merely on the Bajuvarian
stock as it is found in South Bavaria and in Austria: the
Swabian of Augsburg, the Alleman of the Palatinate, the
Frank of the Main, though of widely different blood, call
themselves Bavarians with as much satisfaction as does
the Old-Bavarian at Munich or Landshut, and for no other
reason than that they have been connected with the latter
for three generations through the common dynasty. It is
to dynastic influences that those stocks which present the
most marked characteristics, as the Low-German, the *Platt-
Deutsch*, the Saxon, owe their greater depth and distinct-
ness of differentiation. The German's love of Fatherland
has need of a prince on whom it can concentrate its attachment. Suppose that all the German dynasties were
suddenly deposed; there would then be no likelihood

that the German national sentiment would suffice to hold all Germans together from the point of view of international law amid the friction of European politics, even in the form of federated Hanse towns and imperial village communes. The Germans would fall a prey to more closely welded nations if they once lost the tie which resides in the princes' sense of community of rank.

History shows that in Germany the Prussian stock is that of which the individual character is most strongly stamped, and yet no one could decisively answer the question whether, supposing the Hohenzollern dynasty and all its rightful successors to have passed away, the political cohesion of Prussia would survive. Is it quite certain that the eastern and the western divisions, that Pomeranians and Hanoverians, natives of Holstein and Silesia, of Aachen and Königsberg, would then continue as they now are, bound together in the indisruptible unity of the Prussian state? Or Bavaria—if the Wittelsbach dynasty were to vanish and leave not a trace behind, would Bavaria continue to hold together in isolated unity? Some dynasties have many memories which are not exactly of the kind to inspire attachment in the heterogeneous fragments out of which their states have, as a matter of history, been formed. Schleswig-Holstein has absolutely no dynastic memories, least of all any opposed to the House of Gottorp, and yet the prospect of the possible formation there of a small, independent, brand-new little court with ministers, court-marshals, and orders, in which the life of a petty state should be sustained at the cost of what Austria and Prussia would manage in the *Bund*, called forth very strong particularist movements in the Elbe duchies. The Grand Duchy of Baden has hardly a dynastic memory since the

time of the Margrave Ludwig before Belgrade; the rapid
growth of this little principality under French protection
in the confederation of the Rhine, the court life of the last
princes of the old line, the matrimonial alliance with the
Beauharnais house, the Caspar Hauser story, the revolutionary proceedings of 1832, the banishment of the Grand
Duke Leopold, the citizens' patron, the banishment of
the reigning house in 1849, have not been able to break
the power which subservience to dynasty has in that
country, and Baden in 1866 fought against Prussia and the
German idea because constrained thereto by the dynastic
interests of the reigning house.

The other nations of Europe have need of no such
go-between for their patriotism and national sentiment.
Poles, Hungarians, Italians, Spaniards, Frenchmen would
under any or without any dynasty preserve their homoge-
neous national unity. The Teutonic stocks of the north,
the Swedes and the Danes, have shown themselves pretty
free from dynastic sentiment; and in England, though
external respect for the Crown is demanded by good society, and the formal maintenance of monarchy is held expedient by all parties that have hitherto had any share in government, I do not anticipate the disruption of the nation,
or that such sentiments as were common in the time of the
Jacobites would attain to any practical form, if in the
course of its historical development the British people
should come to deem a change of dynasty or the transition
to a republican form of government necessary or expedient.
The preponderance of dynastic attachment, and the use of
a dynasty as the indispensable cement to hold together a
definite portion of the nation calling itself by the name
of the dynasty is a specific peculiarity of the German Em-

pire. The particular nationalities, which among us have shaped themselves on the bases of dynastic family and possession, include in most cases heterogeneous elements, whose cohesion rests neither on identity of stock nor on similarity of historical development, but exclusively on the fact of some (in most cases questionable) acquisition by the dynasty whether by the right of the strong, or hereditary succession by affinity or compact of inheritance, or by some reversionary grant obtained from the imperial Court as the price of a vote.

Whatever may be the origin of this factitious union of particularist elements, its result is that the individual German readily obeys the command of a dynasty to harry with fire and sword, and with his own hands to slaughter his German neighbours and kinsfolk as a result of quarrels unintelligible to himself. To examine whether this characteristic be capable of rational justification is not the problem of a German statesman, so long as it is strongly enough pronounced for him to reckon upon it. The difficulty of either abolishing or ignoring it, or making any advance in theory towards unity without regard to this practical limitation, has often proved fatal to the champions of unity; conspicuously so in the advantage taken of the favourable circumstances in the national movements of 1848–50. The attachment of the modern Guelf party to the old dynasty I fully understand, and to that party perhaps I should myself have belonged had I been born an Old-Hanoverian. But in that case I should never have been able to escape the influence of the national German sentiment, or be surprised if the *vis majeure* of the collective nationality were relentlessly to annul my liege-loyalty and personal predilection. How to fall with a good grace!

solicitude to solve that problem accords in politics—and not merely in German politics—with other and better justified aspirations; and the Elector of Brunswick's inability to achieve this result impairs in some degree the sympathy which the loyalty of her vassals inspires in me. In the German national sentiment I see the preponderant force always elicited by the struggle with particularism; for particularism—Prussian particularism too—came into being only by resistance to the collective German community, to Emperor and Empire, in revolt from both, leaning first on papal, then on French, in all cases on foreign support, all alike damaging and dangerous to the German community. In regard to the policy of the Guelfic efforts, their earliest historical landmark, the revolt of Henry the Lion before the battle of Legnano, the desertion of Emperor and Empire in the crisis of a most severe and perilous struggle, is for all time decisive.

Dynastic interests are justified in Germany so far as they fit in with the common national imperial interests: the two may very well go hand in hand; and a duke loyal to the Empire in the old sense is in certain circumstances more serviceable to the community than would be direct relations between the Emperor and the duke's vassals. So far, however, as dynastic interests threaten us once more with national disintegration and impotence, they must be reduced to their proper measure.

The German people and its national life cannot be portioned out as private possessions of princely houses. It has always been clear to me that this reflection applies to the electoral house of Brandenburg as well as to the Bavarian, the Guelf, or other houses; I should have been weaponless against the Brandenburg princely house, if in

dealing with it I had needed to reinforce my German national feeling by rupture and resistance; in the predesti-
nation of history,however, it so fell out that my courtier-
talents sufficed to gain the King, and with him by
consequence his army, for the national cause. I have
had perhaps harder battles to fight against Prussian particularism than against the particularism of the other German states and dynasties, and my relation to the Emperor
William I as his born subject made these battles all the
harder for me. Yet in the end, despite the strongly
dynastic policy of the Emperor, but thanks to his national
policy which, dynastically justified, became ever stronger
in critical moments, I always succeeded in gaining his
countenance for the German side of our development, and
that too when a more dynastic and particularist policy
prevailed on all other hands. This, as I was situated at
Nicolsburg, I was only able to effect with the help of the
Crown Prince. The territorial sovereignty of the individual princes had in the course of German history reached
an unnaturally high development; the individual dynasties, Prussia not excepted, had never a better historical
right than under the Hohenstaufen and Charles V to partition the German people among them as their private
property and claim the sovereign's share in its carcass.

The unlimited sovereignty of the dynasties, of the imperial orders, of the imperial cities, and imperial village
communes was won by revolution at the cost of the nation
and its unity. It has always impressed me with a sense of
the unnatural that the frontier line which, lost to view in
moor and heath between Salzwedel and Lüchow, divides
the Lower Saxon population of the Old Mark from the
Lower Saxon population of Brunswick, should yet assign

these two *Platt-Deutsch* speaking populations to two distinct, and, as might in certain circumstances happen, hostile bodies politic, the one ruled from Berlin, the other formerly from London, latterly from Hanover, the right eye as it were fixed on the east and the left eye on the west, so that the peaceable peasants of this district, similar in type and in the intercourse of intermarriage, might be compelled to fire on one another, in the interests on the one hand of Guelfs and Habsburgs, on the other hand of Hohenzollerns. The mere possibility of this shows the depth and strength of the influence of dynastic attachments upon the Germans. That the dynasties have at all times been stronger than press and parliament is established by the fact that in 1866 countries belonging to the *Bund*, whose dynasties lay within the sphere of Austrian influence, disregarded national policy and sided with Austria, those alone which lay under the Prussian guns throwing in their lot with Prussia. Hanover, Hesse, and Hanau were of course not in the latter category, since they thought Austria strong enough to refuse compliance with the Prussian demands, and conquer. In consequence they paid the reckoning, since it proved impossible to reconcile King William to the idea that Prussia at the head of the North German confederation hardly needed an accession of territory. Certain however it is that, as of old, so also in 1866, the material force of the confederate states followed the dynasties and not the parliaments, and that Saxon, Hanoverian, and Hessian blood was spilt, not to advance but to retard the unification of Germany.

The dynasties formed everywhere the points about which the German impulse towards segregation set its crystals in closer array.

CHAPTER XIV

THE MINISTRY OF CONFLICT

In the distribution of offices, for which the choice of candidates was limited, the portfolio of Finance was that which caused the least delay; it was allotted to Charles von Bodelschwingh, who had already held it under Manteuffel from 1851 to 1858. He was brother of Ernst von Bodelschwingh, who had resigned the Ministry of the Interior in March 1848. It was soon manifest indeed that he and Count Itzenplitz, who received the portfolio of Commerce, were not competent heads of their departments. Both limited themselves to appending their signatures to the resolutions of their expert advisers, and perhaps accommodating matters when the conclusions of advisers, half Liberal, half hidebound in narrow departmental ideas, were likely to come into collision with the policy of the King and his ministry. The majority of these highly expert members of the Department of Finance were at heart with the opposition against the ministry of conflict, which they regarded as a brief episode in the progressive liberalisation of the bureaucratic machine; and though the most able of them were too conscientious to hamper the action of the government, yet, when their official sense of duty permitted, they offered a passive resistance, which was at any rate not inconsiderable. This state of things produced a strange situation: von Bodelschwingh, who in respect of his personal convictions constituted the Extreme Right of the ministry, commonly gave his vote on the Extreme Left.

Equally unfit was the Minister of Commerce, Count Itzenplitz, to steer for himself his overladen ministerial bark : he allowed himself to be borne along by the current which his subordinates made for him. Perhaps it would have been impossible to find for the manifold ramifications of the Ministry of Commerce of that day a chief who would have been qualified to lead his subordinates in all the technical matters which fell within his province; but Count Itzenplitz was far less *au fait* in the solution of the problems which came before him than, for example, von der Heydt, and in technical questions fell all but helplessly under the guidance of the experts, Delbrück in particular. Moreover, he was of a yielding disposition and lacked the energy needful for the administration of so great a department. Dishonest practices were imputed to certain prominent colleagues in the Ministry of Commerce. To a man of honour, and such the chief certainly was, this was in the last degree disquieting; yet he hardly knew how to proceed, because the technical assistance of the officials whom he himself suspected seemed to him indispensable. Support for my policy I could not expect from either of the colleagues I am speaking of, whether I estimated their powers of comprehending it or the measure of good-will which they might have to spare for me, a junior President not originally belonging to the service.

I found von Jagow, Minister of the Interior, a minister who, by the animation of his tone, his verbosity and dogmatism in discussion, soon incurred the dislike of his colleagues in such a degree as to cause him to be replaced by Count Frederick Eulenburg. His character is shown by an experience which we had of him after he had left us and been installed in the place of ' Oberpräsident ' at Potsdam. Pending certain negotiations of importance to the city of Berlin he acted as departmental intermediary between the government and the communal authorities. By reason of the urgency of the business the Head Burgomaster was requested to repair to Potsdam, receive by word of mouth the proposals of the ' Oberpräsident ' in regard to a crucial point, and make his report at an evening meeting of the ministry called for the express purpose. The Burgomaster was closeted for two hours with the ' Oberpräsident,' but when he presented himself at the meeting to make his report he explained that he had none to make, because during the two hours that elapsed between his trains he had not been able to address a remark to the ' Oberpräsident.' He had persisted to the verge of discourtesy in attempting to state his question, but had always and with ever increasing energy been silenced by his superior with the words : ' Permit me—I have not yet done ; have the goodness to let me finish what I have to say.' On the score of business the report of the ' Oberbürgermeister ' was vexatious, but by recalling former personal experiences it provoked some merriment.

The talents of my Agricultural colleague, von Selchow, did not correspond to his antecedent reputation in provincial administration. The King had intended to give him the Ministry of the Interior, then of all offices the most important. After a long conversation, in which I made the acquaintance of von Selchow, I begged his Majesty to abandon that idea, because I thought von Selchow unequal to the demands of the office, and proposed in his stead Count Frederick von Eulenburg. Both gentlemen had masonic relations with the King, and had only been offered place in December during the difficulties which attended the completion of the administration. The King had doubts of Count Eulenburg's practical command of the administrative detail belonging to the Home department, and was disposed to give him the Ministry of Commerce, that of Agriculture to Itzenplitz, the Home Office to Selchow. I explained to him at large that, in respect of practical knowledge of departmental work, Eulenburg and Selchow were pretty much on a par, and that in any case that was to be looked for rather from their advisers than from themselves, that in this case I laid more stress on personal endowments, address, and knowledge of men than on antecedent technical training. I was willing to allow that Eulenburg was indolent and fond of pleasure, but on the other hand he was judicious and ready, and if as Minister of the Interior he should by-and-by be called upon to stand foremost in the breach, the need of defending himself and returning the blows which he received would spur him into activity. The King at last gave in to me, and to-day I still think that in the circumstances my selection was right; for however I may myself have from time to time suffered by my friend Eulenburg's want of industry and conscientiousness, yet when he was in the mood for work he was an able coadjutor, and he was always a well-bred gentleman, though not entirely devoid of jealousy and touchiness in regard to me. When he was called upon for more continuous, more self-denying, more strenuous exertions than ordinary, he would fall a prey to nervous disorders. At all events he and Roon were the most eminent members of the ministry of conflict.

Roon, however, was the only one of my later colleagues

who at my entrance upon office knew of its intended consequences and the common plan of operations, and discussed the latter with me. He was unequalled in the
loyalty, staunchness, and resourcefulness with which, before and after my accession to power, he helped to sur-
mount the crisis in which the state had been involved by
the 'new era' experiment. He understood his department
and governed it, was our best speaker, a man of good wits,
and not to be shaken in the sentiments of an honourable
Prussian officer. He shared with Eulenburg his perfect
comprehension of political questions, but was a more consequent thinker, safer, and more circumspect. His private
life was without reproach. My friendship with him dated
from the days of my boyhood—from 1833, when he spent
some time on surveying business at my father's house; and
I have sometimes suffered under his wrath, which readily
rose to a point at which it endangered his health. While he
was holding the office of President, which I had relinquished
to him on account of ill-health in 1873, pushing people like
Harry Arnim and young military officers, the same who
with their allies in the 'Kreuzzeitung' and in the columns
of the 'Reichsglocke' were working against me, reverted
to him, and attempted to estrange him from me. His ten-
ure of the presidency came to an end on the initiative of the
rest of my colleagues without any co-operation on my part.
They missed in him—his irascibility grew with years, nor
was he favourably impressed by our coadjutors in civil business—that formal courtesy which they demanded in intercourse with their colleagues, and made overtures to me,
and confidentially through Eulenburg to the King, for my
resumption of office. The result was that, without my will
and to my regret, chiefly through gossipmongering, there

came to be in Roon's last years not exactly a coldness, but a certain distance between us, and on my side the sense that my best friend and comrade had not confronted the lies and calumnies which were systematically circulated about me as decisively as I hope I should have done if his case had been mine.

The Minister of Religion, von Mühler, nearly resembled his successor, von Gossler, in the manner in which he applied himself to business, except that he was influenced by the energy and amateur participation in affairs of his clever and, when she saw fit, amiable wife, and was probably governed by her stronger will. That, of course, in the first instance, I did not learn by direct observation; it could only be inferred from the impression which the two personages left on my mind in social intercourse. I remember that at Gastein, as early as August 1865, I was compelled to insist to the point of discourtesy on having a private interview with von Mühler in regard to a certain royal mandate before I could succeed in inducing the ' Frau Ministerin' to leave us alone. The occurrence of such a necessity brought in its train misunderstandings which did not indeed intrude into my business relations with him in the course of his practical conduct of affairs, but yet did impair the harmony of our familiar intercourse. Frau von Mühler took her direction in politics not from her husband, but from the Queen, with whom she sought above all things to keep in touch. The atmosphere of the court, questions of precedence, openly declared intimacy with a royal person, exert not seldom an influence on ' Ministerfrauen' which makes itself felt in politics; the personal policy of the Empress Augusta, a policy which usually ran counter to the interests of the state, found in

Frau von Mühler a ready instrument, and von Mühler himself, though a keen-sighted and honourable official, was not decided enough in his convictions to refuse concessions to domestic peace which could only be made at the cost of the state, when they could pass unnoticed.

It was perhaps from his practice as Attorney-General, that the Minister of Justice, Count zur Lippe, had retained his habit of making the most cutting remarks with a smiling face and a supercilious air of superiority; whereby he gave offence both in parliament and to his colleagues. He stood with Bodelschwingh on our Extreme Right, and defended his own line more keenly than Bodelschwingh, because he was sufficiently *au fait* in the details of his department to follow his personal convictions, whereas Bodelschwingh could not manage the business of his office without the willing co-operation of his practical advisers, who in their political views inclined far more to the Left than either their chief or the ministry at large.

The question of constitutional law, which was the subject of the Conflict, and the view thereof taken by the ministry and approved by the King, are set forth in a letter from his Majesty to Lieutenant-Colonel von Vincke at Olbendorf near Grottkau. The letter was noticed at the time in the press, but has never, so far as I remember, been published,[1] though it is the more deserving of publicity, inasmuch as it affords an explanation of the attitude of the King on the question of the indemnity.

[1] It is published in L. Schneider, *Aus dem Leben Wilhelms I*, vol. i. 194-7.

THE MINISTRY OF CONFLICT

New Year's Day 1863 brought to the King a congratulatory letter from Vincke which concluded with the words: 'The people are loyal to your Majesty, but tenacious also of the right which Article 99 of the Constitution unequivocally guarantees to them. God in His grace avert the unhappy consequences of a great misunderstanding!'

The King replied on January 2, 1863: ' To your kind wishes for the New Year I return my best thanks. That the New Year opens no agreeable prospect needs no proof. But how you should run on to the horn of the idea that I do not know the temper of the vast majority of the people is to me incomprehensible; nor can you have read my answers to the many deputations that have presented loyal addresses. Again and again have I repeated that my confidence in my people is unshaken because I know that it is reciprocated; but those who would rob me of my people's love and confidence, them I condemn because their plans can only be carried into effect if this confidence is shaken. And that they deem this an end justifying all means is known to all the world, for only lying, only fraud and falsehood can bring their projects to maturity.

'You continue: " The people demand that effect be given to Article 99 of the Constitution." I should like to know how many of them know the tenor of Article 99, or have even so much as heard of it. That however is neither here nor there, for the clause exists for the government and must be complied with. Who then has made it impossible that effect should be given to it? Have I not made in winter session and renewed in summer session the sacrifice of four millions, and accordingly modified, alas, the military budget? Have I not, alas, made several other sacrifices in order to show that the government is prepared to make advances towards the new House? And what has been the consequence? That the House of Representatives has acted as if I had made no advances towards it, has exerted itself to secure ever more and more concessions, which in the end would have the effect of making government impossible. He who avails himself of his right for such a purpose as that, i.e. who reduces the budget to such a point that the whole business of government comes to an end, is only fit for a madhouse. In what clause of the Constitution is it laid down that only the government is to make concessions, and the representatives never? After I had made mine in unheard-of amplitude it was for the House of Representatives to make theirs. This, however, the House would on no terms do, and the so-called "episode" made it clearer than sunlight that we were to be beset with snare after snare, into which even your kinsmen Patow and Schwerin fell through Bockum-Dolffs's bad behaviour. A further abatement of 234,000 reichsthalers must be made for 1862 in order to carry the budget, though the kernel of the question could not be discussed until 1863; this was expressly stated in print; and when I consent, then for the first time Bockum-Dolffs explains that on their side, that is on the side of his political friends, this consent can only be accepted if a pledge be given forthwith in the committee, and next day in the whole House a measure be introduced, for the reduction of the term of service to two years. And when I refuse to consent, Bockum-Dolffs derides us in his press: "Now think," he says, "of the shamelessness of the government, that it should expect the House to offer peace at the price of

234,000 reichsthalers." And yet was it only by the House that peace was offered? Was any more infamous misrepresentation ever made for the purpose of traducing the government and bewildering the people?

' The House of Representatives has availed itself of its right, and reduced the budget.

' The Upper House has availed itself of its right and thrown out the reduced budget *en bloc*.

' What does the Constitution prescribe in such a case?

' Nothing.

' Since then, as shown above, the House of Representatives so used its right as to bring army and country alike to nought, it became incumbent on me to intervene in the interests of this "nought," and like a prudent head of a household to pilot the household through its straits, and give account afterwards. Who then has made compliance with Article 99 impossible? Not I for certain.

' WILLIAM.'

CHAPTER XV

CONTEMPORANEOUS and not unconnected with the revolution in Italy, a movement began in Poland, the springs of which lay in the distress of the country, the observance by the Church of the national patriotic festivals, and the excitement which prevailed in the rural associations. Towards this movement feeling in St. Petersburg remained for a good while undecided, being dominated in about equal measure by absolutist principles and Polish sympathies. In the higher circles of Russian society the influences which made for Poland were connected with the now outspoken demand for a constitution. It was felt as a degradation that cultivated people like the Russians should be denied institutions which existed in all European nations, and should have no voice in the management of their own affairs. The division of opinion on the Polish question penetrated the highest military circles, and led to a hot dispute between Count Lambert, Governor of Warsaw, and Governor-General Gerstenberg, which terminated with the unexplained death by violence of the latter (January 1862). I was present at his interment in one of the evangelical churches in St. Petersburg. Those Russians who demanded a constitution for themselves pleaded at times in excuse for the Poles that they were not governable by Russians, and that as they grew more civilised they became entitled to a share in the administration of their country.

338

This view was also represented by Prince Gortchakoff, who would have found in parliamentary institutions a sphere in which his eloquence might have gained European éclat, while his craving for popularity rendered him powerless to withstand the liberal tendencies of Russian ' society.' He was the first to sound the note of applause on the acquittal of Vera Sassulitch (April 11, 1878).

The conflict of opinion was very lively in St. Petersburg when I left that capital in April 1862, and it so continued throughout my first year of office. I took charge of the Foreign Office under the impression that the insurrection which had broken out on January 1, 1863, brought up the question not only of the interests of our eastern provinces, but also that wider one, whether the Russian cabinet were dominated by Polish or anti-Polish proclivities, by an effort after Russo-Polish fraternisation in the anti-German Panslavist interest or by one for mutual reliance between Russia and Prussia. The policy of fraternisation found its more sincere adherents among the Russians; the Polish nobility and clergy hardly anticipated any result from it, or proposed it as the definitive end. Hardly a single Pole was there for whom the policy of fraternisation meant more than a tactical move designed to deceive credulous Russians so long as necessity or expediency required. In the Polish nobility and clergy fraternisation with Russians excited, not quite, but almost as unalterable a repugnance as fraternisation with Germans; the greater strength of the latter antipathy being due not merely to race, but to the belief that Germans would never submit to the direction of the common policy by Polish statesmen, whereas Russians might.

For the German future of Prussia the attitude of Rus-

sia was a question of great importance. A philo-Polish
Russian policy was calculated to vivify that Russo-French
sympathy against which Prussia's effort had been directed
since the peace of Paris, and indeed on occasion earlier,
and an alliance (friendly to Poland) between Russia and
France, such as was in the air before the Revolution of
July, would have placed the Prussia of that day in a difficult position. It was our interest to oppose the party in
the Russian cabinet which had Polish proclivities, even
when they were the proclivities of Alexander I.

That Russia herself afforded no security against fraternisation with Poland I was able to gather from confidential intercourse with Gortchakoff and the Czar himself. Czar Alexander was at that time not indisposed to
withdraw from part of Poland, the left bank of the Vistula
at any rate—so he told me in so many words—while he
made unemphatic exception of Warsaw, which would always be desirable as a garrison town, and belonged strate-
gically to the Vistula fortress triangle. Poland, he said,
was for Russia a source of unrest and dangerous European
complications; its Russification was forbidden by the difference of religion and the defective capacity for administration among Russian officials. Were it our task to Ger-
manise Poland, we should be equal to it, because the German population was more cultivated than the Polish. The
Russ had not that sense of superiority which was needful
for ruling the Pole; Russian administration must therefore
be limited to as small a portion of the population as the
geographical situation permitted, i.e. to the line of the
Vistula with Warsaw as *tête de pont*.

I can form no judgment how far the policy thus expounded by the Czar had been maturely considered. It

must have been discussed with statesmen, for I have never known the Czar open his mind to me in regard to a question of policy on his own entirely independent personal initiative. This conversation took place at the time when my recall was already probable, and my expression, not merely polite but entirely truthful, of regret at my recall and willingness to remain at St. Petersburg was misunderstood by the Czar and elicited from him the question whether I were inclined to enter the Russian service. To this I returned a courteous negative, while emphasising my desire to remain at St. Petersburg as Prussian ambassador. It would then have been not displeasing to me if the Czar had taken steps to retain me, for the idea of becoming the instrument of the policy of the ' new era,' whether as minister or as ambassador at Paris or London, without the prospect of helping forward our policy, was by no means seductive. I knew not how at London or Paris I could serve my country according to my convictions, whereas my influence with Czar Alexander and his principal statesmen had its importance for our interests. As for becoming Foreign Minister, I had then just as lief have taken a sea-bath in cold weather; but not all these feelings together were strong enough to induce me to make an attempt to determine my own future or to address a petition to Czar Alexander for such a purpose.

When, after all, I had become minister, domestic took precedence of foreign policy. However, of our foreign relations I was most nearly interested in those which subsisted between us and Russia by reason of my immediate past; and my efforts were directed to assure for our policy, if possible, the continuance of that influence which we possessed in St. Petersburg. It was obvious that, so far as concerned Germany, Prussian policy had no support to expect from Austria. It was not likely that the benevolence with which France regarded our growing strength, and the progress made towards the unification of Germany, would in the long run prove sincere; but that was no reason for neglecting to turn to account the transitory and miscalculated support and furtherance which Napoleon afforded us. With Russia we stood on the same footing as with England, in so far as with neither had we divergent interests of capital importance, and with both were united by an ancient amity. From England we might expect platonic goodwill, with letters and newspaper articles full of good advice, but hardly more. The support of the Czar, on the other hand, as the Hungarian expedition of Nicholas had shown, meant in certain circumstances more than mere benevolent neutrality. That he would be actuated by mere regard for us was not to be supposed; but it was certainly no chimerical idea that in case of attempted French intervention in the German question Czar Alexander would, at any rate by his diplomacy, assist us in defeating it. The bent of this monarch's policy, which justified my calculation, was still manifest in 1870, whereas the friendly neutrality of England was then found compatible with French sympathies. I held, therefore, that every sympathy which, in opposition to many of his subjects and highest officials, Alexander II cherished for us, was on all accounts to be fostered by us as far as was necessary to secure, if possible, that Russia should not take part against us. It was not then possible to forecast with certainty whether and how long the Czar's friendship would remain a realisable political asset. In any case, however, simple common sense enjoined us not to let it fall into the possession of our enemies, whom we might discern in the Poles, the philo-Polish Russians, and, ultimately, probably in the French. Austria was then preoccupied with her rivalry with Prussia on German territory and could the more easily come to terms with the Polish movement because, notwithstanding the memories of 1846 and the price then set on the heads of the Polish nobles, she still retained more of their sympathy and the sympathy of the Polish clergy than either Prussia or Russia.

To harmonise the Austro-Polish with the Russo-Polish plans of fraternisation will always be difficult; but the considerate treatment which in 1863 Austria, in concert with the Western Powers, accorded to the Polish movement showed that she had no fear of Russian rivalry in a resuscitated Poland. Thrice had she, in April, in June, and on August 12, joined with France and England in making representations at St. Petersburg in the interest of Poland. 'We have,' so runs the Austrian note of June 18,[1] 'laboured to ascertain the conditions under which peace and quiet can be restored to the kingdom of Poland, and have come to the conclusion that they may be summed up in the following six points, which we commend to the consideration of the cabinet of St. Petersburg: 1. Complete and universal amnesty; 2. A national representative system participating in legislative functions and invested with an effective control; 3. The appointment of Poles to public offices in such manner that a separate national administration may be formed capable of inspiring confidence in the country; 4. Perfect and entire liberty of conscience, and abolition of the restrictions upon the exercise of the Catholic religion; 5. Exclusive use of the Polish

---

[1] In the French text in the *State Archives*, v. 354 sqq. No. 887.

tongue as the official language for the purposes of administrative and judicial business and public instruction; 6. The establishment of a regular and legal system of recruiting.'

Gortchakoff's proposal that Russia, Austria, and Prussia should unite to determine the destiny of their respective Polish subjects was rejected by the Austrian government with the declaration 'that the accord already established between the three cabinets of Vienna, London, and Paris constituted a bond from which Austria could not now free herself in order to act separately with Russia.' This was the situation in which Czar Alexander informed his Majesty at Gastein by letter in his own hand that he had determined to draw the sword, and sought Prussia's alliance.

It cannot be doubted that the *entente cordiale* then existing with the two Western Powers had contributed to the determination of Emperor Francis Joseph to make the push against Prussia with the Congress of Princes. Of course he would thereby have made a mistake through ignorance of the fact that Napoleon was already weary of the Polish affair and anxious to find a decent pretext for retreat. Count Goltz wrote me on August 31 [1]:

'You will see by what I said to you to-day that Cæsar and I are one heart and soul (in truth he was never, not even at the commencement of my mission, so amiable and confidential as now), that Austria has by her Diet of Princes rendered us a great service in respect of our relations with France, and that (thanks also to the absence of Metternich, and the departure to-day of the exalted lady [2] his friend) we need only a satisfactory adjustment of the

[1] *Bismarck-Jahrbuch*, v. 219 f.   [2] The Empress Eugénie.

Polish differences in order to revert to a political situation
in which we may confront coming events with confidence.

' With the intimations of the Emperor in regard to the
Polish business I have not been able to coincide so far as
I could have wished. He seemed to expect from me an
offer of mediation, but the utterances of the King held me
back. In any event it seems to me advisable to strike
the iron while it is hot; the Emperor's claims are now more
modest than ever, and it is to be apprehended that he may
revert to stronger demands if perchance Austria, by an
increased compliance in the Polish question, should endeavour to repair the disaster of Frankfort. His present
desire is only to get out of the affair with honour; he acknowledges the six points to be bad, will therefore be glad
to shut one eye at the practical performance of them, and
perhaps just as well pleased if no stringent forms compel
him to insist upon their strict execution. My only fear is
that, if the affair continues to be managed as heretofore,
the Russians should deprive us of the credit of settling it
by anticipating our advice by their independent action.
In this connexion the journey of the Grand Duke, who has
not been publicly recalled, seems to me suspicious. How
if Czar Alexander were now to proclaim a constitution,
and notify Napoleon of it by an obligation written in
his own hand? [Cf. Ems, 1870.] This would be better
than the protraction of the dispute, but less to our advantage than if we had said beforehand to Napoleon,
"We are prepared to advise it; would you be satisfied
with it?"'

Fourteen days before the date of this letter this suggestion, that we should advise Czar Alexander to take the
course indicated, had been made point blank by General

Fleury to a member of the Prussian embassy. It was not followed, and the diplomatic campaign of the three Powers came to nought. In the Polish question Austria is confronted by no such difficulties as for us are indissolubly bound up with the re-establishment of Polish independence, difficulties incident to the adjustment of the respective claims of Poles and Germans in Poland and West Prussia, and to the situation of East Prussia. Our geographical position, and the intermixture of both nationalities in the eastern provinces, including Silesia, compel us to retard, as far as possible, the opening of the Polish question, and even in 1863 made it appear advisable to do our best not to facilitate, but to obviate the opening of this question by Russia. Prior to 1863 there were occasions when St. Petersburg entertained the Wielopolskian idea of sending Grand Duke Constantine to Poland as viceroy— accompanied by his beautiful wife, who dressed *à la Polonaise*—and, if possible, giving practical effect to the Polish constitution, which, conceded by Alexander I, subsisted in form in the time of the old Grand Duke Constantine.

The Prussian policy embodied in the military convention concluded by General Gustav von Alvensleben in February 1863 had a diplomatic rather than a military significance.[1] It stood for the victory in the Russian cabinet of Prussian over Polish policy, the latter represented by Gortchakoff, Grand Duke Constantine, Wielopolski, and other influential people. The issue was determined by the personal decision of the Czar, in opposition to the policy of his ministers. An agreement between

[1] Cf. with what follows Bismarck's letter to Count Bernstorff, dated March 9, 1863, *Bismarck-Jahrbuch*, vi. 172 ff.

THE ALVENSLEBEN CONVENTION

Russia and the German foe of Panslavism for joint action, military and political, against the Polish ' Bruderstamm ' movement was a decisive blow to the views of the philo-Polish party at the Russian court; and as such the agreement, though in a military sense little more than a salve, amply accomplished its purpose. It was not positively demanded by the military situation, with which the Russian troops were strong enough to cope. The forces of the insurgents existed in great measure only in the dispatches bespoken from Paris, and manufactured in Myslowitz, dated now from the frontier, now from the seat of war, now from Warsaw, dispatches in some cases quite fabulous, which first appeared in a Berlin journal and then made the tour of the European press. The convention said ' checkmate' in the game which anti-Polish monarchism was then playing against philo-Polish Panslavism within the Russian cabinet.

The Polish question threw Prince Gortchakoff into alternate phases of absolutism and—not exactly Liberalism—but parliamentarism. He thought himself a great speaker, indeed was so, and was fond of imagining the thrill of admiration which his eloquence might propagate through Europe from a tribune in Warsaw or in Russia. It was assumed that liberal concessions, if granted to the Poles, could not be withheld from the Russians; Russian constitutionalists were therefore philo-Polish.

While public opinion with us was busy with the Polish question, and the Alvensleben convention aroused the unintelligent indignation of the Liberals in the Landtag, Herr Hintzpeter was introduced to me at a gathering at the Crown Prince's. As he was in daily communication with the royalties, and gave himself out to me as a man of Conservative opinions, I ventured upon a conversation with him, in which I set forth my views of the Polish question, in the expectation that he would now and again find opportunity of giving expression to it. Some days later he wrote me that the Crown Princess had asked to know the subject of our long conversation. He had re-counted it all to her, and had then reduced it to writing. He sent me the memorandum with the request that I would examine it, and make any needful corrections. I answered that with this request I could not comply. If I did so, it would be consonant with what he himself told me, if I communicated on the question, not with him, but with the Crown Princess, in writing; but I was not at present prepared to go beyond word of mouth.

CHAPTER XVI

THE DANTZIC EPISODE

EMPEROR FREDERICK, son of the monarch whom I designate specifically my master, made it easy for me, by his amiability and confidence, to transfer to him the affection which I had cherished for his father. He was more open than his father had been to the constitutional ideal that I as minister bore the responsibility for the policy of the crown. He was also less hampered by family traditions in adjusting himself to political necessities, domestic and foreign. All assertions of lasting discord in our relations are unfounded. A discord indeed, but only short-lived, was occasioned by the transaction in Dantzic, in speaking of which the publication of the posthumous papers of Max Duncker[1] permits me to use less reserve than would otherwise have been the case. On May 31, 1863, the Crown Prince started for the province of Prussia to review the army there. Before leaving he begged the King in writing to avoid any issuing of regulations. He travelled in the same train with von Winter, Burgomaster of Dantzic, whom he invited into his *coupé*, and afterwards visited on his estate at Culm. On June 2 the Crown Princess followed him to Graudenz; on the day before had appeared the royal press ordinance founded on a ministerial report which was published at the same time. On June 4 his Royal Highness addressed a letter to the

---

[1] R. Haym, *Das Leben Max Dunckers* (Berlin 1891) pp. 292-3.

King, in which he expressed disapproval of this decree, complained that he had not been summoned to the councils in which the step had been discussed, and enlarged on the duties which, in his opinion, his position as heir apparent laid upon him. On June 5 his reception by the civic authorities took place in the town hall of Dantzic. In the course of the ceremony von Winter expressed his regret that present circumstances did not permit the full outspoken utterance of the joy of the town. The reply of the Crown Prince was in part as follows: ' I also lament that I should have come here at a time when a variance has occurred between the government and the people which has occasioned me no small degree of surprise. Of the proceedings which have brought it about I knew nothing. I was absent. I have had no part in the deliberations which have produced this result. But we all, and I especially, I who best know the noble and fatherly intentions and magnanimous sentiments of his Majesty the King, we all, I say, are confident that, under the sceptre of his Majesty the King, Prussia continues to make sure progress towards the future which Providence has marked out for her.'

Copies of the 'Danziger Zeitung,' containing an account of the occurrence, were sent to the offices of Berlin and other newspapers which, owing to its essentially local character, were not accustomed to take in the 'Danziger Zeitung.' The words of the Crown Prince were thus circulated forthwith far and wide, and created, as may well be imagined, a sensation both at home and abroad. From Graudenz he transmitted to me a formal protest against the press ordinance which he requested me to lay before the ministry, subject however to the good pleasure of the King. On the 7th his Majesty returned a grave answer to his complaint of the 4th. He then asked his father's pardon for a step which he had deemed it incumbent on him not to omit in the interest of his own and his children's future, and placed all his offices at the disposal of the King. On the 11th he received the royal answer, which assured him of the forgiveness that he craved, ignored his censure of the ministers and his tender of resignation, and enjoined upon him silence for the future.

While I could not but acknowledge the justice of the King's resentment, I did my best to prevent its manifestation by official or indeed by any publicly recognisable acts. Dynastic interests required me to make it my business to calm the King, and to restrain him from taking any steps which might have recalled the days of Frederick William I and Küstrin. To this end I mainly used the opportunity afforded on June 10 by a drive from Babelsberg to the New Palace, where his Majesty was to inspect the cadet battalion. Lest it should be understood by the servants on the box, the conversation was carried on in French. I succeeded in applying to the father's irritation the healing balm of state policy, which, in view of the impending struggle between prerogative and parliament, enjoined that differences within the royal house should be muffled, ignored, buried in silence; and that the King, both as King and as father, should be especially solicitous that his interests should not suffer in either character. ' Deal tenderly with the boy Absalom,' I said in allusion to the fact that country parsons were already beginning to preach on 2 Samuel xv. 3, 4. ' Let your Majesty decide nothing in wrath; state policy only can rightfully determine your conduct.' The King seemed to be particularly impressed when I reminded him that in the conflict between Frederick William I and his son the sympathy of contemporaries and posterity was with the latter, and that it was not advisable to make the Crown Prince a martyr.

After the affair had been at least apparently disposed of by the above-mentioned correspondence between the father and son, I received from Stettin a letter from the Crown Prince dated June 30, a letter censuring my entire policy in strong terms. It lacked sympathy and consideration for the people, it was supported by very doubtful constructions of the constitution, would render the constitution worthless in the eyes of the people, and force the people to transgress it. On the other hand, the ministry would advance from one strained interpretation to another, and finally would advise the King to an open breach. He would pray the King to permit him while this ministry remained in office to take no further part in its deliberations.

The fact that after this utterance on the part of the heir apparent I held on in the course I had taken shows conclusively that I set no store by remaining in office after the change of sovereign, which, it was likely enough, might very soon take place. For all that, the Crown Prince compelled me to make an express declaration to this effect in a conversation to which I shall have to refer later on.

To the King's surprise, on June 16 or 17, a paragraph appeared in the 'Times' to the following effect: 'While travelling on military duty, the Prince allowed himself to assume an attitude antagonistic to the policy of the Sovereign, and to call in question his measures. The least that he could do to atone for this grave offence was to retract his statements. This the King demanded of him by letter, adding that, if he refused, he would be deprived of his honours and offices. The Prince, in concert, it is said, with her Royal Highness the Princess, met this demand with a firm answer. He refused to retract anything, offered to resign his honours and commands, and craved leave to withdraw with his wife and family to some place where he would be free from suspicion of the least connection with affairs of state. This letter is described as a remarkable performance, and it is added that the Prince is to be congratulated on having a consort who not only shares his Liberal views, but is also able to render him so much assistance in a momentous and critical juncture. It is not easy to conceive a more difficult position than that of the princely pair placed, without a single adviser, between a self-willed sovereign and a mischievous cabinet on the one hand, and an incensed people on the other.'

Attempts were made to discover the purveyor of this article, but without definite result. Circumstantial evidence threw suspicion on Meyer, counsellor to the embassy. The more detailed communications made to the ' Grenzboten' and the ' Süd-deutsche Post' by Brater, a member of the House of Representatives, seem to have come through the channel of a petty German diplomatist,' who was in the confidence of the Crown Prince and Princess. This confidence he retained, and a quarter of a century later abused by the indiscreet publication of manuscripts entrusted to him by the Prince. Of the truth of the Crown Prince's assertion that the publication of the ' Times' article was entirely without his cognisance I have never entertained a doubt, not even after reading

[1] Geffcken.

what he wrote to Max Duncker on July 14,[1] that he would
hardly be surprised if, on Bismarck's side, means had been
found to procure copies of his correspondence with the
King.   I believed that the prime responsibility for the
publication was to be sought in the same quarter, to which,
in my belief, the Prince owed the bent of his political
views.   What I observed during the French war, and
later what I have gathered from Duncker's papers, have
confirmed the view which I then took.   For a quarter of
a century a whole school of political writers had extolled
what, without any thorough comprehension of it, they
called the English constitution, as a model to be imitated
by continental nations.   What wonder then that the
Crown Princess and her mother overlooked that peculiar
character of the Prussian state which renders its administration by means of shifting parliamentary groups a sheer
impossibility?   What wonder that this error bred the
further mistake of anticipating for the Prussia of the nine-
teenth century a repetition of the civil broils and catastrophes of the England of the seventeenth century unless the
system by which they were terminated were introduced
among us?   I was informed at the time that in April 1863
memoranda criticising the domestic condition of Prussia, carefully prepared by President Ludolf Camphausen
at the instance of Queen Augusta and by Baron von
Stockmar at the instance of the Crown Princess, were
laid before the King.   I have not been able to determine
precisely whether this report was true or false; but that
the Queen, to whose *entourage* counsellor Meyer belonged,
was then full of apprehension of catastrophes similar to
those which befell the Stuarts, I knew for certain; indeed,

[1] *Leben Dunckers*, p. 308.

in 1862 it was already plainly apparent to me in the dejected
frame of mind in which the King returned from his wife's
birthday fête at Baden.[1] The party of progress, then daily
anticipating a victorious termination to its struggle with
prerogative, availed itself of the opportunities which the
press and individual leaders of opinion afforded to place
the situation in the light best calculated to influence
female minds.

In August the Crown Prince paid me a visit at
Gastein. There, less under the sway of English influences, he spoke of his conduct like one conscious of a
native want of independence, and full of veneration for his
father. Modestly and gracefully, he traced his error to
its source in his imperfect political training and aloofness
from affairs; in short, he used the unreserved language of
one who sees that he has done wrong and seeks to excuse
himself on the score of the influences under which he had
lain. In September, after we had returned to Berlin, the
King with me by Baden, the Crown Prince direct from
Gastein, the influences and apprehensions which had dictated his action in June regained the upper hand. On the
day following the dissolution of the House of Representatives, he wrote me:

' Berlin, 3/9/63.

' I have to-day imparted to his Majesty the views
which I detailed to you in my letter from Putbus [more
accurately Stettin] and which I begged you not to disclose
to the King until I had so done. A momentous decision

[1] See above, p. 314.

355

was yesterday taken in the council; in the presence of the
ministers I would not in any way oppose his Majesty; to-
day I have done so; I have expressed my views, I have set
forth my grave apprehensions as to the future. The King
now knows that I am the determined foe of the ministry.

'FREDERICK WILLIAM.'

The dispensation from attendance at the cabinet councils craved by the Crown Prince in his letter of June 30
now came up for discussion. The relations of the two royal
persons, as they then still stood, appear from the following
letter of von Bodelschwingh, dated September 11:

'I know of the sad occasion*of your journey, but know
not at what hour to expect your return, or whether I may
soon thereafter hope to have speech of you. I therefore
inform you by writing, that, in consequence of the command of his Majesty conveyed to me through the aide-de-
camp, I went about your business in the following way.
I informed the aide-de-camp of the Crown Prince of your
hasty departure and its occasion, and prayed him to notify
the same to his Royal Highness in case your request of
an audience should have been laid before him, or decision
been already taken thereon. His Majesty, so Prince
Hohenlohe told me, has not seen fit to say a word to the
Crown Prince either about your departure or the matter of
the audience.'

The King had decided that the Crown Prince should
continue to attend the cabinet councils, as he had done
since 1861, and had commissioned me to inform him of
the fact. I suppose that the audience craved for this pur-

* The death of my mother-in-law. I was absent from Berlin from the
6th to the 11th.

pose was not had; for I remember that a mistake which the Crown Prince made—presenting himself in the council chamber on a day when the cabinet did not meet—served to introduce the necessary explanation. I asked him why he held so aloof from the government; in a few years he would be its master; and if his principles were not ours, he should rather endeavour to effect a gradual transition than throw himself into opposition. That suggestion he decisively rejected, apparently suspecting me of a desire to pave the way for my transfer into his service. The refusal was accompanied by a hostile expression of Olympian disdain, which after all these years I have not forgotten; to-day I still see before me the averted head, the flushed face, and the glance cast over the left shoulder. I suppressed my own rising choler, thought of Carlos and Alva (Act 2, sc. 5), and answered that my words had been prompted by an access of dynastic sentiment, in the hope of restoring him to closer relations with his father, in the interest alike of the country and the dynasty which the estrangement prejudiced; that in June I had done what I could to induce his father to decide nothing in wrath, because in the interest of the country and in view of the struggle with the parliament I wished to preserve harmony within the royal family. I said that I was a loyal servant of his father, and desired that on his accession to the throne he might find, to supply my place, servants as loyal to him as I had been to his father. I hoped he would dismiss the idea that I aimed at some day becoming his minister; that I would never be. His wrath fell as suddenly as it had risen, and he concluded the conversation in a friendly tone.

To the request to be relieved from further attendance

at the cabinet councils he adhered firmly, and in the course of September addressed to the King another memorandum, inspired perhaps in some degree by foreign influence, in which he unfolded his reasons in a way which seemed like a sort of justification of his conduct in June. It occasioned a private correspondence between his Majesty and myself which concluded with the following brief note:

'Babelsberg: November 7, 1863.

'Herewith I send you my answer to my son the Crown Prince's memoir of September. For your better guidance I return you the memorandum together with your notes, of which I made use in my answer.'

I took no copy of the memorandum; its contents, however, can be gathered from my marginal notes, which are as follows:

P. 1. The claim that a caveat by his Royal Highness ought to outweigh the gravely and carefully considered decisions of the King arrogates for his own, as compared with his royal father's position and experience, an undue importance. No one could suppose that his Royal Highness had any part in the ordinances, for everybody knows that the Crown Prince has no vote in the cabinet, and that the official position which former usage accorded to the heir apparent is now unconstitutional. The *démenti* at Dantzic was therefore superfluous.

P. 2. His Royal Highness's freedom of action is not impaired by his attending cabinet councils, listening and expressing his opinion, and thus keeping himself *au courant* with affairs of state, as it is the duty of every heir apparent to do. The discharge of this duty, if publicity be given to it in the newspapers, must produce in all quarters a good opinion of the conscientiousness with which the Crown Prince prepares himself for his high and serious vocation. The words 'with hands tied' and so forth have no meaning.

P. 2. It is quite impossible that the country should identify his Royal Highness with the ministry, for the country knows that the Crown Prince is not summoned in order that he may concur officially in the decisions. Alas! the attitude of opposition to the crown which his Royal Highness has assumed is known well enough in the country, and will be disapproved by every head of a household throughout its length and breadth, without distinction of party, as a revolt against that paternal authority which cannot be disregarded without doing violence to natural feeling and established usage. His Royal Highness could not be more gravely damaged in public esteem than by the publication of this memorandum.

P. 2. As it is not the vocation of the heir apparent to raise the standard of opposition against his royal father, the position of his Royal Highness is indeed false throughout. His 'duty' is therefore to retire from it, which can only be done by reverting to a normal attitude.

P. 3. The conflict of duties does not arise, for the former duty is self-imposed; the care for the future of Prussia is a burden which lies, not on the Crown Prince, but on the King, and whether 'mistakes' are made or not, and on what side, the future will make known. Where the 'judgment' of his Majesty comes into collision with that of the Crown Prince, the former must always be decisive; so there is no conflict, his Royal Highness himself acknowledges that in our constitution there is 'no room for opposition on the part of the heir apparent.'

BISMARCK

P. 4. The right of opposing in council does not exclude the duty of submission to his Majesty as soon as a resolution is come to. Ministers oppose whenever there is a divergence of view, but submit* to the decision of the King, though it fall to them to give effect to the policy they have combated.

P. 4. If his Royal Highness is aware that the action of ministers is sanctioned by the King he cannot conceal from himself that the opposition of the heir apparent is directed against the ruling monarch himself.

P. 5. A campaign against the will of the King is an enterprise which the Crown Prince is neither called upon to undertake nor justified in undertaking, precisely because he has no official status. Any Prince of the royal house whose views differed from the King's might, with as good a right as the Crown Prince, claim for himself the ' duty ' of going into open opposition against the King in order thereby to secure ' his own and his children's ' eventual succession against the consequences of alleged mistakes on the part of the King's government, i.e. in order to safeguard the succession after the style of Louis Philippe, in the event of the King losing his throne by a revolution

P. 5. It is for the Minister-President to give more precise account of his utterances at Gastein.

P. 7. It is not as ' adviser ' of the King, but for his own instruction and preparation for his future vocation, that the Crown Prince is summoned by his Majesty to attend cabinet councils.

P. 7. An attempt to ' neutralise ' the measures of the

* Here in the margin are added in the King's own hand the words : ' if they conscientiously can.'

government would be open revolt and insurrection against the Crown.

P. 7. No open attack on the part of the democracy, no secret 'gnawing' at the roots of the monarchy, is so dangerous as the relaxation of the bonds which still knit the people with the dynasty by the spectacle of an heir apparent in openly-declared opposition and discord in the bosom of the dynasty bruited abroad of set purpose. When the authority of the father and the King is assailed by the son and the heir apparent, to whom shall it still remain sacred? When for present revolt from the King a far-sighted ambition may safely anticipate a future reward, the relaxation of those bonds will redound to the future King's own disadvantage, and from the maimed authority of the present government will spring a yet more degenerate growth. Any government is better than one divided against itself and maimed, and the shocks which it is in the power of the present Crown Prince to occasion might shake the very foundations of the edifice in which he will himself in the future have to dwell.

P. 7. By the customary law of Prussia, which has not been materially altered by the Constitution, the King rules, not his ministers. It is only legislative, not governmental functions that are shared with the Chambers, before which the King is represented by the ministers. It is thus still the law, just as before the Constitution, that the ministers are his Majesty's servants and his chosen advisers, but not the rulers of the Prussian state. Even therefore by the Constitution the Prussian monarchy is not yet on a par with that of Belgium or England. Rather with us the King still rules personally, and his authority

is limited in its exercise only by some other power, i.e.
only within the legislative sphere.

P. 8. Publication of state secrets is an offence against
the criminal law. What is to be treated as a state secret
depends upon the regulations made by the King for the
secrecy of the service.

P. 8. Why does the Crown Prince attach such importance to the appreciation of his position by ' the country
at large'? If his Royal Highness gives conscientious
expression to his convictions in the council he does all
that his conscience can require of him. He has no official
position in state affairs, he is in no way called upon to
give public expression to his views; no one who has even
a superficial acquaintance with our administrative institutions will impute to his Royal Highness concurrence with
the decisions of the government merely because he is without a vote, and therefore attends the proceedings of the
council without power to make effective opposition.

P. 8. ' Do not appear better;' herein lies just the false-
ness of the position in that too much importance is attached to appearance; all really depends on *being* and
being able, and these results are only to be gained by serious and sober work.

P. 9. The part taken by his Royal Highness in the
councils is no ' active' one, inasmuch as he gives no vote
in divisions.

P. 9. To summon people and confer with them on
affairs of state without authorisation by his Majesty would
be an infringement of the criminal law. His Royal Highness's right to the free utterance of his opinions will certainly not be limited; on the contrary, its exercise is
desired; but it does not extend beyond the council, where

alone it can influence the decisions to be taken. The claim, on the other hand, to ' lay everything frankly before the country' can only be prompted by a desire to gratify the sense of self-importance, and if conceded might easily have the effect of fomenting discontent and insubordination, and so prepare the way for the revolution.

P. 10. The presence of his Royal Highness at the cabinet councils will undoubtedly render the task of the ministry more difficult, and complicate the problems with which they have to deal. But can his Majesty absolve himself from the duty of securing for the Crown Prince by all possible human means a practical training in the public business and the laws of his country? Would it not be a perilous experiment to allow the future King to lose touch with affairs of state, though the weal of millions depends upon his conversance with them? In the memorandum before me his Royal Highness displays ignorance of the fact that the Crown Prince's participation in cabinet councils carries with it no responsibility, is only intended for his own instruction, and under no circumstances imposes the obligation of voting. Disregard of this circumstance is the basis of his entire reasoning. Were the Crown Prince conversant with affairs of state he would not have threatened the King with the publication of the proceedings of the council, i.e. with a breach of the law, not to say the criminal law, in the event of the King not falling in with his Royal Highness's wishes. And that only a few weeks after his Royal Highness himself had censured in severe terms the publication of his correspondence with his Majesty.

P. 11. The reproach here referred to is one which certainly touches every man in the nation very closely; no one imputes such a design to his Royal Highness, but the *on dit* certainly is that others who cherish such a design hope to accomplish it by means of the unconscious co-operation of the Crown Prince, and that the hatchers of nefarious plots to subvert the government by force have now a better prospect of success than formerly.

P. 12. The request for timely notice of the business to be discussed at the councils has always been recognised as reasonable, and will always be complied with; indeed, frequent expression has been given to the wish that his Royal Highness would permit himself to be kept more exactly *au courant* than was heretofore possible. That would mean that his Royal Highness's place of residence should always be known and always be within reach, that he himself should always be accessible to ministers, and that his discretion should be unimpeachable. Especially necessary, however, is it that the intermediary advisers, with whose aid alone his Royal Highness can be authorised to busy himself with the consideration of pending affairs of state, should be adherents, not of the opposition, but of the government, or at least impartial critics without intimate relations with the opposition in the Diet or the press. The question of discretion is that which presents most difficulty, especially in regard to our foreign relations, and must continue so to do until his Royal Highness and her Royal Highness the Crown Princess have fully realised that in ruling houses the nearest of kin may yet be aliens, and of necessity, and as in duty bound, represent other interests than the Prussian. It is hard that a frontier line should also be the line of demarcation between the interests of mother and daughter, of brother and sister; but to forget the fact is always perilous to the state.

THE DANTZIC EPISODE

P. 12. The 'last cabinet council' (on the 3rd) was not a cabinet council. The ministers merely received a summons to an unexpected audience of his Majesty.

P. 13. To lay the memorandum before the ministry would give it an official character which deliverances on the part of heirs apparent have not in themselves.

CHAPTER XVII

THE FRANKFORT DIET OF PRINCES

THE earliest attempts along the road by which alliance with Austria was eventually reached in 1879 were made while Count Rechberg was Minister-President and subsequently Minister for Foreign Affairs (May 17, 1859, to October 27, 1864). Since the personal relations in which I stood to him in the Federal Diet might have helped to further such attempts, and at one moment certainly did further them, I insert here two experiences which I had with him at Frankfort.

After a sitting in which I had annoyed Rechberg he stayed behind with me in the Chamber, and vehemently reproached me for my incompatibility: I was *mauvais coucheur*, a picker of quarrels; referring to cases in which I had defended myself against encroachments of the chair. I replied that I did not know if his anger was merely a diplomatic move or if it were meant seriously; but that his manner of expressing it was of a highly personal nature. ' We cannot,' I said, ' dispatch the diplomatic business of our states with pistols in the Bockheim wood.' Thereupon he replied, with great violence: ' Let us drive there at once; I am ready to start this minute.' With that I considered we had forsaken diplomatic ground. I answered without violence: ' Why should we drive? There is space enough in the palace garden here; Prussian officers live over the way, and there are Austrian

366

officers in the neighbourhood. The whole affair can be settled in a quarter of an hour. I must ask you to allow me to write a few lines concerning the origin of the quarrel, and I expect you to sign the note with me, that my King may not deem me a bully whom the diplomatic business of his master leads to a duel.'

While I was writing, my colleague walked up and down behind me with hasty strides. During that time his anger evaporated, and he regarded more calmly the situation that he had brought about. I left him with the words that I would send Herr von Oertzen, the Mecklenburg ambassador, to him, as my second to negotiate further. Through Oertzen's mediation the quarrel was made up.

It is interesting too to mention how I afterwards gained the confidence of this irascible though honourable man, and perhaps, when we had both become ministers, his friendship. During a business visit which I paid him, he left the room to make some change in his dress; he put into my hands a dispatch which he had just received from his government and asked me to read it. I convinced myself from the contents that Rechberg had made a mistake, and had given me a document that certainly related to the matter in question, but which was intended for his eyes alone; it had obviously been accompanied by a second document which was to be shown. When he returned I gave him back the dispatch with the remark that he had made a mistake and that I would forget what I had read; as a matter of fact I preserved an absolute silence in regard to his blunder, and neither in dispatches nor in conversation did I make even an indirect use of the secret document or of his slip. Thenceforth he placed in me every confidence.

The attempts made at the time of Rechberg's ministry would, if successful, have led to a union of all the German powers on the basis of a dual government, to an empire of seventy millions in Central Europe with a twofold apex. Schwarzenberg's policy pointed somewhat the same way, but there was to be only a single apex—Austria; while Prussia would probably have been reduced to the rank of a middle state. The congress of princes in 1863 was the last attempt at this. If the Schwarzenberg policy in the posthumous form of the congresss had ultimately succeeded, the employment of the Federal Diet for the purpose of repression would then, so far as the internal policy of Germany was concerned, presumably have come to the front upon the lines of the constitutional revisions which the *Bund* had already started upon in Hanover, Hesse, Luxemburg, Lippe, Hamburg, and other places. By the same analogy the Prussian constitution might have been hauled over the coals, if the King had not laid his plans too well.

Under a dualistic apex, with Prussia and Austria equal in authority, a consummation that worked out as a result of my closer relations with Rechberg might have been attained; our internal constitutional development would not necessarily have been threatened with extinction in the slough of federal reaction, or by the one-sided furtherance of the absolutist aims of individual states; the jealousy of the two great states would have been the safeguard of the constitutions. Prussia, Austria, and the middle states would, under the system of the dual apex, have clearly been left to compete for the favour of suffrages in the whole nation, as well as in individual states, and the friction thence arising would have preserved our public life from

such benumbing as followed the days of the Mainz commission of inquiry. The period of activity of the Austrian Liberal press in rivalry with Prussia, although only
in the sphere of phrases, made it perfectly clear, even at
the beginning of the 'fifties, that the undecided struggle
for hegemony had its uses in quickening our national
feelings, and in furthering our constitutional development.

But the reform in the *Bund* that Austria endeavoured
to obtain with the aid of the ' Diet of Princes ' in 1863
would have left little room for rivalry between Prussia,
Austria, and parliamentarism. The pre-eminence of Austria in the then purposed reforms would have been secured,
on the basis of the apprehension of Prussia and of parliamentary conflicts felt by the ruling houses, by means of a
permanent and systematically founded majority in the
Diet.

The consideration in which Germany was held abroad
depended, under both forms of government, the dual, and
that of Austria alone, on the degree in which both the
one and the other preserved a firm unity in the nation as
a whole. The developments of Danish affairs proved that
directly Austria and Prussia were united, they represented
a power in Europe that none of the other nations would
be likely to attack with a light heart. So long as Prussia, even though she might be supported by the strongest
expression of public opinion on the part of the German
people, the middle states included, had the matter in hand
alone, she made no progress, and only led the way to conclusions like the armistice of Malmö and the convention
of Olmütz. As soon as Austria, under Rechberg, was
successfully won over to act in unison with Prussia, the

weight of the two German states was sufficient to prevent
any desires of interference on the part of the other Powers. In the course of her more recent history, England
has always felt the need of allying herself with one of the
military Powers of the Continent, and has sought to satisfy that need, from the point of view of English interests
at the moment, sometimes at Berlin and sometimes at
Vienna. A sudden transition from one point of support
to the other, as happened in the Seven Years' war, has not
seemed to her a reason for cherishing any nice scruples
against the charge of leaving old friends in the lurch.
But when the two courts were united and allied, English
policy did not find it too advantageous to take up a hostile
attitude towards them, in alliance, it might be, with one
of the Powers most dangerous to her—France and Russia.
The moment, however, there had been a split in the
Austro-Prussian alliance, the interference in the Danish
question of the European elders in convention assembled,
led by England, would have followed. If, therefore, our
policy was not again to leave the track, insistence on an
understanding with Vienna was of the utmost importance;
therein lay our protection from Anglo-European interference.

On December 4, 1862, I had openly shown my hand
to Count Karolyi, with whom I was on confidential terms.
I said to him:

' Our relations must become either better or worse
than they now are. I am prepared for a joint attempt to
improve them. If it fails through your refusal, do not
reckon on our allowing ourselves to be bound by the
friendly phrases of the Diet. You will have to deal with
us as one of the Great Powers of Europe; the paragraphs

in the Vienna decrees have no power to hinder the progress of German history.'[1]

Count Karolyi, a man of honourable and independent character, doubtless reported exactly what we had said confidentially when alone. But since the Olmütz and Dresden time, and the period of Schwarzenberg's predominance, an erroneous opinion had obtained at Vienna; it had become customary to consider us weaker, and especially more timid, than we are apt to be, as well as to rate in the long run too highly the importance of royal kinship and personal regard in questions of international politics.

The older military presumptions at any rate went to show that if the war of 1866 had been entered on in 1850, our prospects would have been hazardous. But to count on our timidity as late as the 'sixties was an error which left out of the reckoning the change in the occupant of the throne.

Frederick William IV would have determined upon mobilisation as easily as in 1850, or as his successor in 1859, but scarcely upon actual warfare. In his reign there was always the danger that tergiversations similar to those under Haugwitz in 1805 might have led us into a false position; even after an actual breach, people in Austria would have stepped over all our muddling attempts after mediation, and passed with decision to the order of the day. Disinclination to break with the paternal traditions and with old-standing family relations was as strong with King William as with his brother; but so soon as, under the guidance of his honour, whose sensitiveness lay as

---

[1] Cf. the dispatch of January 24, 1863, in which Bismarck gives an account of his interviews with Karolyi on December 4 and 13, 1862, *State Archives*, viii. p. 55 ff. No. 1,751.

much in his German sword-belt as in his consciousness
of being a monarch, he felt compelled to decisions which
weighed heavily on his heart, you felt certain that if you
stuck to him in no danger would he leave you in the
lurch. Vienna made too little account of this change in
the supreme direction, and too much of the influence
which had formerly been customarily exercised on the
Berlin decisions by what was called public opinion as gen-
erated by press agents and subsidies, and would further
be exercised through the interposition of royal relatives
and of correspondents of the royal family.

Vienna likewise overrated such weakening effect as
our domestic conflicts might have had on our foreign policy and our military capabilities. Manifold symptoms,
from Blind's attempt at assassination and the criticism of
it in progressive journals * to the public manifestoes of
great corporate communities and to the result of the elections, testify that the disinclination to cut the Gordian
knot of German politics with the sword was equally strong
and widespread in 1866. But these currents of feeling
did not get into our regiments and their efficiency in action; and on the battlefield lay the final decision. Even
the symptomatic fact that diplomatic notes in connexion
with the Court were, through the intervention of von
Schleinitz, once Foreign Minister, and at that period
Minister of the Household, going to and fro at Berlin
while the first actions were being fought in Bohemia, had
not the slightest influence on the military side in the
management of the war.

* In the Berlin picture-shops hung a lithograph in which the *attentat*
was represented with the devil catching bullets destined for me with the
words : ' He belongs to me !' Cf. *Political Speeches* x. 123 (Speech of
May 9, 1884).

If the Austrian cabinet had not erroneously estimated facts, and had taken at its right value the confidential overture made by me to Count Karolyi in 1862; if it had modified its policy in the direction of seeking an understanding with Prussia instead of trying to coerce her by means of majorities and other influences, we should probably have seen, or at any rate made trial of, a period of dualistic policy in Germany. It is certainly very doubtful if, without the clearing effect of the experiences of 1866 and 1870, such a system could have developed peacefully in a sense acceptable to German national sentiment, and with permanent avoidance of internal dissensions. The belief in the military superiority of Austria was too strong, both at Vienna and at the Courts of the middle states, for a *modus vivendi* on the footing of equality with Prussia. The proof that this was the case at Vienna lay in the proclamations that were found in the knapsacks of the Austrian soldiers, together with the new uniforms ordered for the entry into Berlin. The contents of those documents betrayed the certainty with which the Austrians had counted on the victorious occupation of the Prussian provinces. The refusal to entertain the latest Prussian proposals for peace, made through the brother of General von Gablenz, and the reason of it, namely, the finance minister's requirement of a contribution from Prussia, as well as the readiness announced at that time to treat after the first battle, demonstrates the certainty with which a victory in this was reckoned on.

The joint result of these representations working in

a similar direction was the opposite of any advance on the part of the Vienna cabinet towards a desire for the dual rule; Austria passed to the order of the day over the head of Prussia's proposal in 1862, and with the diametrically opposite course of initiating the convocation of the Frankfort 'Diet of Princes,' by which King William and his cabinet were surprised at Gastein at the beginning of August.

According to Fröbel,[1] who regards himself as the originator of the congress of princes, and who doubtless was initiated in the preliminaries, the rest of the German princes were not aware of the Austrian scheme until they received the invitation dated July 31. It is, however, likely that von Varnbüler, who was subsequently Wurtemberg minister, had been in some degree admitted to the secret. In the summer of 1863 that able and hardworking politician showed an inclination to renew the relations that had formerly existed between us through the intervention of our common friend, von Below of Hohendorf. He engaged me to meet him on July 12, and at his desire the interview took place secretly at a little place in Bohemia west of Carlsbad. The only impression I retained of the interview was that he wished rather to sound me than to offer suggestions on the German question. The economic financial questions on which he in 1878 gave me the valuable assistance of his special knowledge, and of his powers of work, were already occupying a foremost place in his ideas, and he especially leaned to a Great-German policy with a corresponding customs union.

[1] *Julius Fröbel: ein Lebenslauf.* Stuttgart, 1891. Part ii. pp. 252, 255.

THE FRANKFORT DIET OF PRINCES

At Gastein, on August 2, 1863, I was sitting under the fir-trees in the Schwarzenberg gardens by the deep gorge of the Ache. Above me was a nest of titmice, and watch in hand I counted the number of times in the min- ute the bird brought her nestlings a caterpillar or other insect. While I was observing the useful activity of these little creatures, I saw King William sitting alone on a bench on the Schillerplatz on the opposite side of the gorge. When the hour drew near to dress for dinner with the King, I went to my lodgings and there found a note from his Majesty informing me that he would await me on the Schillerplatz in order to speak to me about the meeting with the Emperor. I made all possible haste, but before I reached the King's apartments an interview had taken place between the two Sovereigns. If I had spent less time over my observations of nature, and had seen the King sooner, the first impression made on him by the Em- peror's communications might have been other than it was.

He did not instantly feel the slight implied by this sudden attack, by this invitation, we might almost say by this summons *à courte échéance*. He probably favoured the Austrian proposal because it contained an element of royal solidarity in the struggle against parliamentary Liberalism, by which he himself was just then hard pressed at Berlin. Queen Elizabeth, whom we met at Wildbad on our journey from Gastein to Baden, was urgent with me to go to Frankfort. I replied: ' If the King does not otherwise decide I will go and perform his business there, but I will not return as minister to Berlin. ' The prospect seemed to disturb the Queen, and she ceased to contest my views with the King.

Had I dropped my resistance to the King's efforts to

go to Frankfort, and, according to his wish, accompanied him thither in order, during the congress, to convert the rivalry of Austria and Prussia into a common warfare against revolution and constitutionalism, Prussia would have remained outwardly what she was before; under the presidency of Austria she would, no doubt, by means of federal decisions, have been able to get her Constitution revised in the same way as happened with those of Hanover, Hesse, and Mecklenburg, and at Lippe, Hamburg, and Luxemburg, but would thereby have closed the road to German nationality.

It was not an easy task to decide the King to stay away from Frankfort. I exerted myself for that purpose during our drive from Wildbad to Baden, when, on account of the servants on the box, we discussed the German question in the small open carriage in French. By the time we reached Baden I thought I had convinced my master. But there we found the King of Saxony, who was commissioned by all the princes to renew the invitation to Frankfort (August 19). My master did not find it easy to resist that move. ·He reflected over and over again: 'Thirty reigning princes and a King to take their messages!' Besides, he loved and honoured the King of Saxony, who moreover of all the princes had personally most vocation for such a mission. Not until midnight did I succeed in obtaining the King's signature to a refusal to the King of Saxony. When I left my master, both he and I were ill and exhausted by the nervous tension of the situation; and my subsequent verbal communication with the Saxon minister, von Beust, bore the stamp of this agitation.[1] But the crisis was overcome,

[1] Cf. Beust, *Aus drei Vierteljahrhunderten*, i. 332, 333; v. Sybel ii. 532.

and the King of Saxony departed without, as I had feared, visiting my master again.

On the return journey from Baden-Baden to Berlin (August 31) the King passed so near Frankfort that his decision not to take part in the congress became known to every one. The majority, or at least the most power-ful, of the princes felt very uncomfortable at this when they thought of the scheme of reform which, if Prussia held aloof, left them standing alone with Austria in a connexion where they got no protection from the rivalry of the two Great Powers. The Vienna cabinet must have thought of the possibility that the other Federal princes would agree in the congress to the proposals made on August 17, even when they had finally been left alone with Austria in the reformed federal relation. Otherwise it would not have been demanded of the princes who re-mained at Frankfort that they should accept the Austrian proposals and carry them into practice without the consent of Prussia. But at Frankfort the middle states did not de-sire either a solely Prussian or a solely Austrian leadership; they wanted to hold as influential a position as possible as arbiters in the sense of the Triad, by which each of the two Great Powers would be driven to compete for the votes of the middle states. To the demand of Austria that they should conclude without Prussia they replied by referring to the necessity of fresh negotiations with Prussia and by announcing their own inclination to such a course. The form of their reply to the wishes of Austria was not smooth enough not to excite some irritation at Vienna. The effect on Count Rechberg, prepared by the friendly relations in which our acting as colleagues at Frankfort had ended, was to make him say that the road to Berlin was not longer or more difficult for Austria than for the middle states.

The ill-temper engendered by the refusal was, according to my impressions, chiefly responsible for the impulse which led the Viennese cabinet to make a agreement with Prussia inconsistent with the Federal Constitution. This new turn of affairs suited Austrian interests, even if it should last for some while. To this end it was most requisite that Rechberg should remain at the oar. If by that means a dual leadership of the German federation was restored, which the other states would not have refused so soon as they were convinced that the understanding was honourable and likely to last, then in face of the Austro-Prussian understanding the edge would have been taken off the desire on the part of individual South German ministers for a Rhenish federation—a desire that, whatever Count Beust may say in his Memoirs, was most clearly expressed at Darmstadt.

A few months after the Frankfort congress, King Frederick VII of Denmark died (November 15, 1863). The failure of the Austrian advance, and the refusal of the other Federal states to enter into closer relations with Austria, alone caused the idea of a dual policy of the German Powers to be closely deliberated at Vienna, in consequence of the opening of the Schleswig-Holstein question and succession, and with more prospect of realisation than there had been in December 1862. Count Rechberg, in his annoyance at the refusal of the members of the federation to pledge themselves without the co-operation of

Prussia, simply faced about, with the remark that an understanding with Prussia was easier for Austria than for the middle states.[1]

In this he was right for the moment, but, for a permanence, only if Austria was prepared actually to treat Prussia as holding equal right in Germany, and to reward Prussia's support of Austria's European interests in Italy and the East, by permitting the free exercise of Prussian influence, at least in North Germany. The beginning of the dual policy gave her a splendid opportunity for action in the joint battles on the Schlei, in the joint invasion of Jutland, and the joint treaty of peace with Denmark. The Austro-Prussian alliance maintained itself even under the weakening effect of the ill-temper of the other Federal states, in sufficient preponderance to keep in check all the counter-efforts of ill-temper on the part of the other Great Powers, under whose protection Denmark had thrown down the glove to united Germany.

Our closer connexion with Austria was first endangered by the violent pressure of military influences on the King, urging him to cross the frontier of Jutland even without Austria. My old friend Field-Marshal Wrangel sent the King telegrams, not in cipher, containing the coarsest insults against me, in which remarks were made, referring to me, about diplomatists fit for the gallows.* I succeeded, however, at that time in inducing the King not to move a

---

[1] Cf. Beust, *loc. cit.*, i. 336.

* In consequence of this episode, we were personally estranged for many years. We did not speak when we met at Court, until on one of the many occasions when we were neighbours at table, the Field-Marshal said, smiling in a shamefaced way: 'My son, can you not forget?' 'How can I possibly forget what I have gone through?' I replied. After a long pause he returned: 'Can you not even forgive?' 'With my whole heart,' I answered. We shook hands and were friends again as in the old days.

hair's-breadth in advance of Austria, especially not to give the impression at Vienna that Austria was being dragged along by us against her will. My friendly relations with Rechberg and Karolyi enabled me to restore the understanding about the invasion of Jutland.

In spite of this success, the attempt at dualism reached its culminating point, and began to decline, at an interview which took place between the two monarchs attended by their ministers, Rechberg and myself, at Schönbrunn on August 22, 1864. In the course of the conversation I said to the Emperor of Austria:

'Destined by our history for one political community, we should both do better business if we held together and accepted the leadership of Germany, which we shall not lose, when once we are united. If Prussia and Austria take upon themselves the task of furthering not only the interests common to both, but also each the interests of the other, the effects of the alliance of the two great German Powers will be far-reaching in its operation, both in Germany and in Europe. To Austria, as a state, it matters little what form is given to the Danish duchies, but a great deal what her relations are with Prussia. Does not this undoubted fact prove the convenience of a policy benevolent to Prussia, consolidating the alliance existing between the German Powers, and awakening in Prussia gratitude towards Austria? If our joint acquisition was situated in Italy instead of in Holstein, if the war which we have conducted had placed Lombardy at the disposal of the two Powers instead of Schleswig-Holstein, it would not have occurred to me to induce my King to oppose any resistance to any wishes of our ally, or to claim an equivalent, had there not been at the time an equivalent to be disposed of. But to cede to him an old Prussian province for Schleswig-Holstein would scarcely be possible, even if the inhabitants wished it; at Glatz, however, even the Austrians settled there had protested against it. I felt that the profitable results of the friendship between the great German Powers were not ended with the Holstein question, and that, although now situated at the very farthest distance from the domain of Austrian interests, they might on another occasion be much nearer, and that it would be useful for Austria to act generously and obligingly towards Prussia now.'

It seemed to me that the prospect I had sketched was not without effect on the Emperor Francis Joseph. He spoke indeed of the difficulty in regard to public opinion in Austria if the present situation ended without an equivalent, if Prussia made so large a gain as Schleswig-Holstein. He ended, however, with the question whether we were actually determined to demand and incorporate that possession. My impression was that, if he should be assured of a firm connexion with Prussia in future, and of the support of analogous desires on the part of Austria by Prussia, he did not consider it impossible to yield to us his pretensions to the territory resigned by Denmark. He proposed in the first place for further discussion the question whether Prussia really was firmly determined to make the duchies Prussian provinces, or whether we should be content with certain rights in them such as were formulated afterwards in the so-called February conditions. The King did not answer; I broke the silence by replying to the Emperor: 'I am exceedingly glad that your Majesty has submitted the question to me in the presence of my gracious master; I hope to have the opportunity of learning his views.' So far I had, in fact, received no plain statement from the King, either verbally or in writing, about his Majesty's final pleasure respecting the duchies.

The *mise en demeure* by the Emperor resulted in the King saying, with some hesitation and embarrassment, he had no right to the duchies and could therefore make no claim to them. By this utterance, in which I plainly perceived the influence of the King's relatives and of the Court Liberal party, I was, so far as the Emperor was concerned, put *hors de combat*. I at once took up the cause of the preservation of the union between the two great German Powers, and a short paper adequate for that purpose, in which the future of Schleswig-Holstein remained undecided, was drawn up by Rechberg and myself, and sanctioned by the two Sovereigns.

My idea of dualism was that it would have resembled the circumstances that at present exist, with the difference, however, that Austria would have kept federal influence over the states which, with Prussia, now form the German Empire. Rechberg was won over to the strengthening of the preponderance of Central Europe by means of such an understanding between the two states. This arrangement, compared with what had gone before, and in regard to the circumstances at the time, would at all events have been a step forward toward better things, but would have promised to be permanent only so long as confidence in the leading persons on both sides remained undisturbed. When I left Vienna on August 26, 1864, Count Rechberg told me that his position had been attacked; through the discussions of the ministry and the Emperor's attitude towards them, he could not but fear that his colleagues, especially Schmerling, intended to drop him overboard if he did not at least give the assurance that he would within a definite time enter on negotiations concerning a customs union, a matter with which the Emperor was principally occupied. I had no scruples against such a *pactum de contrahendo* because I was convinced that it would be unable to haggle me into any concessions that went beyond the bounds of what seemed to me possible, and because the political side of the question stood in the forefront. I regarded a customs union as an impracticable Utopia on account of the differences in the economic and administrative conditions of both parties. The commodities which formed the financial basis of the customs union in the north do not come into use at all in the greater part of Austro-Hungarian territory. The difficulties which the differences in habits of life and in consumption between North and South Germany, brought about even now within the Zollverein, would be insurmountable, if both districts were to be included in the same customs-boundary with the eastern provinces of Austria-Hungary. A fairer scale of distribution, or one more corresponding with the existing consumption of dutiable goods, could not be arrived at; every scale would be either unfair to the Zollverein, or unacceptable to public opinion in Austria-Hungary. There is no common measure of taxation for the Slovack or Galician with his few wants on the one side, and on the other for the inhabitant of the Rhenish provinces and of Lower Saxony. Besides, I did not believe in the trustworthiness of the service on a great part of the Austrian frontier.

Convinced of the impossibility of a customs union, I had no hesitation in doing Count Rechberg the desired service in order to keep him in his post. When I set out

383

for Biarritz on October 5, I felt quite secure that the King
would stand by my vote; and even to this day I am not
clear as to the motives that induced my colleagues—Karl
von Bodelschwingh, the Minister of Finance, and Count
Itzenplitz, the Minister of Commerce, and their free-trad-
ing *spiritus rector* Delbrück—to work on the King during
my absence with such determination about a matter somewhat out of his province, so that through our refusal Rechberg's position was, as he had anticipated, shaken, and he
was replaced as Foreign Minister by Mensdorff, who was
in the first place Schmerling's candidate, until he was
himself driven out of office by reactionary and Catholic
influences. The King, firm as he was in domestic politics, allowed himself in that case to be influenced by the
doctrine advocated by his wife—that popularity was the
means of solving the German question.

Herr von Thile wrote to me to Biarritz about a conference of members of the Foreign Office, and of the Ministry of Commerce, which was held on October 10,
1864:

'I found confirmed afresh in to-day's conference what
indeed has been long known, that experts, with all their
special delicacy, which I gladly recognise, in their han-
dling of the professional side, sadly disregard the political
side, and, for instance, treat the possibility of a change of
ministers at Vienna as a trifle. Itzenplitz vacillates in his
views very much. I repeatedly succeeded in making him
confess that Article 25, *finaliter et realiter*, pledges to
nothing. But each time a reproving look from Delbrück
frightened him back to his specialist position.'

Two days later, on October 12, Abeken, who was with
the King at Baden-Baden, informed me that he had not

succeeded in gaining the King over to Article 25; his Majesty shrank from the 'shrieks' that would be raised over such a concession to Austria, and said among other things: 'We should perhaps prevent a ministerial crisis at Vienna, but should create one at Berlin; if we conceded Article 25, Bodelschwingh and Delbrück would probably resign.'

And again, two days later, Count Goltz wrote to me from Paris:

'If Rechberg's position is decidedly shaken (that it is so with the Emperor I decidedly doubt), the necessity will arise for us to anticipate here the beginnings of a purely Schmerling ministry.'

Not without significance for the value of the dualist policy was the question upon what measure of steadfastness in maintaining this line of policy we could reckon on the part of Austria. When we recalled the suddenness with which Rechberg, in his irritation, broke with the middle states when they would not follow him, and allied himself with us without them and against them, the possibility could not be disregarded that non-agreement with Prussia in single questions might lead us unexpectedly to a new evolution. I have never had to complain of any lack of uprightness on Count Rechberg's part, but he was, as Hamlet says, 'splenetic and rash' to an unusual degree; and if the personal irritation of Count Buol about the unfriendly demeanour of the Emperor Nicholas, rather than about political differences, had sufficed to keep Austrian policy firmly and permanently on the lines of the

well-known ingratitude of Schwarzenberg ('nous éton-
nerons l'Europe par notre ingratitude'), no one could shut
his eyes to the possibility that the far weaker cement between Count Rechberg and myself might be washed away
by any sort of tidal wave. The Emperor Nicholas had
a much stronger foundation for a belief in the trustworthiness of his relations with Austria than we had at the time
of the Danish war. He had done the Emperor Francis
Joseph a service such as scarcely any monarch had ever
done a neighbouring state, and the advantages of mutual
reliance in the monarchical interest against revolution, of
the Italians and Hungarians as well as of the Poles of
1846, made the alliance with Russia weigh heavier in the
scale for Austria than the alliance with Prussia possible
in 1864. The Emperor Francis Joseph has an honourable nature, but the Austro-Hungarian ship of state is
of so peculiar a construction that its oscillations, to which
the monarch must adapt his attitude on board, can hardly
be reckoned on in advance. The centrifugal influences of
individual nationalities, the interlacing of the vital interests which Austria has simultaneously to represent towards Germany, Italy, the East, and Poland, the ungovern-
ableness of the Hungarian national spirit, and, above all,
the incalculable way in which confessional influences
cross political decisions, lay on every ally of Austria the
duty of being prudent, and of not making the interests of
its own subjects entirely dependent on Austrian policy.
The reputation for stability which the latter had won
under the long rule of Metternich is not tenable according to the composition of the Habsburg monarchy, and,
according to its internal motive forces, not in agreement
at all with the policy of the Vienna cabinet before the

Metternich period, and not entirely with that which followed it. If, however, the reaction of changing events and situations on the decisions of the Vienna cabinet is not permanently calculable, it is certainly open to every ally of Austria not to refrain absolutely from cultivating relations out of which other combinations may, in case of necessity, be developed.

CHAPTER XVIII

LEWIS II, KING OF BAVARIA

ON our way from Gastein to Baden-Baden we visited
Munich. King Max had already started for Frankfort, having deputed his wife to receive the guests. I do not think
that Queen Mary, with her retiring disposition and her
scanty interest in politics, had any very active influence
on King William or on the decisions of which he was
then full. At the regular meals which we took during
our stay at Nymphenburg on August 16 and 17 the Crown
Prince, afterwards Lewis II, sat opposite his mother,
and next to me. It seemed to me that his thoughts were
far away from the table, and only now and again did he
remember his intention to talk to me; our conversation
did not go beyond the ordinary Court subjects. But even
so I thought I recognised in his remarks a talent, a viva-
city, and a good sense realised in his future career. In the
pauses of the conversation he looked past his mother to the
ceiling, now and again hastily emptying his champagne
glass, the filling of which was, as it seemed to me by his
mother's directions, somewhat slowly performed; thus it
happened that the Prince very often held his glass over his
shoulder, behind him, where it was hesitatingly refilled.
Neither then nor later did he overstep the bounds of moderation in drinking, but I had the feeling that his surroundings bored him, and that the champagne aided the play of

his independent fancy. He made a sympathetic impression on me, although I must confess, with some vexation, that my efforts towards a pleasant conversation with him at table were unsuccessful. That was the only time I met King Lewis face to face, but from his accession soon after (March 10, 1864) I remained in friendly relations with him, and in a comparatively brisk correspondence, that lasted until his death, he always impressed me as a businesslike, clear-headed ruler, full of the German national spirit, but caring greatly for the preservation of the federal principle of the Constitution of the Empire, and of the constitutional privileges of his country. I remember, as something outside the domain of practical politics, his uppermost thought in the Versailles negotiations, that the German Empire, with the federal presidency, should alternate between the Prussian and Bavarian houses. The doubts as to how that unpractical idea was to be made practical were put an end to by the negotiations with the Bavarian representatives at Versailles, and by the result of them, according to which the rights which he exercises to-day were conceded in principle to the president of the federation, and thus to the King of Prussia, before the title of Emperor was discussed.

I insert here some examples of my correspondence with King Lewis, which display the real characteristics of the unfortunate prince, and possess also in themselves an intrinsic interest. The technical forms of address are only given in the first letters.

BISMARCK

From Prince Bismarck to King Lewis

'Versailles : November 27, 1870.[1]

' Most serene and mighty King, most gracious Lord,
—For the gracious overtures which, by command of your
Majesty, Count Holnstein has made to me, I hereby tender my most respectful thanks. My feeling of gratitude
towards your Majesty rests on a foundation deeper and
broader than the personal one in the official position in
which I am called on to rate at their true value your
Majesty's high-spirited resolutions, by which your Majesty,
both at the beginning and in the finishing of this war, has
given the deciding touch to the unity and power of Germany. It is not, however, my duty, but that of the
German people and of history, to thank the Serene Bavarian House for your Majesty's patriotic policy and for the
heroism of your army. I can only assure you that so long
as I live I shall be your Majesty's attached and devoted in
all honourable gratitude, and shall esteem myself at all
times fortunate if it is granted me to be of service to your
Majesty. In the question of the German Emperor I have
ventured to place before Count Holnstein a short paper on
the German question, founded on the train of ideas that,
according to my feelings, are stirring the German stock.
The German Emperor is the compatriot of all of them;
the King of Prussia is a neighbour, to whom, under that
name, rights do not appertain which have their basis only
in voluntary assignment by German princes and stocks. I
believe that the German title for the presidency makes
the concession of it easier, and history teaches that the

[1] After the rough draft, which seems to have received some additions in
the fair copy.

great princely houses of Germany never regarded the existence of the Emperor elected by them as derogatory to
their position in Europe.

'v. BISMARCK.'

From King Lewis to Prince Bismarck

'Hohenschwangau : December 2, 1870.

' My dear Count,—I note with the liveliest pleasure
that, notwithstanding urgent and manifold business, you
have found leisure to express your feelings towards me.

' I tender you my most cordial thanks therefore; for I
attach a high value to the devoted feelings of a man
towards whom the gaze of the whole of Germany is directed with joyful pride.

' My letter to your King, my loved and honoured
uncle, will reach his hands to-morrow.

' I wish, with my whole heart, that the proposal I have
set before the King may meet with the fullest response
from the other members of the federation to whom I have
written, as well as of the nation. It is satisfactory to me
to be conscious that at the beginning of this glorious war,
as at the conclusion, I was, in virtue of my rank in Germany, in the position to make a decisive step in favour of
the national cause. But I hope, and hope with assurance,
that Bavaria will in the future preserve her position, for it
is surely consistent with a loyal unreserved federal policy,
and will be most safe to obviate a pernicious centralisation.

' Great, undying is that which you have done for the
German nation, and, without flattery, I may say that you
hold the most eminent place among the great men of our
century.

'May God grant you many many years, that you may

391

continue to work for the weal and prosperity of our common Fatherland. With my best salutations, I remain, my dear Count, always

' Your sincere friend,

' LEWIS.'

From Prince Bismarck to King Lewis

' Versailles : December 24, 1870.[1]

' Most serene King, most gracious Lord,—Your Majesty's gracious letter, which Count Holnstein delivered to me, emboldens me to offer to your Majesty my thanks for its gracious contents, and my dutiful good wishes for the approaching new year. Seldom, indeed, has Germany awaited from any new year the fulfilment of national aspirations with the same confidence as from the year that lies before us. If these hopes are realised, if United Germany attains by her own forces to the power of guaranteeing her peace abroad within well-secured frontiers, without at the same time prejudicing the free development of individual members of the federation, then the deciding position which your Majesty has gained at the new shaping of our common Fatherland will remain to all time unforgotten in the history and in the gratitude of the Germans.

' Your Majesty rightly presumes that I expect no salvation from centralisation, but I perceive in that very maintenance of rights which the federal constitution secures to individual members of the federation the form of development best suited to the German spirit, and, at the same time, the surest guarantee against the dangers to which law and order might be exposed in the free movement of

[1] After the rough draft, some changes in style were made in the fair copy.

the political life of to-day. The hostile position taken up
by the Republican party throughout Germany in regard to
the re-establishment, through the initiative of your Majesty
and the Federal princes, of the imperial dignity, proves that
it is conducive to Conservative and Monarchical interests.

'Your Majesty may rest assured that I shall esteem
myself happy if I succeed in preserving your Majesty's
good opinion.

'v. B.'

From King Lewis to Prince Bismarck

'Hohenschwangau : July 31, 1874.

'My dear Prince,—It would not only be of the greatest
interest to me, but it would also afford me the liveliest
pleasure to speak with you and give verbal expression to
the very high esteem I feel for you. To my sincere grief
I learn that the horrifying attempt at assassination,[1] for
the failure of which I shall ever be thankful to God, has
had a bad effect on your health, so precious to me, and
upon the course of your cure.

'It would therefore be presumptuous on my part were
I to ask you at once to take the trouble to come to me,
now that I am staying in the mountains. I thank you
from the bottom of my heart for your last letter, which
filled me with sincere pleasure. I place my firm trust in
you, and believe, as you expressed yourself to my minister,
von Pfretzschner, that you will stake your political influence on making the federal principle form the basis of the
new order of things in Germany. May Heaven preserve
your precious life to us for many years! Your death, as

[1] Kullmann's on July 13, 1874.

well as that of my honoured Emperor, would be a real misfortune for Germany and for Bavaria. With my most heartfelt salutations, with particular esteem, and deep-seated confidence, I remain always

'Your sincere friend,

' LEWIS.'

From Prince Bismarck to King Lewis

'Kissingen : August 10, 1874.

' Most serene King, most gracious Lord,—On the point of finishing my cure, I cannot leave Kissingen without once more respectfully thanking your Majesty for all the kindness which you have shown me here, and particularly for your gracious letter of the 31st ult.

' I am most fortunate in the confidence therein expressed in me by your Majesty, and I shall strive always to deserve it. But apart from personal guarantees your Majesty may securely reckon on those comprised in the very constitution of the Empire. That constitution rests on the federal basis accorded it in the treatises of federation and cannot be violated without breach of treaty. Therein the constitution of the Empire differs from every national constitution. Your Majesty's rights form an indissoluble part of the constitution of the Empire, and rest on the same secure basis of law as all the institutions of the Empire. Germany, in the institution of its Federal Council, and Bavaria, in its dignified and intelligent representation on that council, have a firm guarantee against any deterioration or exaggeration of efforts in the direction of unity. Your Majesty will be able to place the fullest confidence in the security of the treaty-guarded law of the constitution, even when I no longer have the honour of

serving the Empire as chancellor. With deep respect, I
remain

'Your Majesty's faithful servant,

'v. BISMARCK.'

'Friedrichsruh: June 2, 1876.

' Baron Werther informs me of your Majesty's kindness in placing at my disposal, for my visit to Kissingen,
horses and carriages from the royal stables. I hope I shall
be able to follow my physician's advice and to seek again
this summer the cure which, as your Majesty has done me
the honour to remember in your order of April 29, I found
so beneficial two years ago.

' Turkish affairs look menacing and may entail pressing
diplomatic work; but among the European Powers, Germany will permanently, or at all events longer than the
others, remain in the most favourable position for keeping
aloof from the complications with which an Eastern question
may threaten the peace. Therefore I do not give up the
hope that I shall be able in a few weeks to go to Kissingen, and respectfully beg your Majesty to accept my heartfelt thanks for your gracious provisions for my comfort.

'v. BISMARCK.'

From King Lewis to Prince Bismarck

'Berg: June 18, 1876.

' I am sincerely delighted to learn that the hope of visiting Kissingen expressed in your letter of the 2nd inst. is
now fulfilled.

' I heartily welcome you to my country, and am happily
confident that your health, which is so precious to the

395

Empire, will be again restored by means of Bavarian waters.

' May the desire for the preservation of peace, common to all German princes, be realised, and may you thereby, my dear Prince, be granted plentiful refreshment from laborious work and disturbing anxieties.

' Meanwhile, I salute the Princess, and send you my most cordial regards, remaining, with the sentiments known to you, always

' Your sincere friend,

' LEWIS.'

From Prince Bismarck to King Lewis

' Kissingen : July 5, 1876.

' . . . . Unfortunately politics do not leave me all the repose needed for a course of baths. The barren labours of diplomatists are caused rather by the general unrest and impatience, than by any actual danger to peace, for Germany at least. Barren those labours must necessarily be so long as the struggle within the Turkish borders does not grow to anything decisive. However the decision may turn out, a reciprocally sincere understanding between Russia and England will be always possible if—and for as long as—Russia does not strive to gain possession of Constantinople. Very much more difficult in the long run will be the adjustment of Austro-Hungarian and Russian interests. So far, however, the two imperial Courts are still in agreement, and in regarding the preservation of this agreement as a main task for German diplomacy, I know I can reckon on your Majesty's approval. It would seriously embarrass Germany if she had to choose between two such closely allied neighbours; for I feel sure that I am acting in accordance with the ideas of your Majesty, and of all German princes, if in our policy I advocate the principle that Germany of her own will should only take part in a war for the preservation of undoubted German interests. As long as the Turkish question develops within the frontiers of Turkey it touches, in my most humble opinion, no German interests worth fighting about. Even a conflict between Russia and one or both of the Western Powers may develop without necessarily drawing Germany into sympathising. But in this matter much more difficulty is presented by the case of Austria and Russia becoming disunited, and I hope that the meeting of the two monarchs at Reichstadt may bear good fruit in confirming their friendship. Happily the Emperor Alexander wishes for peace and recognises that Austria's situation in regard to the Southern Slavonic movement is more difficult and more constraining than that of Russia. For the latter foreign interests, for Austria vital domestic interests, are at stake.

'v. BISMARCK.'

From King Lewis to Prince Bismarck

'Hohenschwangau : July 16, 1876.

'I received with the greatest delight your news of the obviously favourable course of the cure. I thank you many times for the joyful tidings and heartily hope that you may soon be free from the troublesome consequences of the exhaustion due to the use of the Kissingen waters.

'I am also deeply obliged, my dear Prince, for your clear exposition of the political situation. The far-seeing, statesmanlike survey, which is noticeable in your views regarding the position of Germany towards the present still somewhat threatening developments abroad, has my complete admiration, and I surely need not assure you that your powerful efforts to preserve peace have my warmest sympathy and my unbounded confidence. May the fortunate issue of the German policy and the gratitude of the German princes and stocks find you, my dear Prince, in possession of complete health and vigour.

' To that heartfelt wish I add most cordial salutations and the assurance of the real esteem and of the firmly-rooted confidence with which I, my dear Prince, am always

' Your sincere friend,

'LEWIS.'

From Prince Bismarck to King Lewis

' Kissingen : June 29, 1877.

. . . . .

' So much business during my course of treatment was unavoidable because, through the difficulties which it made relative to the appointment of some one to act in my place, and against which I was not then well enough to contend, the Reichstag compelled me to keep the counter signatures in my hands even during my holiday. This was one of the weapons by which the majority in the Reichstag sought to obtain the introduction of the institution which they understand under the designation "responsible minister to the Empire;" against that I have always stood on the defensive, not in order to remain sole minister, but in order to guard the constitutional rights of the Federal Council, and of its exalted constituents. Only at the cost of the latter could imperial ministries, if obtained, be endowed with the powers of conducting business, and therewith a step would be taken in the direction of centralisation, in which, as I believe, we should seek in vain the salvation of the future of Germany. It is in my humble judgment, not only the constitutional right, but also the political task of my non-Prussian colleagues in the Federal Council to support me openly in my opposition to the introduction of such an imperial ministry, and thereby to make it perfectly clear that so far I have not taken the field for the ministerial despotism of the chancellor, but for the rights of the members of the federation, and of the ministerial competence of the Federal Council. I have already expressed myself in this sense to Pfretzschner. I venture to assume that my views have corresponded with your Majesty's, and I am convinced that your Majesty's representatives in the Federal Council, themselves in combination with other colleagues, will by their support relieve me of a part of the struggle against the pressure in the Reichstag for a responsible imperial ministry.

' If, as I hear, your Majesty's choice has fallen on Herr von Rudhart, I may, considering all I know of him from Hohenlohe, be with all respect thankful, and I can make sure in advance of being able to discuss with him, with confidential candour, not only the domestic, but also the foreign business of the Empire, a thing that in dealing with your Majesty's representative is necessary for me, both on business and on personal grounds. For the moment our position with regard to other countries of Europe remains the same as throughout the winter, and the hope that war will not touch us as strong as ever. The confidence of Russia in the trustworthiness of our neighbourly policy has visibly increased, and with it the prospect of averting such developments as might compel Austria, in her own interests, to interfere. Our endeavours to keep

both empires friendly have been successful. Our friendship with England has so far not suffered thereby, and the
rumours set afloat in that Court by political intriguers, that
Germany may have designs about the acquisition of Holland, could only have met with transitory approval among
ladies in high social circles; the calumniators were not
tired, but the believers appear at last to be becoming so.
Under these circumstances the foreign policy of the Empire is in a position to turn its unimpaired attention to the
volcano in the West, which for three hundred years has so
often littered Germany with its eruptions. I have no confidence in the assurances which we receive from there, and
can give the Empire no other advice than to await a possible fresh attack, well equipped and with ordered arms.

' v. BISMARCK.'

From King Lewis to Prince Bismarck

'Berg: July 7, 1877.

' I am compelled on this occasion, my dear Prince, to
tell you with what lively regret I heard, a little while ago,
the news of the possibility of your retirement. The
greater my personal respect for you, and my confidence in
the federal basis of your activity as a statesman, the more
deeply should I have felt the disaster of such an event for
me and for my country.

' To my real joy it has not taken place, and I hope,
from the bottom of my heart, that your wisdom and activity may long be preserved to the Empire, and to Bavaria,
its loyal member. You have also, my dear Prince, my
deepest thanks for the satisfactory information regarding
prospects of peace, and for the assurance that von Rudhart, my destined envoy to Berlin, will be received by you

with confidence and goodwill.   In the position assumed by you towards the question, constantly cropping up, of responsible imperial ministries you show yourself to be the strong refuge of the rights of the Federal princes, and it is with a real relief of mind that I receive your word that the salvation of Germany in the future is not to be sought in centralisation such as would follow from the creation of such ministries.   Rest convinced that I shall omit nothing in order to secure to you at all future times the public and entire support of my representative in the Federal Council, in the struggle for upholding the basis of the constitution of the Empire, a line of action in which plenipotentiaries of other princes will certainly join.*

'Lewis.'

From Prince Bismarck to King Lewis

'Kissingen : Aug. 12, 1878.

'May I venture to lay at your Majesty's feet my most respectful thanks for the gracious orders given to the royal stables this year again for my sojourn here, and for the gracious recognition which your minister, von Pfretzsch-ner, delivered by your instructions?   Politics are for the time brought by the congress to a conclusion, whose fit-ness as regards Germany your Majesty is pleased to acknowledge in your gracious letter.   Our own peace remains intact, the danger of a breach between Austria and Russia is removed, and our relations with both our friendly neighbour empires are maintained and made firmer.   I am particularly glad that we have succeeded in actually strengthening, both in the cabinet and among the people of the Empire, the comparatively recent confidence

* This was not verified in the case of Rudhart.

of Austria in our policy. I can be convinced of your
Majesty's approval of my future labours to keep the foreign policy of the Empire in the direction indicated, and
to use corresponding action upon the Porte and elsewhere
at the present time, so as to lighten as far as possible, by
the diplomatic support, the difficult task which Austria,
somewhat late, it is true, has undertaken.

' More difficult at this moment are the problems of home
politics. Since the death of Cardinal Franchi my negotiations with the Nuncio are completely at a standstill while
instructions are awaited from Rome. Those which the
Archbishop of Neocæsarea brought demanded the re-establishment of the *status quo ante* 1870 in Prussia, *de facto*,
if not actually by treaty. Such concessions of principle
are impossible on both sides. The Pope does not possess
the means with which to render us the required reciprocal
services. The Centre party, the press hostile to the state,
the Polish agitation, do not any of them obey the Pope,
even if his Holiness were willing to command those elements to support the government. The forces united in
the Centre party are now indeed fighting under the Papal
flag, but are in themselves hostile to the state, even if the
flag of Catholicism were to cease to cover them ; their connexion with the Progressives and Socialists on the basis of
hostility to the state is independent of the dispute with
the Church. In Prussia, at least, the electoral districts
in which the Centre party is recruited, with the exception of the Westphalian and Upper Silesian nobility, who
are led by the Jesuits, and by them badly brought up
on purpose, were in opposition even before the dispute
with the Church. Under these circumstances the See of
Rome cannot possibly offer us an equivalent for the con-

cessions it desires from us, especially since the Pope has at present no control over the influence of the Jesuits in German affairs. The powerlessness of the Pope without this support has been proved especially in the by-elections when Catholic votes were given to Socialist candidates against the will of the Pope, and when Dr. Moufang, at Mainz, publicly took pledges in that sense. The negotiations here with the Nuncio cannot go beyond the stage of mutual reconnoitring; they have convinced me that a settlement is not yet possible; but I ought, I think, to avoid breaking them off altogether, and the Nuncio appears to have the same desire. At Rome they obviously consider us more in need of help than we are; they overrate the support which they, with the best will, have the power to afford us in parliament. The elections to the Reichstag have pushed its centre of gravity farther to the right than was supposed. The preponderance of the Liberals is lessened, and even in a greater degree than appears in the figures. At the time of motion for dissolution I was in no doubt that the electors were more friendly to the government than were the deputies, and the consequence has been that many of the deputies, who, notwithstanding their opposition attitude, were again elected, only attained that end by promising to favour the government. If they fail to keep that promise, and a fresh dissolution follows, the electors will no longer have faith in them, and they will not again be elected. The result of this loosening of relations with the Liberal and Centralising parties will be, in my respectful opinion, a firmer cohesion of the federated governments one with the other. The growth of the Social-Democrat danger, the yearly increase of the menacing bands of robbers with whom we share our larger towns as dwelling-places, the refusal of support against this danger on the part of the majority in the Reichstag, renders obligatory on the German princes, on their governments, and on all supporters of order in the Empire, a solidarity of self-defence for which the demagogy of the orators and of the press will be no match so long as the governments remain united and resolute as they are at present. The aim of the German Empire is the protection of law; parliamentary activity was regarded at the establishment of the existing federation of princes and cities as a means of attaining the aim of federation, not as an end in itself. I hope that the attitude of the Reichstag will exempt the federated governments from the necessity of ever drawing practical consequences from that position. But I am not sure that the majority of the Reichstag now elected will correctly express the undoubtedly loyal and monarchical leanings of the German electors. Should that not be the case, the question of a new dissolution comes into the order of the day. I do not think, however, that a right moment for the decisions will occur this autumn. At a new appeal to the electors the question of economic and financial reform will, as soon as it is rightly understood by the people, be a comrade in federation with the federated governments, but to this end its discussion in the Reichstag is necessary, and that cannot be before winter. The need of increased revenue through indirect taxation is felt in all the federated states, and it was unanimously recognised by their ministers at Heidelberg. The opposition to it of parliamentary theorists finds, in the long run, no response in the producing majority of the population.

' I most humbly beg your Majesty to accept with gracious indulgence this brief sketch of the situation, and to honour me further with your Highness's favour. . . .

'v. BISMARCK.'

From King Lewis to Prince Bismarck

'I offer you my sincere thanks for that interesting exposition of the present political situation which you did me the attention of sending me from Kissingen, and also for the points which your policy at large has laid down as aims for the immediate future. It is my most earnest wish that Kissingen and the after-cure may leave you in possession of the gigantic strength which the execution of your plans requires, and on which the ensuing session of the Reichstag will make heavy demands. May your vigorous operations be, as hitherto, blessed to the salvation of Germany, and may you be spared for many years to all of us who have the welfare of Germany at heart. I yield also to the firm hope that whenever the question of exorcising the Social-Democrat danger arises, the federal governments will always remain united and coherent.

'I beg you to express my deep respect to the Princess, and to give my best remembrances to your son, Count Herbert.

'Repeating my cordial thanks for your interesting and most welcome letter, I remain, my dear Prince, with the assurance of my particular esteem, regard, and confidence, always

'Your sincere friend,

'LEWIS.'

'Hohenschwangau : July 29, 1879.

'My dear Prince Bismarck,—The favourable result of the discussions in the Reichstag on your great financial

project affords me the welcome opportunity of heartily con-
gratulating you. It needed your extraordinary vigour and
energy to come off victorious in the fight with the views
of adversaries, and the thousands of selfish interests which
opposed themselves to your plan. The German lands
stand under a fresh obligation to you, and press with reani-
mated hope towards the goal of material welfare which
forms the indispensable basis of man's life as a citizen.

'May your sojourn at Kissingen be again successful
in removing the effects of the fatigues and labours of the
past months. To that heartfelt wish I join the assurance
of the particular regard with which I am

'Your sincere friend,

'LEWIS.'

From Prince Bismarck to King Lewis

'Kissingen : August 4, 1879.

'Your Majesty has made me very fortunate by the
gracious acknowledgment which your letter of the 29th
ult. contained for me. I am particularly grateful for the
indulgence which you vouchsafe to the difficulties which
the party passions in the federation, together with private
interests, placed in the way of the reforms planned by the
federated governments.

'In economic matters, touching the protection of German labour and production, we have, I venture to submit,
in the immediate future, not to strive for something more
than we have attained, but rather to watch its practical
operation; and this again cannot be ascertained with certainty in the coming year, because the postponement decided on by the Reichstag of the date of the new tariff offers
foreign countries further opportunity for swamping the

German market without paying duty. The hoped-for salu-
tary effect on the raising of our material prosperity will
only become appreciable after the expiration of next year.

' In the region of finance, however, I believe that in
an early sitting of the Reichstag the attempt to open out
further sources of revenue for the federated governments
will be renewed, since the sources of revenue cover perhaps the deficit of our budget, but do not suffice to make
reforms in direct taxation possible, or to afford support to
the needy local administrations.

' In political affairs the result of the proceedings of the
federated governments has so far borne out my expecta-
tions, and the defective grouping and composition of our
political parties and fractions of parties seem, through the
discussions about them, to have suffered a lasting blow.
For the first time the Centre party has begun to take a
constructive part in the legislation of the Empire. If the
gain is to be permanent, only experience can teach. The
possibility is not excluded that, if no understanding is
come to with the See of Rome, the party will return to its
former purely critical attitude of opposition. According
to outward appearances the prospect of an understanding
with Rome is no nearer than last year. But I may perhaps attach some hopes to the fact that the papal nuncio,
Jacobini, officially expressed to the ambassador, Prince
Reuss, the wish to enter into negotiations, for which he
has plenary power from Rome. I do not know the scope
of that power, but I have declared myself willing, at the
desire of the nuncio, to meet him and discuss the matter in
the course of this month at Gastein.

' The National Liberal party will, I hope, through the
last Reichstag session, be borne towards their division

into a monarchical and a progressive—that is a republican—party. The attempt of the former President von Forckenbeck to bring the legislative authorities of the Empire under the direct control of a German federation of cities, and the inflammatory speeches made by Lasker and Richter to the unpropertied classes, have made the revolutionary tendencies of those members so clear and palpable that no further political association with them is possible on the part of adherents of the monarchical form of government. The plan of a federation of cities with its permanent committee at the seat of the Reichstag was modelled on the summoning of the *fédérés* from the French provincial towns in 1792. The attempt met with no response from the German people, but it serves to show how material for Convention deputies is to be found among our progressive members. The preparers of the Revolution are recruited pretty exclusively from the learned proletariat in which North Germany is richer than South. They are the educated, highly cultured gentlemen, who, without property, without industry, without business, live either by their salary as civil or local servants, or by the press, or frequently by both; in the Reichstag they form considerably more than half of the members, while among the electors they form only a small percentage. These are the gentlemen who provide the revolutionary ferment, and who lead the Progressive and National Liberal groups, and the press. In my humble opinion the splitting-up of their group forms an essential task of the preservative policy, and the reform of economic interests is the ground on which the governments can more and more approach that goal.

' I respectfully thank your Majesty for your kind wishes

regarding the treatment I am undergoing, from which, according to my impressions hitherto, I hope to find, as in former years, a cure for the damage to my health caused by the winter.   An essential part of the good result is due to the ease with which your Majesty has made it possible for me to enjoy the fine air of the neighboring forests.   The magnificent horses from your Majesty's stables make it easy to reach every point of the beautiful environs of Kissingen, a comfort doubly acceptable since age has robbed me of my walking powers.   Your Majesty will graciously accept my sincerest thanks for this comfort, and for the consideration for me to which the granting of them testifies.

'v. BISMARCK.'

'Kissingen : August 7, 1879.

'In consequence of the interest which your Majesty takes in the progress of the negotiations with Rome, I venture to lay before you transcripts of the following documents :

' 1. The letter of the Pope to his Majesty the Emperor of May 30.

' 2. The reply to it of June 21.

'3. The still unanswered letter of the Pope to his Majesty of July 9.

'v. BISMARCK.'

From King Lewis to Prince Bismarck

' Berg : August 18, 1879.

' My dear Prince,—I thank you most cordially for both your welcome letters of the 4th and 7th inst., in which you give me such interesting information about the state of parties, and the situation of the matter at issue with

409

Rome. Your negotiations with Rome have even now
been successful since the considerably improved relations
to the Curia had a decided influence on the Centre party,
and through it, on the success of your work in financial
reform. May your strenuous efforts to create a large Conservative party be likewise favoured with success. It is
my earnest wish, my dear Prince, that health and strength
may be preserved to you for mastering your great and important tasks, and it was with real pleasure that I learned
from your letter that your sojourn at Kissingen promised
the best results.

' Rest assured, my dear Prince, of my particular
esteem, and of the complete esteem and confidence with
which I am always

'Your sincere friend,

'Lewis.'

'Berg : September 1, 1880.

' My dear Prince,—The congratulations which you so
politely offered me on my double celebration, and on
jubilee for the seven hundredth anniversary of my house,
gave me real pleasure.[1] I heartily thank you for the well-
tested sentiments of affection which are of so high value to
me and to my country, and upon which, as hitherto, I place
my sincere confidence for the future. With the close relations in which you, as the great and renowned Chancellor,
stand to me, it was of especial interest to me to learn that
my ancestors had already had occasion to esteem and distinguish your family. The satisfactory news which you, my
dear Prince, give me of your health is most gratifying, and
I repeat how gladly I perceive that Bavarian waters should

[1] There is unfortunately no copy of the letter.

410

assist in the preservation of the admirable strength which you expend upon the welfare of the German states. With entire satisfaction I derived from your letter confidence in the certainty of peace, and I am grateful for the assurance of a report on the political situation.

'Accept, my dear Prince, assurances of my warmest sympathy and of the particular esteem for you and yours with which I am always

' Your sincere friend,

' LEWIS.'

' Hohenschwangau : August 10, 1881.

' My dear Prince,—The good result of the cure at Kissingen fulfils my sincere wishes, and I hope that the compulsory rest will also cure the neuralgic pains which, to my great sorrow, are, you tell me, still troubling you. The exposition of the foreign and domestic situation, for which I have to thank your welcome and esteemed letter, was in the highest degree interesting to me. The great things which you achieve in both departments are the objects of my admiration. I am as sensible of the prospects of peace as of your firm stand against the lust after government by parliamentary majorities which is now cropping up in Bavaria also, although from another quarter. I shall take care that their goal, which is not compatible with the monarchical principle, and would produce endless disturbance and discord, is not attained. I am looking forward with the greatest interest to the approaching elections. If, however, the result is not according to our wish, I still firmly believe that your perseverance will succeed in establishing the financial and economic basement needed for placing the welfare of the German land,

411

and especially the situation of the working men, on a more satisfactory footing; of the honest co-operation of my government you may be certain. On the other hand, my dear Prince, I am confidently convinced that in the carrying out of your great ideas, you start from the federal principle on which the Empire and the independence of the individual states depend.

'I was heartily glad to learn that you were within the frontier of Bavaria. I hope that you will visit my country for many many years yet, and I send you, my dear Prince, with best wishes for the future, the assurance of the particular confidence and complete esteem with which I always remain

' Your sincere friend,
' LEWIS.'

' Berg : August 27, 1881.

' My dear Prince,—I return you my warmest and most cordial thanks for the great pleasure your congratulations on my birthday afforded me. They, as well as the whole contents of your letter, give me a fresh proof of the sentiments of attachment on which I always with pleasure wholly rely. I hope that during your stay at Varzin you will have rest and fine weather, so that you will be able, in the enjoyment of perfect health, to go and occupy yourself as you are longing to do with your great tasks.

'Meanwhile, my dear Prince, I send you and yours my best remembrances, and with particular esteem remain always

' Your sincere friend,
' LEWIS.'

LEWIS II, KING OF BAVARIA

'Schloss Berg : September 2, 1883.

' My dear Prince,—The kind letter which you were attentive enough to address to me from Kissingen gave me the liveliest pleasure. While I return you most cordial thanks for the congratulations on my double celebration therein expressed, I must not omit to tell you, my dear Prince, of the deep interest with which I followed the exposition enclosed in your letter of the political situation. To my great satisfaction, I was able to gather from it that there are at present no serious signs that cause apprehension of immediate danger to the peace of Europe. If, at the same time, the situation in Russia, and the unusual stationing of troops on the western frontier of Russia, are calculated to awaken some anxiety, I indulge in the hope that the fortunate understanding between Germany and Austria, which offers so powerful a pledge of peace for the Continent, and your wise and foreseeing policy, will be successful in averting a warlike issue, and that the peaceful intentions of the Emperor of Russia, clearly and publicly uttered a short time since, on the solemn occasion of the coronation at Moscow, will aid in assuring that victory. Receive, my dear Prince, with my warmest thanks for your always welcome letter, the expression of my pleasure that your health, which has been so long ailing—a fact that caused me deep sorrow—has, through the use of the Kissingen cure, and thanks to the excellent medical treatment, begun to improve. It is my most sincere wish that you may soon regain vigorous health, so that Germany may long be gladdened by the feeling of safety which her confidence in the activity and prudence of her great statesman inspires. Once again, my dear Prince, I repeat in

413

these lines the assurance of the admiration and unchangeable affection towards you which ever animates me. With
warmest remembrances

<blockquote>
' I am always
  ' Your sincere friend,
    ' LEWIS.'
</blockquote>

' Elmau : September 27, 1883.

' My dear Prince Bismarck,—I have had the pleasure
of receiving your letter of the 19th, and thank you warmly
for your communications as well as for forwarding the
accompanying document from St. Petersburg. I have
studied both with the lively interest attached to everything that comes to me from you. But the most cheering thing your letter brought me was the news of your
progress towards recovery, which will, I hope from my
heart, lead to the complete restoration of your health.
The hope thus founded that you, newly strengthened
and refreshed, will be able completely to devote yourself
in the future to the high task of your statesmanlike calling, enables me to regard with greater unconcern the
further development of the political situation. Regarding more particularly the relations between Germany and
Russia, I note with satisfaction the report of General von
Schweinitz that there can at least be no doubt as to
the Russian Emperor's sincere love of peace, and that
of his chief ministers. That reassuring fact, in con-
junction with the pleasant relations now happily prevailing between Germany and Austria—relations which,
to my great joy, are confirmed afresh by your letter—
helps to strengthen the hope of a continued preservation
of peace.

414

LEWIS II, KING OF BAVARIA

' Accept, my dear Prince, with repeated expressions of my warmest wishes for the complete restoration of your strength, the assurance of the particular esteem with which I am

' Your sincere friend,

' LEWIS.'

END OF THE FIRST VOLUME

COSIMO CLASSICS

COSIMO is an innovative publisher of books and publications that inspire, inform and engage readers worldwide. Our titles are drawn from a range of subjects including health, business, philosophy, history, science and sacred texts. We specialize in using print-on-demand technology (POD), making it possible to publish books for both general and specialized audiences and to keep books in print indefinitely. With POD technology new titles can reach their audiences faster and more efficiently than with traditional publishing.

> ➢ **Permanent Availability:** Our books & publications never go out-of-print.

> ➢ **Global Availability:** Our books are always available online at popular retailers and can be ordered from your favorite local bookstore.

COSIMO CLASSICS brings to life unique, rare, out-of-print classics representing subjects as diverse as *Alternative Health, Business and Economics, Eastern Philosophy, Personal Growth, Mythology, Philosophy, Sacred Texts, Science, Spirituality* and much more!

COSIMO-on-DEMAND publishes your books, publications and reports. If you are an Author, part of an Organization, or a Benefactor with a publishing project and would like to bring books back into print, publish new books fast and effectively, would like your publications, books, training guides, and conference reports to be made available to your members and wider audiences around the world, we can assist you with your publishing needs.

Visit our website at www.cosimobooks.com to learn more about Cosimo, browse our catalog, take part in surveys or campaigns, and sign-up for our newsletter.

And if you wish please drop us a line at info@cosimobooks.com. We look forward to hearing from you.